Public Management and Complexity Theory

Routledge Critical Studies in Public Management

EDITED BY STEPHEN OSBORNE

The study and practice of public management has undergone profound changes across the world. Over the last quarter century, we have seen

- increasing criticism of public administration as the over-arching framework for the provision of public services,
- the rise (and critical appraisal) of the 'New Public Management' as an emergent paradigm for the provision of public services,
- the transformation of the 'public sector' into the cross-sectoral provision of public services, and
- the growth of the governance of inter-organizational relationships as an essential element in the provision of public services

In reality these trends have not so much replaced each other as elided or co-existed together— the public policy process has not gone away as a legitimate topic of study, intra-organizational management continues to be essential to the efficient provision of public services, whist the governance of inter-organizational and inter-sectoral relationships is now essential to the effective provision of these services.

Further, whilst the study of public management has been enriched by contribution of a range of insights from the 'mainstream' management literature it has also contributed to this literature in such areas as networks and inter-organizational collaboration, innovation and stakeholder theory.

This series is dedicated to presenting and critiquing this important body of theory and empirical study. It will publish books that both explore and evaluate the emergent and developing nature of public administration, management and governance (in theory and practice) and examine the relationship with and contribution to the over-arching disciplines of management and organizational sociology.

Books in the series will be of interest to academics and researchers in this field, students undertaking advanced studies of it as part of their undergraduate or postgraduate degree and reflective policy makers and practitioners.

Public Management and Complexity Theory

Richer Decision-Making in Public Service

Mary Lee Rhodes, Joanne Murphy,
Jenny Muir, and John A. Murray

Routledge
Taylor & Francis Group
New York   London

First published 2011
by Routledge
270 Madison Avenue, New York, NY 10016

Simultaneously published in the UK
by Routledge
2 Park Square, Milton Park, Abingdon, Oxon OX14 4RN

Routledge is an imprint of the Taylor & Francis Group, an informa business

Typeset in Sabon by IBT Global.
Printed and bound in the United States of America on acid-free paper by IBT Global.

Library of Congress Cataloging-in-Publication Data
   Public management and complexity theory : richer decision-making in public services / by Mary Lee Rhodes . . . [et al.]. — 1st ed.
      p. cm. — (Routledge critical studies in public management ; 6)
   Includes bibliographical references and index.
   1. Public administration—Ireland—Case studies.   I. Rhodes, Mary Lee.
   JF1351.P826 2010
   352.3'3—dc22
   2010017286

ISBN13: 978-0-415-45753-8 (hbk)
ISBN13: 978-0-203-84160-0 (ebk)

Contents

Figures

Tables

Abbreviations and Acronyms

ADM	Area Development Management Ltd
BCH	Belfast City Hospital
BHTF	Ballymun Housing Task Force
BNC	Ballymun Neighbourhood Council
BRL	Ballymun Regeneration Ltd.
CAS	Complex Adaptive System
CCDB	City and County Development Boards [ROI]
CEC	Commission of the European Communities (now known as the European Commission)
CHA	Connswater Housing Association
CNR	Catholic/Nationalist/Republican
CPO	Compulsory Purchase Order
CRA	Clonard Residents' Association
DCC	Dublin City Council
DFP	Department of Finance and Personnel [NI]
DoHC	Department of Health and Children [ROI]
DHSSPS	Department of Health, Social Services and Public Safety [NI]
DoCRGA	Department of Community, Rural and Gaeltacht Affairs [ROI]
DoEHLG	Department of the Environment, Heritage and Local Government [ROI]
DoELG	Department of Environment and Local Government, now known as DoEHLG [ROI]
DSD	Department for Social Development [NI]
EPES	Electronic Prescribing and Eligibility System
EHR	Electronic Health Record
ERHA	Eastern Regional Health Authority [ROI]
ESRI	Economic and Social Research Institute
EU	European Union
EUSSPPR	European Union Special Support Programme for Peace and Reconciliation (the official name of PEACE I, II programmes)
FDI	Foreign Direct Investment
FGU	Fatima Groups United

FRB	Fatima Regeneration Board
GDP	Gross Domestic Product
GP	General Practitioner
GPIT	General Practitioner Information Technology (National project to iImprove IT usage amongst GPs [ROI])
GVA	Greater Village Area
GVRT	Greater Village Regeneration Trust
HCIS	Healthcare Information Systems
HeBE	Health Board Executive [ROI]
HIQA	Health Information Quality Authority [ROI]
HL7	Messaging protocol for healthcare information requirements; accredited by the American National Standards Institute (ANSI)
HP	Hewlett Packard
HPSS	Health and Personal Services Structure [NI]
HSE	Health Services Executive [ROI]
ICT	Information & Communications Technology
ILO	International Labour Organization
INTERREG	EU cross-border co-operation funding programme
IT	Information Technology
LA	Local Authority
MARA	Mersey Street Area Residents' Association
MBW	*Making Belfast Work*
MHC	Mental Health Commission [ROI]
MLA	Member of the Legislative Assembly [NI]
MP	Member of Parliament [UK]
NDP	National Development Plan [ROI]
NGO	Non-Governmental Organization
NHS	National Health Service [NI]
NI	Northern Ireland
NIAO	Northern Ireland Audit Office
NIHE	Northern Ireland Housing Executive
NIO	Northern Ireland Office
NIPAC	Northern Ireland Public Accounts Committee
NISRA	Northern Ireland Statistics and Research Agency
NRS	Neighbourhood Renewal Strategy
OCS	Order Communication System
OECD	Organization for Economic Cooperation and Development
OFMDFM	Office of the First Minister and Deputy First Minister
PEACE I	EU Special Support Programme for Peace and Reconciliation (1995–1999) - See also EUSSPPR
PEACE II	EU Programme for Peace and Reconciliation in Northern Ireland and the Border Region of Ireland (2000–2006) - See also EUSSPPR
PPP	Public—Private Partnership

PRINCE2	PRojects In Controlled Environments, version two
PSA	Project Specific Agent
PUL	Protestant/Unionist/Loyalist
QUANGO	QUasi-Autonomous Non-Governmental Organization
RABIU	Regional Acquired Brain Injury Unit ICT
RAPID	Revitalising Areas through Planning, Investment and Development
ROI	Republic of Ireland
RWS	Remedial Works Scheme
SBP	South Belfast Partnership
SBPB	South Belfast Partnership Board
SDU	Northern Ireland Department of Health, Social Services and Public Safety's Service Delivery Unit
SRO	Senior Responsible Officer
TD	Member of Parliament [ROI]
TMS	Theatre Management System
UK	United Kingdom
UR	Urban Regeneration
URBAN	Instrument within EU Cohesion Policy, dedicated to the regeneration of urban areas and neighbourhoods
URS	Urban Renewal Scheme

Acknowledgements

The authors would like to acknowledge the support of the Higher Education Authority of Ireland, whose generous grant enabled the research reported here. They would also like to thank Dublin City Council and the Northern Ireland Housing Executive for their support in facilitating the research on urban regeneration projects in Dublin and Belfast.

The authors acknowledge the following people for their significant contribution to this research:

Fabian Armendariz of the National College of Ireland for his contribution to the Healthcare Information Systems case studies;

Professor Colleen Grogan of the University of Chicago for her contribution to the analysis of the healthcare environment in Ireland;

Dr Paul Haynes of the Polytechnic University of Valencia for his contribution to the Urban Regeneration case studies.

In addition, the authors would like to thank Liz Powell and Joan Murphy for their unflagging efforts in editing, diagramming and proofing without which this book would never have seen the light of day.

Introduction
The Case for CAS

Jeffrey Weber recently observed that 'the academic discipline of public administration is drifting and largely ignored, because so often the ideas are stale and impractical for they are based on a faulty understanding of existence' (Weber 2005: 266). Weber is just one of the many voices calling for a reinvigoration of public administration theory; Jan-Erik Lane highlighted the already long simmering dissatisfaction of theorists in 1993 when he wrote 'public administration as an academic discipline has more or less crumbled during the recent decades . . . replacing it there is now a proliferation of concepts, frameworks and theories' (Lane 1993: vii).

Some of the blame for the frustration with theory and its apparent irrelevance to practitioners must be laid at the door of those who develop theories of public administration in the first place. Since the demise of the 'bureaucratic model' in the mid-twentieth century, the discipline of public administration has split into many different sub-strands, with economists, political scientists, sociologists and management theorists developing alternative theories to explain the workings of the administrative state. Frederickson and Smith (2003) detail eight different theories of public administration that are actively pursued. These are: political control of bureaucracy; bureaucratic politics; (public) institutional theory; public management; postmodern theory; decision theory; rational choice; governance. Pierre and Peters (2000) suggest that 'governance' had eight different 'perspectives'—different to those described by Frederickson and Smith—namely: top-down authority of the state; autopoiesis and network steering; cybernetic processes; potential (policy) instruments for steering; institutional analysis; rational choice; policy networks; neo-Marxism and critical theory. Richard Stillman, in the 7th edition (and 25th year) of his highly regarded textbook, *Public Administration: Concepts and Cases*, opts for a 'Chinese menu' approach of 15 different topics and an introduction in which he says that public administration is 'the eminently practical science' that is 'continuously "bubbling up" with multiple new perspectives for understanding, defining and dealing with salient public issues of the here-and-now by means of its own brand of interdisciplinary hands-on conceptual creativity' (Stillman 2000: 29). In a recent exploration of theories of public governance, Stephen Osborne suggests that there are five 'strands' or perspectives (socio-political governance; public policy governance; administrative governance; contract governance; network governance) with the 'potential to assist our understanding of the complexity of the challenges [in public management] and as a reflection of the reality of the working lives of public managers today' (Osborne 2010: 6). While there are clearly ongoing efforts to bring the theory of public management in line with practice, there is still little in the way of greater coherence emerging from these efforts.

In the same article in which he suggests that public administration theory is drifting and no longer relevant to practitioners, Weber proposes that theories of 'complexity' may hold the key for reinvigorating the discipline and helping to increase the coherence of theory across the many perspectives that have been brought to bear on the problem(s) of public administrators. Several others join him in this view, including those from public administration (Boston 2000, Blackman 2001, Chapman 2002, Teisman and Klijn 2008) and organizational complexity (Anderson 1999, Stacey and Griffin 2006, Dennard *et al.* 2008). There are numerous articles and conference papers exploring the potential application of complexity theory (or theories) to public administration and policy. Two recent compilations on the topic (Stacey and Griffin 2006, Dennard *et al.* 2008) provide wide-ranging examples, models and theoretical propositions, and there have been several special issues of journals exploring the same space (c.f. *Public Administration Quarterly* 2005, vol. 29: 3, *Public Management Review* 2008: vol. 10: 3).

In a series of articles that contributed to the research reported here, ML Rhodes and colleagues (Rhodes and MacKechnie 2003, Rhodes and Murray 2007, Rhodes 2008, Muir and Rhodes 2009) develop the case for applying a particular strand of complexity theory, complex adaptive systems (CAS) theory, to public administration and public service systems in particular. The perspective on systems embodied in CAS theory, and its efforts to model and understand such systems seemed to offer an intellectual framework with which to observe and seek to understand, in a fresh manner, the functioning of public management systems. The complexity of such systems is generally accepted. The multiplicity, intensity and non-linearity of interactions seem, intuitively, to accord with CAS characteristics, as do their adaptive characteristics. Since outcomes are seldom fully predictable in public management, yet may nonetheless serve their purpose well, concepts such as self-organization and emergent order seem like reasonable characterizations. The inherent potential in complexity theory for addressing the policy and management challenges facing practitioners, as well as for integrating the various theoretical strands in public administration into a coherent framework, is what inspired the research that informs this book.

However, there are few research programmes that explicitly set out to determine the merits of this relatively new approach for interrogating, understanding and explaining empirical examples of public administration and management, in order to identify patterns arising from (or specific to) the complex nature of tasks and relationships inherent in these organizational phenomena and to develop hypotheses for theory and practice.

The research programme engaged in by a team of researchers from Northern Ireland and the Republic of Ireland set out to do this very thing. The authors apply a CAS framework to a series of case studies in public sector management in Ireland to generate new insights into the issues, processes and participants in public service domains. The case studies were carefully chosen to allow for analysis across similar cases as well as to highlight how varying circumstances and/or specific policy and practice choices might influence participant behaviour and/or system outcomes. Urban regeneration and information systems development in healthcare settings were the two public management challenges chosen for this study because of the broad interest these activities generate, the different organizational levels and range of participants involved, the highly differentiated objectives between the two areas and the existence of multiple cases that could be examined. Furthermore, cases were selected from the two governmental jurisdictions in Ireland, the Republic of Ireland in the south and the UK region of Northern Ireland, which provided data on subtle political and historical differences that proved useful in identifying how different social and political contexts do or do not influence participant behaviour and outcomes. This book is the result of research into these two separate domains of activity undertaken in Ireland between January 2004 and June 2007.

The original objectives of the research were:

To contribute to the understanding of factors that enable more effective public service decision making;

and

To apply a complexity 'lens' to the analysis of public service cases in order to achieve the first objective.

Initially, the researchers left open the question of selecting among the various complexity frameworks to apply to the case data, but as the research progressed it became clear that a CAS framework fit the data and also facilitated analysis and discussion of issues with practitioners, policy-makers and academics. In the following chapter, the section 'Complex Adaptive Systems Framework' sets out the specifics of this framework.

Following this introduction, Chapter 1 sets out the basic research objectives, research framework, context and case data upon which the rest of the book is based. Chapters 2 and 3 apply the CAS framework to the cases to demonstrate how these two policy domains may be perceived as consisting of the basic elements of CAS, namely system, environmental factors, environmental rules, agents, processes and outcomes. Chapter 4 brings this analysis together to argue that a CAS perspective is relevant to public administration activity and that theory and practice can benefit from the CAS perspective. Part II of the book (Chapters 5 to 9) develops this argument through a detailed exploration of the CAS dynamics present in the case studies in the context of issues of current relevance to public managers and academics. These include issues of boundary-setting, stakeholder involvement, role of the private sector and tensions between 'core' and 'locale' in public policy and implementation. Part II concludes, in Chapter 9, with the key findings and a reflection of the value of applying a complexity lens to the selected public service domains.

1 Setting the Stage for a CAS Analysis

In this chapter, the research approach and projects studied are described in order to set the stage for the subsequent analyses of Part I and Part II of this book. The first two sections cover the research approach with particular attention on the elements of the research framework, i.e., complex adaptive systems (CAS). Sections 3 and 4 provide an overview of the projects studied and the relevant context(s) in the two jurisdictions of Ireland in which the research took place.

RESEARCH APPROACH

The research approach adopted was a comparative case study of decision-making in a particular policy domain (Eisenhardt 1989, Yin 1993, Yin 2002, Barzelay *et al.* 2003, Carlile and Christensen 2006). Eisenhardt provided an outline of the basic steps to be followed for case-based theory building, while Barzelay *et al.* provided useful conceptual guidance for case studies in public policy—in particular the concept of 'social mechanisms' that inform decisions being made. Examples of social mechanisms include the attribution of past success or failure to particular decisions, rules, institutions and/or public perceptions. These considerations informed the interview and survey guidelines and the generation and analysis of case material. Yin's rich vein of methodological research, classification and examples of case studies was helpful in clarifying the specific details of the research across Eisenhardt's eight steps (detailed below), and Carlile and Christensen provided the starting point for the general question to be explored and the relevant constructs. Their succinct statement of the central question to be explored in any management research, i.e., 'what actions by managers [actors] will lead to the results they seek, given the circumstances in which they find themselves?' (Carlile and Christensen 2006: 4) provided the basic categories to be analyzed in each case over the course of the research project. The four categories were actors, actions, circumstances and outcomes.

It must be acknowledged that none of the approaches above was designed with a complexity framework in mind and the initial case data collection process did not incorporate a CAS framework into the data collection protocols. The CAS framework ultimately used to interpret the case data was developed by the authors over the course of the research, as the literature on complexity in the social sciences in general and public policy and administration in particular developed and matured. In essence, the development of the CAS framework was a separate, but overlapping, research exercise, which informed the analysis steps of the case research, and which was enhanced by this and other research activities undertaken in parallel. The specific elements of the research process are summarized below—organized as per Eisenhardt's eight steps of theory-building case research.

1. Define the Question

Carlile and Christensen's (2006) statement of the central question in management provided the basic question and constructs of actions, actors, circumstances and outcomes to be described in the case studies. Barzelay *et al.* (2003) contributed the concept of social mechanisms in public administration by which actors attribute success or failure (in terms of outcomes) to particular actions, actors or circumstances.

2. Select the Cases

The selection of cases was a structured process based on Yin's (2002) advice for undertaking comparative case study research. Cases were chosen to represent a range of public management activity using criteria developed by the project team including: (a) political jurisdiction (Dublin/Belfast); (b) organizational 'level' (intra- versus inter-organizational); (c) stage in the project lifecycle (beginning, middle, end), (d) the range of agents involved; and (e) the size of the projects. The purpose of using these criteria to select projects was to highlight key features of agent behaviour under different conditions and at different points in time.

3. Use Multiple Data Collection Methods and Different Researchers, if Possible

Several different strategies were employed to ensure that different types of data, as well as diverse perspectives, were used in the research. Firstly, practitioners' perspectives were gathered using different approaches: for the inter-organizational (urban regeneration) domain, a research advisory group was created, drawn from practitioners and academics with expertise in one or more of the main organizational sub-sectors (the private sector, the non-profit sector, the public sector, the community sector and the policy sector[1]). In the intra-organizational analysis (healthcare information systems) different perspectives were captured by targeting interviewees from different functional areas. Secondly, a range of social science disciplines was represented in the research team, which included researchers from social policy, economics, strategy, organizational theory and sociology. Finally, in addition to the case study protocol, a mail survey of decision-makers in approximately 400 different organizations was used to gather further information on the factors that influence strategic decisions.

4. Overlap Data Collection and Analysis

Semi-structured interviews were conducted with project participants representing the various constituencies involved in the projects and documents relating to the projects were reviewed. 48 interviews were conducted, with approximately 60 per cent being in urban regeneration and 40 per cent in healthcare/information technology (IT). These interviews spanned 12 cases, six each in the two policy domains.

Interviews and case studies were written up by different researchers and both were sent back to interviewees for their review and commentary. In the cases of interviews, over half of all interviewees provided feedback, including corrections and further explanations. Urban Regeneration data collection and analysis were completed, and findings were presented at conferences and written up in academic journals to generate additional critique and to refine the analysis approach for the healthcare information systems research.

5. Perform Within- and Cross-Case Analyses

The case analyses were undertaken with two goals in mind. The first was to assess whether and to what extent the cases conformed to a CAS model— i.e., could these activities be viewed as complex adaptive systems in a consistent manner across projects and domains. Secondly, the case narratives were interrogated by researchers with different backgrounds to determine if there was evidence of the system dynamics inherent in CAS, i.e., path-dependency, adaptation, emergence and bifurcation.

The within- and cross-case analyses produced by the research team were reviewed with the advisory group in the case of Urban Regeneration and with the other researchers and selected experts in the field in the case of healthcare information systems.

6. Shape Hypotheses through Iterative Analysis, Search for Evidence of the 'Why' Behind the 'What'

The hypothesis that projects in public administration that take the form of projects may be perceived as complex adaptive systems was shaped and tested through the case analyses and the multiple reviews by the research team, interviewees, members of the advisory group, conference participants and journal referees. Confirmation and critique were both incorporated into the developing theory. Patterns of CAS dynamics identified by different researchers were written up and reviewed by other members of the research team.

7. Compare with Literature—Search for Conflicting Hypotheses/Tests

The emerging hypothesis that public administration activities that take the form of projects may be perceived as complex adaptive systems was developed and challenged through a comparison with literature on complexity and complex systems, as well as to historical literature on and critiques of systems theory and public administration. In addition, the classification of systems elements in the cases were informed by theory from a range of disciplines including housing, healthcare, organizational theory, strategy, information systems management, economics, sociology and political science.

8. Closure Comes When Marginal Improvement from Next Case Becomes Small

Twelve cases were carefully selected to represent a range of public administrative activity and contexts—while at the same time maintain some ability to compare the cases as examples of a distinct phenomenon. Through the process described above, the case for CAS as a viable analytic framework on which to base governance theory for public administration was constructed. This characterization of public administration as CAS has undergone extended and rigorous review by practitioners and academics in numerous forums. Additional research is advised to explore in more detail the dynamic properties of these systems, but this will require a different approach to research.

THE COMPLEX ADAPTIVE SYSTEMS (CAS) FRAMEWORK

The CAS framework presented in this section was developed in parallel with the research described above, although the two theory-building activities merged into an integrated effort over the second half of the project. At the outset, the authors considered several potential frameworks for tackling complexity in public management (Lynn *et al.* 2000, Barzelay *et al.* 2003, Haynes 2003, Koppenjan and Klijn 2004), but in the end, the complex adaptive systems framework was selected as being most promising. The use of complexity theory in the social sciences has been developing over the last decade and there are numerous special issues of journals across the spectrum of social sciences dedicated to this topic (*Organization Science* 1999 vol. 10: 3, *Population and Environment* 2000, vol. 22: 2; *Public Administration*

Quarterly 2005 vol. 29: 3; *Public Management Review* 2008 vol. 10: 2). Among the many different disciplines developing theories of complexity for their area(s) of interest, a common objective lies in understanding systems that consist of agents whose interactions result in self-organization, adaptation, path-dependency, emergence and bifurcation. These latter properties distinguish a CAS from other types of system and these were evident in the cases studied. The second half of this book explores the nature of these properties in detail and seeks to demonstrate the relevance of this framework to the development of public administration theory and practice.

In their simplest form, CAS models seek to identify those agents in a system that act and interact in the pursuit of their individual or collective objectives, and to study how agent behaviour and the interdependencies among agents result in systemic outcomes (Anderson 1999). In truth, a CAS model will look very much like the open systems models developed decades ago and applied to a wide range of natural and social systems with mixed results. Like these earlier models, a CAS model will incorporate feedback from the system's environment as well as from the outcomes created by the actions of the agents within the system itself. Figure 1.1 is the original CAS model used by the research team and based on work by several researchers in organizational complexity such as Kauffman (1993), Holland (1998), Anderson (1999), and Stacey (2001). This simple framework informed the preliminary exploration of the cases and was used in several early articles and conference papers on the urban regeneration domain (Rhodes and MacKechnie 2003, Rhodes and Haynes 2004, Rhodes 2005, Rhodes and Murray 2007, Rhodes 2008).

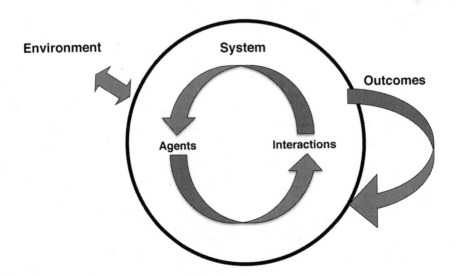

Figure 1.1   General CAS modelling framework.

However, as the research progressed and other academics explored the application of complexity theory to social phenomena, the CAS model was enhanced to incorporate relevant details proposed and observed in the field of public management and to address concerns raised by other academics at conferences and in journal article reviews. The principal impact of these enhancements was on the concepts of the 'environment' and 'interactions'. The environment was the more complicated area of enhancement as the different component elements of 'rules' and 'factors', along with the important distinction between the exogenous and endogenous environment became apparent. Koppenjan and Klijn's (2004) discussion of rules in public sector networks was particularly helpful in clarifying what constituted rules, as was Scott's (1995) more general typology—although the importance of 'rules' in human complex systems models was clearly stated by Holland (1995, 1998). The difference between the exogenous and endogenous environments is also related to Holland's– as well as Gell-Mann's (1994)—characterization of human complex adaptive systems in their description of how agents go about interpreting their environment through a process of schema-building. In addition, research by colleagues and others in public administration and housing further suggested that 'perceptions' formed by agents in interpreting their environment and in interacting with each other are what drives action and outcomes. As the research evolved, the concept of a single, albeit multifaceted, environment morphed into a more nuanced concept of an (endogenous) environment within an (exogenous) environment (see Figure 1.2). The endogenous environment is created by the schema-building agents acting and interacting within the system and, as we shall see in the following chapters, creating their own shared *and* contested representation of factors and rules that influence decisions.

The modification made to the concept of 'interactions' was far simpler, driven by the impossibility of cataloguing all of the possible interactions among agents within the cases studied. In reviewing the developing literature over the course of the project, it was clear that the potential range of interactions of interest was not narrowing, but was expanding as researchers from different disciplinary backgrounds brought their own conceptual frameworks and interests to the CAS table. As the members of the research team came from different disciplinary backgrounds themselves, there was little appetite for narrowing the scope of potential interactions of interest, but there was still a need to bring some structure to the analysis of the cases. In the end, the team agreed to shift from the concept of 'interactions' to that of 'processes' for the purpose of analyzing the cases. Processes—defined as a related collection of actions and interactions perceived by actors as leading to an outcome—encompass the concept of interactions, but focused the attention of the researchers on those interactions that related to the business at hand, namely the pursuit of individual and collective objectives through the agents' participation in

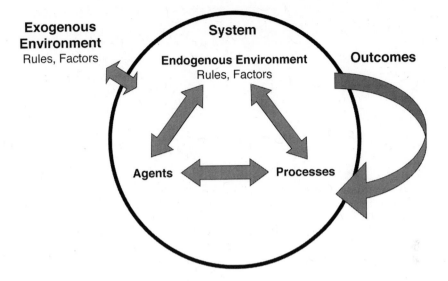

Figure 1.2   Core systems elements underpinning a CAS analysis.

the project. As the cases were analyzed, patterns of interactions among agents within and across processes were identified, as were patterns of individual actions across agents and projects. Figure 1.2 shows the resulting basic systems framework ultimately used to analyze the cases as CAS, and the figure is followed by definitions of the six basic CAS elements. It is this framework that is used to organize the analyses of urban regeneration and healthcare information systems presented in the following chapters.

Definitions of the Six Core CAS Elements

1. System

The definition of the 'system', as distinct from the definition of its component parts, is principally concerned with the nature of the boundaries that separate the system from its environment. In systems theory, this would generally be referred to as the 'scope' of the system. In public management systems, these boundaries generally take the form of policy domains (e.g. housing, healthcare, transport, etc.), geographic boundaries and/or participant stakeholders. In addition, with respect to public administration projects like those studied here, there are generally boundaries having to do with time and cost. This conceptualization of the system is very close to the concept of 'arena' defined as 'the place or filed where actors meet and play their [policy] game' (Koppenjan and Klijn, 2004: 50).

2. Environmental Factors

Environmental features are those features of the environment that affect the behaviour of the agents and the outcomes of the system. Note that the *exogenous* environment (that which exists outside of the scope of the system) may be described by any number of features, and we have used the 'PESTEL' framework from management strategy as a guideline for the analysis. However, these factors may or may not feature in agents' decision-making (in spite of the fact that these factors ultimately do influence outcomes) and so there is a need to distinguish the exogenous environment from the *endogenous* environment. The latter includes only those factors that participating agents perceive as important to their decision-making. Furthermore, there may be additional factors to those found in the exogenous environment that affect decision-making, such as the level of competition or cooperation between agents and/or characteristics of the agent themselves such as leadership capacity, access to resources and organizational structure.

3. Environmental Rules

Rules are the laws, codes, assumptions and norms that govern how agents behave. A well known typology of rules is Scott's (1995) list of cognitive, normative and regulative rules, which addresses the degree to which the rules are explicitly stated and subject to shared understanding. However, this classification was difficult to use effectively in analyzing the cases. A more practical lens with which to observe rules in practice was described by Kopenjan and Klijn (2004) who suggested two main types of rules in public administration networks: 'interaction rules', including who can participate and how they can or must interact in particular policy arenas; and 'arena rules', which establish the nature of the policy game that will be played out in the arena. In the case of the public management projects studied during this research process, the Kopenjan and Klijn classification provided the basic typology, but within each of their categories, two subcategories were identified. Under the 'interaction rules', those rules regarding which agents could or should participate were distinguished from those relating to the processes (actions and interactions) in which they could undertake. Under 'arena rules' a differentiation was made between rules relating to the benefits and costs of actions ('payoffs') and rules about the time or place in which actions were expected to be undertaken. Hence, four categories of rules were used to analyze the cases: Agents; Processes; Payoffs; and Time/place.

4. Agents

Agents are individuals representing themselves, or a group of which they are a part, who are engaged in processes *within the scope of the system* to accomplish individual or joint objectives. In the case of healthcare information systems projects, agents consisted of individuals representing functional groups, including clinical, managerial, technical specialists and consultants. In the case of urban regeneration, the agents were individuals representing organizations, and included firms, non-profit agencies, public sector agencies and community groups.

5. Processes

Processes are a related collection of actions and interactions among agents perceived by these agents to be purposeful—i.e. leading to a desired outcome. It is the processes engaged in by agents that connect their behaviour (constrained or facilitated by rules and the environment) with the outcomes of the system.

6. Outcomes

Outcomes are the 'results' or 'impact' of the system as understood by the agents participating in the system. Here we are following Pollitt and Bouckaert's (2004) definition of outcomes, and their distinction between outputs and outcomes. Outputs are the products of processes engaged in by actors, while outcomes are the 'results' or 'impacts' of those outputs on the environment in which the agents are acting. As an example, an output is the production of new houses, while an outcome is the impact of this housing on standards of living, levels of homelessness, house prices etc. It must be noted, however, that the feedback loop indicated in Figure 1.2 is far more complicated in practice than it appears, as agents respond to and measure themselves against outputs (and even process objectives) as much as, or more than, to outcomes.

The six elements defined above represent only the basic requirements for a phenomenon to be interpreted as a CAS framework. The six core elements (system, environmental factors, environmental rules, agents, processes and outcomes) are features of any number of open systems frameworks, so their presence is a necessary, but not sufficient indicator of CAS behaviour. In order for a phenomenon to be characterized as CAS, there must also be evidence of the unique dynamics of complex systems, i.e. self-organization, adaptation, path-dependency, emergence and bifurcation. These dynamics are what make complex systems models so interesting to social scientists, as they have been observable for some time in studies of human behaviour but, until recently, have been difficult to link to any coherent framework that would provide the basis for testable theory. Developments in complexity science and modelling capacity have supported a groundswell of activity with researchers at the Santa Fe Institute acting as a focal point and dissemination agent in this area. The definitions of each of these dynamic characteristics of CAS is provided below, along with additional references relating to these concepts for the reader who wishes to explore the underlying theory in more depth. The definitions are drawn from work by researchers associated with the Santa Fe Institute along with other well known academics writing in this area. The evidence of these dynamics in the cases studied, and their implications for public management theory and practice, are what occupies the second part of this book.

Dynamics of CAS

Self-organization is at the core of complex adaptive systems and refers to the ability of systems to emerge spontaneously from the interaction of agents following their own 'local' rules and responding to feedback from other agents and their environment (Kauffman 1993, 1995). The interaction of these agents over time results in patterns and regularity (rule-based behaviour) without the intervention of a central controller. 'A defining feature of complexity is that self-organization is a natural consequence of interactions between simple agents' (Anderson 1999: 222).

Adaptation is defined as the changes made by agents in response to the actions of other participants, environmental conditions or emergent systems characteristics and is generally conceived of as a feature of goal-seeking behaviour of agents in a complex adaptive system (Kauffman 1993, Holland 1995). There are several different mechanisms by which agents can adapt, one of the most popular of which is based in evolutionary theory and typified by Beinhocker's (2007) phrase: 'differentiate, select, amplify'. Whatever the mechanism, the ability of agents to adapt to each other and to changes in the environment is a fundamental aspect of CAS theory

Emergence at its simplest is the creation of new properties (Emmeche *et al.* 1997), that is, properties that could not be predicted based on the antecedent actions or component elements of the phenomena that led to or comprise the resulting (emergent) phenomenon. Emergence also implies properties that are at a higher level of abstraction than the antecedent actions and/or elements (de Wolf and Holvoet 2005); for example, the emergent properties of housing markets arising from the buying and selling of houses over time. Finally, the emergent phenomena identified in this book are consistent with Holland's (1998) definition of emergence in that they are recurring, although not necessarily predictable, patterns across multiple instances of the system examined and 'involve patterns of interaction that persist despite a continual turnover of the constituents' (Holland 1998: 7).

Path-dependency refers to the tendency for systems to lock into a particular set of behaviours and/or outcomes early on in their lifecycle due to conditions in the environment and/or the nature of the agents and their early interactions. Furthermore, complex adaptive systems are characterized by their sensitivity to initial conditions (Prigogine 1997), which are the specific characteristics of the environment and/or the agent-participants at the time of the system's start-up. In the case of organizational systems, the relationship between initial conditions and path-dependency may be understood as a dynamic of organizational contingency theory (Donaldson 2001).

Bifurcation is a dynamic associated with dissipative structures theory (Prigogine and Stengers 1984, Prigogine 1997). Dissipative structures are phenomena that maintain their existence through the constant input of energy from their environment, existing in a kind of semi-equilibrium state, importing energy to maintain their shape for a while but then suddenly collapsing into disorder before reaching a 'bifurcation point', after which a new form is adopted and becomes the new equilibrium state of the system. The new structure of the system cannot be predicted from the previous state, but is created through spontaneous self-organization of the elements that make up the phenomenon. Models of dissipative structures are most often applied in the natural sciences, although the concept of 'punctuated equilibrium' in organizational change (Romanelli and Tushman 1994) is similar to the ideas of Prigogine.

The dynamic properties of CAS as they appeared in the cases are examined in Part II of this book.

IRISH CONTEXT FOR PUBLIC ADMINISTRATION PROJECTS

The first two sections of this chapter covered the research objectives and approach underpinning the analysis presented in this book. The next two sections will provide the context for and overview of the cases analyzed. This section provides an overview of the Irish context and compares the two jurisdictions (the Republic of Ireland and Northern Ireland) on several dimensions. Drawing on Pollitt and Bouckaert's (2004) framework for analyzing the context for public management reform, we present the information under three headings: history and politics; socio-economic forces; and governance/administrative structures.

History and Politics

The two Irish jurisdictions were formed in 1921, when the island of Ireland was partitioned as a result of the Government of Ireland Act 1920. Twenty-six of the 32 counties became a British dominion, the Irish Free State, in 1922, and an independent Republic of Ireland in 1949. The other six counties remained as an integral part of the United Kingdom. Since 1921, the Free State/Republic has been governed peacefully, with minor constitutional amendments over the years (Gallagher 1999) but following the basic model of an *Oireachtas* (Parliament) consisting of an elected *Dáil Éireann*, a selected *Seanad*, and an elected President. The Irish Constitution, *Bunreacht na hÉireann*, dates from 1937, and has the unusual feature that every constitutional amendment requires the consent of the people, which has always been by referendum (Gallagher 1999).

In 1973, both the Republic of Ireland and the United Kingdom, including Northern Ireland, joined the European Economic Community, now the European Union (EU). The subsequent partnership ethos of the EU was to have a particular impact on the governance of the Irish Republic, through the development of the concept of social partnership, which was established in 1987 and has survived ever since. The structure consists of a series of economic and social policy agreements between the private sector, trades unions, the agriculture sector and the community and voluntary sector 'pillars'. Social partnership has established a tradition of problem solving which has also been applied at local level (Walsh 2001) and contributed to economic growth through controlling wages and achieving legitimization of government policies (Kirby 2004). Although well thought of in many quarters, the structure has been subject to some criticism (Meade 2005) and has recently faltered under the pressure of the economic crisis in Ireland.

After Partition, the six Northern counties became known as Northern Ireland and remained part of the UK along with England, Scotland and Wales (Great Britain). As is widely known, the governance arrangements for Northern Ireland have been problematic ever since, and the continuing theme of contested territory was important for this research. Northern Ireland was ruled by its own Parliament, dominated by unionist politicians, until 1972. During this time, legislation prevented Westminster's House of Commons from debating matters within the competence of the Northern Ireland Government, a convention that was not challenged until the 1960s. Between 1972 and 1998 Northern Ireland was governed from Westminster against the backdrop of the 'Troubles', in which over 3,000 people died. It is notable that this violent and prolonged expression of territorial conflict affected the Irish Republic in different and less divisive ways, although the Irish Republic's politicians worked with their Northern Ireland and British counterparts over the years to try to bring about a solution.

Following the signing of the Good Friday Agreement in 1998, widely perceived as the beginning of the end of the 'Troubles', the Northern Ireland Act 1998 made provision for Northern Ireland to have its own elected assembly with a wide range of devolved powers, under a more comprehensive UK devolution settlement which also included a Scottish Parliament and a Welsh Assembly. However, the political process in Northern Ireland did not run smoothly after this, and the Northern Ireland Assembly and Executive was suspended between October 2002 and May 2007, i.e. for most of the period covered by this research. During this time, responsibility reverted to a team of Northern Ireland Ministers and a Secretary of State, reporting to the Westminster Parliament. There was no large-scale return to violence during suspension, although local conflict and territorial divisions remained. In contrast, the historic division between Protestant and Roman Catholic across the island had little significance in the Republic of Ireland by the end of the twentieth century.

The conflict and divisions in Northern Ireland referred to above require further explanation, as they were an important aspect of the urban regeneration case studies and also affected the healthcare information systems environment, although to a lesser degree. There was no equivalent set of issues in the Irish Republic; indeed, the scale and intensity of the Northern Ireland conflict are rare across the world.

The deep divisions between Protestant and Roman Catholic communities in the north-western part of Ireland date from the mid-eighteenth century, well before Partition. Over the years, religious background has remained the key, signifying feature of the conflict, supplemented by a number of other distinguishing characteristics such as area of residence, school attended, sports followed, national identification (British or Irish) and political party supported. Conflict did not end with the signing of the Good Friday Agreement although the nature of the conflict changed—at the time of the research, low level violence in areas of contested space known as 'interfaces' continued, along with the continued existence of 'peace' walls to separate adjacent Protestant and Catholic communities, and domination of some working-class areas by paramilitary groups officially on ceasefire (Jarman 2004, Shirlow and Murtagh 2006). These overt features of conflict are found in the poorer areas of Northern Ireland, and particularly in Belfast; middle-class divisions are more subtle.

Residential segregation has been identified in Belfast since the 1880s (Boal 1995). It has been particularly marked in social housing, both in Northern Ireland as a whole (Northern Ireland Housing Executive 1999) and especially in Belfast, where 91 per cent of Housing Executive estates contained more than 80 per cent of either Protestant or Catholic households (Shuttleworth and Lloyd 2008). There has been a reluctance to concede territory to the 'other side'—and recently, in some areas, to minority ethnic groups—and areas are marked by painted kerbstones, militaristic or historical murals on house gable ends and flying of national and paramilitary flags. The implications of such stark and severe territorial boundaries are important for social housing allocations policy and for the allocation of urban regeneration funds. The alienation of Protestant working-class communities from the State, identified from the 1980s onwards (Finlay 2001), provides an additional important contextual factor in two of the urban regeneration case studies. The acknowledged problems of additional deprivation and lack of access to services in communities living in interface areas (Shirlow 2001, Murtagh 2002) have led to duplication and inefficient use of services, with an estimated additional cost of £1.5bn annually (Deloitte 2007).

Finally, the 'Troubles' and continuing sectarian conflict had a direct impact on the mental and physical health of Northern Ireland's population (O'Reilly and Browne 2001, Jordan *et al.* 2006), with people in poor areas affected regardless of religious affiliation (Campbell 2003). For example, those affected by the 'Troubles' were almost twice as likely to experience mental health problems (34 per cent) than those who were not (18 per cent) (NISRA 2002). The, already high, rate of 16.3 suicides per 100,000 in 1996 increased to 23.4 in 2005 (Northern Ireland Statistics and Research Agency 2005).

Socio-Economic Forces

The socio-economic contexts of the two jurisdictions also differed widely. In the Irish Republic, the research took place against the background of the 'Celtic Tiger' economic growth of the 1990s to mid-2000s, based on knowledge-intensive industries such as information technology and pharmaceuticals (Kirby 2002). In 1995, the Irish Republic's gross domestic product (GDP) was 12 per cent below the Organization for Economic Cooperation and Development (OECD) average and by 2003 it was 22 per cent above (Nolan and Maître 2007). Significant changes in *per capita* GDP in the Republic of Ireland were recorded at this time (Table 1.1). Unemployment decreased considerably in the late 1990s and remained at around 4.4 per cent (International Labour Organization (ILO)[2]) during 2004–2007. Northern Ireland's GDP was adversely affected by the 'Troubles' in terms of private investment, but cushioned against peaks and troughs by a high level of subsidy for public services (Considine and O'Leary 1999). During the research period, GDP *per capita* increases were around half that of the Irish Republic, although the gap was closing by 2007, as evidenced in Table 1.1 (First Trust, 2005, 2006, 2008); although employment lagged in Northern Ireland, after 2002, unemployment was roughly the same in both jurisdictions, Table 1.2 (CSO 2003, 2008).

In spite of the difference in economic performance, poverty and social exclusion have been key issues in both jurisdictions. Along with the specific urban regeneration, housing and health policies to be discussed in subsequent chapters, both jurisdictions had strong policy commitments to tackling poverty and policies to address social exclusion more generally.

A comparison of four of the EU's Laeken indicators[3] on poverty and inequality in Table 1.3 show that the two Irish societies are broadly similar on income inequality. Northern Ireland has a greater proportion of jobless households, with the difference between the two jurisdictions being particularly striking in the case of adults. It is also notable that the highest EU ranking is at just over the halfway mark, indicating a comparatively poor performance in both cases.

There is a general acknowledgement that the Northern Ireland 'Troubles' exacerbated long-term unemployment, economic inactivity, social isolation and poverty (Department of Health, Social Services and Public Safety (DHSSPS) 2004), thus contributing to social exclusion. The verdict on the impact of the Irish Republic's 'Celtic Tiger' economic growth is more mixed, with some expressions of concern being raised about increasing poverty and social divisions (Kirby 2002 and Kirby 2004); whereas Whelan *et*

Table 1.1   Percentage per capita Gross Domestic Product Increases 1998 and 2004–2007, Republic of Ireland and Northern Ireland

	1998	2004	2005	2006	2007
Republic of Ireland	10.8%	4.5%	4.7%	5.7%	5.3%
Northern Ireland	1.8%	2.8%	2%	2.5%	3%

Source: Gottheil (2003), First Trust (2005, 2006, 2008).

Table 1.2   Unemployment rates, Republic of Ireland and Northern Ireland, 1998–2006

	1998	2000	2002	2004	2006
Republic of Ireland	7.8%	4.3%	4.2%	4.5%	4.5%
Northern Ireland	7.1%	7.0%	5.5%	4.8%	4.4%

Source: Central Statistics Office, ROI 'Ireland North and South: A Statistical Profile' 2003, 2008.

Table 1.3   Poverty and Inequality in the Two Jurisdictions and Comparisons within the EU, 2004

Laeken Indicator	RoI	NI	ROI position in EU [†]	NI-position in EU
Percentage at risk of poverty[*]	21%	20%	22nd	20th
Income inequality ratio [§]	5%	5.4%	15th	19th
Percentage in jobless households (aged under 18)	12%	18%	19th	24th
Percentage in jobless households (aged 18–59)	8%	14%	12th	23rd

Source: Kenway et al. (2006); data relates to 2004.
Notes:
[*] 'At risk of poverty' defined as individuals with an income below 60 per cent of the median income.
[§] The ratio is that of the top 20 per cent share of income divided by the bottom 20 per cent.
[†] The ranking is out of 25, representing membership in 2004.

al. (2006) argue that inequality became no worse, presenting evidence that the poorest in society did benefit from economic growth.

The economy and culture of both jurisdictions were affected by other international influences and by the globalized economy. Aspects of globalization include: domination of international financial markets; importance of the knowledge economy; ease of transnational communication through technological innovation; corporations operating on a global scale; transnational state organizations such as the EU and the G7; common global cultural flows; and new geographies including reduced importance of national boundaries.

In the two Irish economies, globalization occurred through governments attracting foreign direct investment (FDI) in a way that embedded multinational firms into the local economy, and by integrating local firms into global markets (Ó Riain 2000). At the time of the research, this process was further advanced in the Irish Republic as it has been held back in the North due to the 'Troubles' (Kirby 2002). Investment from the United States was important in the 'Celtic Tiger' economic boom (Gottheil 2003), and has also been crucial in Northern Ireland. The Irish Republic scores highly on the AT Kearney Globalization Index, which measures economic flows, technological capacity, political engagement and worldwide personal contacts; for example, in 2005 Ireland was ranked second (behind Singapore) whereas the UK, including Northern Ireland, was twelfth. In the North, the state-funded InvestNI (http://www.investni.com/) claimed some success in attracting multi-national companies to the province, and some local firms were doing well in accessing global markets (Cooke *et al.* 2003).

Governance and Administrative Structures

While there were significant differences in the overall political contexts of the two jurisdictions, the basic governance structures had many similarities. The single transferable voting system, proportional representation, operating in the Republic of Ireland, and in local elections in Northern Ireland, is widely seen as resulting in high level political involvement in quite low level, local issues –as well as political 'clientelism'.[4] Furthermore, the administrative infrastructure in both jurisdictions followed the basic template of the British Civil Service, whose role is to provide advice to ministers and to implement policy decisions. In both jurisdictions, the period of the research saw a rise in the number and influence of special advisors and consultants to the government and 'the use of partisan political advisors is now firmly entrenched'[5] (Pollitt and Bouckaert 2004: 294). Local government in both jurisdictions is relatively weak in relation to central government, partly due to the nature of the voting/political system, but also due to legislation specifically restricting the role of local government in favour of implementing agencies that are independent (but government-funded) or report directly to central government departments. This was particularly true in the case of housing in Northern Ireland and healthcare in both jurisdictions.

EU membership has had a profound influence in both jurisdictions, primarily, perhaps, in the Irish Republic. Here, changes have included the introduction of a regional tier of government and new planning processes such as the National Development Plan, linked to the social partnership processes described in the earlier section on governance. Anti-poverty and social exclusion policies were greatly influenced by EU agreements, as were equality polices. The EU provided both jurisdictions with a large export market and a flexible labour force from other EU countries. EU funding and policies have been important in both urban regeneration and healthcare policy areas, with funding more important for urban regeneration and policies (including information systems and data protection) more important for healthcare.

For urban regeneration, funding was available for programmes to tackle social exclusion under the Structural Funds from 1998 onwards (Ó Riain 2000), such as the URBAN and INTERREG programmes in both jurisdictions, and Area Partnerships in the Irish Republic (Walsh 2001). The additional PEACE programmes (Special Support Programmes for Peace and Reconciliation) ran from 1994 onwards in Northern Ireland and the border counties of the Irish Republic (Hughes *et al.* 1998). The objectives of the PEACE programmes were: 'to promote the social inclusion of those at the margins of economic and social life; [and] to exploit the opportunities and address the needs arising from the peace process in order to boost economic growth and stimulate social and economic regeneration' (Greer 2001: 73). The programmes included a requirement for partnership governance arrangements (Geddes and Bennington 2001).

The principle of partnership governance was to prove particularly influential in the Irish Republic at both the local and national level, but local partnership structures were also introduced in Northern Ireland (Hughes *et al.* 1998). Urban regeneration and planning policy in both jurisdictions were contextualized and influenced by the advisory European Spatial Development Perspective, which in 1999 agreed to three objectives for planning policy: 'economic and social cohesion; conservation of natural resources and cultural heritage; and more balanced competitiveness of the European territory' (Commission of the European Communities (CEC) 1999: 10). The EU's Charter of Fundamental Rights includes the right to 'housing assistance' (CEC 2000, Article 34).

For health and healthcare systems, there has been a small amount of cross-border project funding (Clarke 2007), but the primary influence of the EU has been in policy terms. Access to healthcare services has long been viewed as a shared value among member states and is included in the Charter of Fundamental Rights (CEC 2000: Article 35). Perhaps the most visible health-related policy has been the ban on smoking in public places, which came into effect in March 2004 in the Irish Republic and in April 2007 in Northern Ireland.

The White Paper *Together for Health* set out principles for member states' activity on healthcare, recognized the importance of new technologies in healthcare and made a commitment to supporting innovation in healthcare systems. A system of European Community Health Indicators 'with common mechanisms for collection of comparable health data' was also proposed (CEC, 2007: 4). The EU's support of the eHealth Project in 2007 was in line with this larger strategy. The project developed a database of key national eHealth policy documents, a database of key national contact points for eHealth research and technology development and it produced several extended reports about current eHealth issues including one on Ireland (Ryan *et al.* 2007). The Charter of Fundamental Rights includes stipulations on the protection of personal data (CEC 2000: Article 8), and an EU Directive on Data Protection (95/46/EC) also influenced the data protection policies of the two jurisdictions. The development of cross-border markets in healthcare, and successful legal challenges to refusals by states to allow citizens to take up care in an EU member state (Rich and Merrick 2006) have implications for data sharing, common information systems and data protection.

PROJECT SUMMARIES

As discussed in the beginning of this chapter, the research strategy was to choose a number of projects in each jurisdiction for the two policy domains that displayed a specific set of different characteristics to facilitate comparison and analyses. In both jurisdictions three projects were chosen, each in different stages of development roughly corresponding to beginning, middle and end. In addition, projects were selected to represent large, medium and small projects and the research group sought to find projects that differed along a continuum of complexity in terms of the number and type of actors involved. In the case of the intra-organizational projects in healthcare information systems, large projects were those with national scope, medium projects had regional or multi-organizational scope and small projects addressed only the organization's requirements. In all but one case, however, the project was being managed out of one organization.

The projects chosen are listed in Table 1.4 with their classification in each of the three variables indicated, followed by a brief description of each project.

Urban Regeneration Projects

Northern Ireland– Clonard/*Cluain Mór*: The Clonard/*Cluain Mór* project is the largest of the Northern Ireland urban regeneration projects studied and also represents a completed project in this study. The Clonard area of West Belfast was targeted for redevelopment by the Northern Ireland Housing Executive (NIHE) after the publication of the first *Making Belfast Work* (MBW) strategy[6] in 1988 as it had long been an area of significant economic and social deprivation as well as civil unrest, including the infamous Bombay Street incident, in which the houses along Catholic Bombay Street had been burned to the ground by Protestants following sectarian clashes and rioting in 1969. The targeted area consisted of 650 'kitchen' or 'parlour' houses—terraced houses with two rooms on each of two floors. The area was (and continues to be) largely Catholic and Nationalist, with

Table 1.4   Projects Studied and Their Characteristics—All

Urban Regeneration			
	Size	Stage	Complexity
Republic of Ireland: Dublin			
Ballymun	Large	Middle	High
Fatima Mansions	Medium/Large	Beginning	Medium
Hardwicke Street	Small	End	Low
Northern Ireland: Belfast			
Clonard/*Cluain Mór*	Large	End	Medium
Connswater	Medium	Middle	Low
Roden Street/Greater Village	Small	Beginning	High

Healthcare Information Systems			
	Size	Stage	Complexity
Republic of Ireland: Dublin			
Electronic Health Record (EHR)	Large	Beginning	High
HealthLink	Medium/Large	Middle	Low
Order Communication System (OCS)	Small	End	Medium
Northern Ireland: Belfast			
Electronic Prescribing and Eligibility System (EPES)	Large	Beginning	High
Regional Acquired Brain Injury Unit (RABIU)	Medium	End	Low
Theatre Management System (TMS)	Small	Middle	Medium

*Note that this case study followed the development of a pilot of the system in a single hospital. This was part of a much larger project to roll out theatre management systems across all acute hospitals in Northern Ireland.

a tight-knit community and strong voluntary and community organizations and at the time prior to regeneration was nearly 100 per cent owner occupied.

Upon hearing rumours of the possible redevelopment, area residents came together to form the Clonard Residents Association (CRA) with a local retired builder as chair. The NIHE proposal to demolish 650 dwellings and replace these with 200, necessitating the relocation of many residents, was met with dismay by the residents and it was clear to all involved that additional nearby housing would need to be found or built in order to gain the approval of the community. Throughout 1992 and 1993 the CRA met frequently to discuss plans and to communicate issues, concerns and desires to the NIHE. Negotiations between various government departments got underway to see if a solution could be found to the problem of additional housing, and the adjacent vacant site of the old Mackies metal works factory was identified as a potential housing site. With the promise of approximately 300 new houses to be built on the Mackies site, the vesting[7] order for the Clonard site as originally planned was approved in 1994.

Phase I of the Clonard project got underway in 1995 with the renovation of a nineteenth century convent building into 45 sheltered accommodation units. While this building had originally been scheduled for demolition as part of the redevelopment, comments by a British direct rule minister to NIHE officials that he hoped the building could be saved resulted in plans being redrawn. Then, in 1996, the new build programme for all social housing was moved from the NIHE to Northern Ireland Federation of Housing Associations. This resulted in the introduction of a new player– Oaklee Housing Association—one of the largest and most successful housing associations in Northern Ireland. In spite of Oaklee's reputation, there was considerable concern in the community about the moving of responsibility for the project from the NIHE to Oaklee, which could have derailed the constructive relationship among the stakeholders. However, Oaklee successfully engaged with residents through housing management clinics and personal visits from a dedicated staff member to local residents to discuss their individual plans and concerns. Phase II of the Clonard project was completed by Oaklee in September 2000 and included 56 social dwellings.

The *Cluain Mór* development progressed rapidly after the agreement to use the Mackies site for housing was made and the third and fourth phases of the project– including construction of an additional 26 social dwellings and 87 private dwellings– began in January 2001 and were completed in mid-2002. In fact, *Cluain Mór* effectively became the 'new' Clonard with most of the original residents moving to this new development. As a result, the degree of engagement between residents of *Cluain Mór*, NIHE/Oaklee and the architect in charge was perceived as significantly greater than in the original Clonard site. The good relationships between stakeholders, the use of the Mackies site and the placement strategy were regarded as very successful and very few neighbourhood complaints were received. Overall, the Clonard/*Cluain Mór* development is deemed to be a success by the majority of stakeholders.

Northern Ireland–Connswater: The Connswater area is located in the 'Island' Ward of East Belfast, which contains Queen's Island and the industrial site of Harland and Woolf ship builders; builders of the *Titanic* and one of the iconic industries of Northern Ireland. For over 100 years this area was a thriving industrial part of the city, with docks, factories, transport depots, markets and, of course, ship building. Since the 1970s, however, the area had been in decline, culminating with the shutting down of the shipyards during the period of the research.

This area has consistently been identified as having some of the worst levels of poverty and deprivation in Northern Ireland, emerging as the 34th worst out of 582 wards in Northern Ireland in terms of the Noble indicators[8] in the period studied. Furthermore, for the indicator relating to housing quality and the physical environment included in Noble, the Island Ward is among the ten worst. The area is strongly unionist and virtually all the residents are Protestant. While there continues to be some demand for property in the area, with low vacancies, the population is aging and the school roll is dropping.

In 1998, based upon the findings in the Northern Ireland House Condition Survey of 1996, the NIHE determined that approximately 500 terraced houses in the Connswater area should be targeted for regeneration. However, in order to avoid speculative buying in advance of regeneration, the decision was not made public until the redevelopment plan was well advanced and vesting was applied for in 1999. The first time that local residents or politicians were notified of the redevelopment plans was the distribution of leaflets informing the community of the application for the vesting order.

In response, residents and politicians formed the Mersey Street Area Residents Association (MARA) in September 1999 to discuss local concerns about redevelopment and to generate ideas as to how the community could make its concerns known to the authorities. MARA received funding assistance and support from both the East Belfast Partnership Board (via the East Belfast Community Development Association and the International Fund for Ireland.[9] By April 2001, MARA succeeded in putting together a document detailing the concerns of local residents and business, including a 'ten-point plan' for future engagement with the NIHE. The document addressed a range of issues, including specific physical requirements for housing and area layout, a request for affordable housing and consultation and development process recommendations. In addition to the points in the ten-point plan, residents raised serious concerns about the decision to close the Mersey Street Primary School in the face of declining enrolment.

The vesting order was approved by the Department for Social Development (DSD) in early 2000 and Phase I of the project was begun, and completed, in late 2001. This phase consisted of the relocation of tenants, the demolition of existing dwellings and the construction of 33 new social dwellings. Connswater Housing Association, a non-profit housing organization that had been operating in the area since 1976, was contracted to build and manage the new dwellings.

Phase II of the project began in April 2002 and, of the ten points raised by MARA, nine were incorporated into this second phase. Only the request to build affordable housing for purchase by local residents and the relocation of the primary school (raised later as an issue by the residents) remained under discussion at the time the research was concluded. The second phase included the construction of 55 new dwellings and was scheduled for completion in early 2006.

Northern Ireland– Roden Street/Greater Village Area: The Roden Street/ Greater Village Area project represents a mix of project types: a small 'pilot' project (Roden Street) nested within a much larger project (Greater Village Area). The original focus of the research was on the Roden Street element of the project, but interesting threads relating to the Greater Village Area (GVA) were felt to be relevant to the overall research aims and so these were included. Roden Street is a small street in south Belfast that runs perpendicular to the Donegall Road—a large main street that has long been a point of reference in Belfast. It is in a well known Loyalist area with numerous murals and active paramilitaries, although the population has been changing recently with many long-time residents moving out of the area and immigrants, students and new employees of the local hospitals moving in. Overall, the population in the area has been dropping precipitously, with the local Blackstaff Ward losing over 20 per cent of its population in ten years, between the censuses of 1991 and 2001. Adding to the difficulties for the area, the Blackstaff Ward is rated one of the worst in the country in terms of the Noble index of multiple deprivation. Nevertheless, in terms of location, Roden Street and the Greater Village Area are considered to be prime real estate, close to the centre of the city, two major hospitals, Queen's University and many other amenities.

For many years prior to the Roden Street project, the area had been considered by the Northern Ireland Housing Executive to be in need of redevelopment. However, an NIHE proposal to develop the larger GVA was rejected by the community in the mid-1990s, due in part to the perception that there was a 'conspiracy' to depopulate the area to make it less volatile and to clear the way for private redevelopment. In 1999, in order to gain some momentum for redevelopment, a small project to redevelop the Roden Street area was proposed by the NIHE, comprising the demolition of 111 dwellings (60 per cent owner-occupied, 20 per cent private rental and 20 per cent social) and replacing these with 26 new social housing units.

Around this time, a great deal of organizational activity was getting underway in the local community sector. Building on the significant funding available from the DSD under the MBW strategy, the South Belfast Partnership Board (SBPB) was established in 1998 as one of four partnership boards in the city, with the objective of generating creative ideas and facilitating integrated programmes to address economic, social, physical and community issues in their respective areas. Each board is made up of the same number of representatives from the various stakeholder groups: eight from community, eight political representatives, five statutory and four private sector representatives.

In 1999, one year after the SBPB was formed, the Greater Village Regeneration Trust (GVRT) was established with the support of the NIHE and the SBPB. The initial aim of the GVRT was to canvass community groups, private firms and residents about the requirements for redevelopment in the area. Members of the board of the GVRT were drawn from local community groups and private firms as well as including political activists and elected representatives. In March 2002, the GVRT's framework proposal for the redevelopment of the area was launched by the then Minister for Social Development, Nigel Dodds.

In spite of (or perhaps due to) the positive developments with respect to community involvement, and although many of the dwellings that were planned to be demolished were derelict and/or unoccupied, there were still difficulties in getting a number of residents to agree to proposal for the redevelopment of Roden Street. For this reason, the vesting application, which had been lodged in 1999, was not approved by the DSD until the end of 2002, following protracted legal and administrative efforts. In early 2003, Fold Housing Association (Fold) was contracted to undertake the development, and demolition of derelict housing got underway, however planning permission was not received until November 2004. In 2005, a 'sod-turning' ceremony on the Roden Street site was held and construction finally began on the 26 social housing dwellings to be built and managed by Fold. At the time of conclusion of the research, the buildings were scheduled for completion in mid-2006.

In the meantime, the NIHE published its draft proposal in 2004 for the redevelopment of the larger Greater Village Area (1,500 dwellings). The GVA proposal included five alternatives for consideration, ranging from a minor rehabilitation programme to a '95 per cent demolish/redevelop' approach estimated to cost £107 million. However, the GVRT reacted with disappointment to the long-awaited proposal, as it felt that it did not reflect the desires of the community documented in the framework proposal that had been launched with such fanfare in 2002. In response, the GVRT swung into action and produced a sixth alternative, which the NIHE agreed to include, with its original five alternatives, in the consultation packs sent out to all residents in the area. The NIHE asked the GVRT to run the consultation process but, at the conclusion of the research period, only 30 per cent of all residents had responded (with the majority split between the NIHE '95 per cent demolish/redevelop' alternative and the GVRT proposal). However, the NIHE required an 80 per cent response rate from the residents in order to progress to the next stage (application for vesting). This, unusually high, response rate was probably required due to the painful experiences of the first GVA proposal and the protracted Roden Street vesting process. The GVRT doubted the achievability of the target response rate, so the outlook in 2005 was bleak for completion of the GVA project.

Republic of Ireland—Ballymun: Ballymun is the largest of the three projects in Dublin and the largest of all of the projects in the study. Much has been written about this area[10] and the many features of the project cannot possibly be addressed in this brief summary. The regeneration project (which, at time of writing, was still underway) began in 1997 with the establishment of Ballymun Regeneration Ltd (BRL), a semi-state company-owned jointly by the Department of Finance and Local Authority. The 13 board members of BRL include the City Architect, Director of Traffic, and Managing Director of BRL (all from Dublin City Council), two local councillors, three community representatives, four representatives from various statutory agencies (including the secretary of the local university) and an independent chairman appointed by Dublin City Council. The project has been funded through the Area Regeneration Programme, along with funding from the Department of the Environment, Heritage and Local Government, various urban renewal schemes and partnerships as well as targeted funding for particular programmes such as childcare, health and social supports. Overall, the project covers an area of about 1.5 square miles and 5,200 dwellings (of which 2,800 are in flat complexes and 2,400 are houses), with about 20,000 people living in the area.

The history of Ballymun is integral to understanding the regeneration project. Ballymun was created in the mid-1960s as Ireland's first (and last) high-rise social housing project, comprising both 15-storey 'tower' blocks and eight-storey 'slab' blocks. This was an ambitious design as traditionally homes in Ireland were houses, rather than flats. Built on the outskirts of the city, near the airport, Ballymun was a symbol of progress in Irish urban planning and development and was designed to address the serious shortage of urban housing at that time. However, 'it flew in the face of everything Irish politicians believed about housing' and was 'an unrepeated experiment in modernity' (Power 1993) that was widely condemned as a failure early on in its history. Problems with construction, a lack of amenities in the area, poor housing management by the local council, economic recession, social change, drug-dealing and misguided housing policy combined to turn the area into a black-spot of unemployment, crime, anti-social behaviour, vacant dwellings and boarded-up shops. By 1986, turnover in the council housing had reached nearly 50 per cent and that year was seen as a 'year of crisis' in the area (Somerville-Woodward 2002).

The difficulties in the area over the years had the effect of generating significant expertise amongst residents in lobbying, campaigning, working together and forging relationships with public and private sector organizations to address the festering problems. From broken lifts to bank closings, playgrounds to pools, the Ballymun residents organized almost constant protests about crises in their community. In fact, Somerville-Woodward (2002) suggests that Ballymun became something of a training ground for local activists in the 1980s, and the demonstrated need to engage productively with residents led Dublin Corporation, now called Dublin City Council,[11] to move the functions of housing management and rent collection for the estate to a local office—the first decentralization of this function in the state. The first Housing Task Force for an urban estate was set up in Ballymun in 1987 with a membership comprising local TDs (elected representatives), members of the Ballymun Community Coalition, the Combat Poverty Agency and officials from Dublin Corporation and the Eastern Health Board. (Now the 'Eastern Regional Health Authority.

One of the first projects undertaken by the Housing Task Force was to ensure that Ballymun was included on Dublin Corporation's list of estates scheduled for major remedial works in 1988. The proposed regeneration was budgeted at between IR£50–70 million[12] and planned for 11 phases over ten years. A novel element of the proposed programme was the level of community involvement that was to be a feature of all physical/social improvements. After the first phase of the refurbishment was completed in 1993, the Department of the Environment and Local Government insisted that an evaluation be carried out to see if the project (which had cost double the original estimate) was achieving value for money. The resulting report from Craig Gardner/Price Waterhouse (1993) turned out to be a watershed in the history of the area, as it included the clearance and redevelopment of the entire estate among its five alternatives for completion of the project. The feeling of the community and Dublin Corporation at the time was to opt for a conservative approach and, following a period of consultation, the option of a balance of refurbishment and some demolition of the worst of the tower blocks, replacing these with housing more in keeping with Irish preferences was selected.

However, by 1996, the 'Celtic Tiger' economy was in full flight and the 'rainbow coalition'[13] was in power with an aggressive social agenda. The then Minister for the Environment, Brendan Howlin, and Minister of State for Housing and Urban Renewal, Liz McManus, suggested that, since the cost of refurbishment was extremely high and would need to be redone in approximately another 15 years, it would be more sensible to opt for a plan that would rectify the mistakes of the past and put Ballymun on the path to a completely new future. The Ballymun Housing Task Force accepted this challenging opportunity with enthusiasm, and a new entity– BRL –was created in 1997 to oversee the design and implementation of a whole new town. It was agreed that Dublin Corporation would remain as the landlord of all social housing in the area and would retain the responsibility for those infrastructural elements that were under its remit (e.g., roads, lighting, sewage), but BRL would be responsible for the integrated planning and development of the area.

The 1998 Master Plan proposed by BRL was an ambitious 10-year regeneration plan encompassing physical, social, economic, environmental, cultural and process elements. Progress under each of these headings was to be tracked by the Monitoring Committee of the Board and reported every one to two years as a requirement of the Urban Renewal Scheme/Integrated Area Programme. Because of the plethora of objectives, it is difficult to gauge the status of the project as a whole, but in terms of the housing elements, by the end of 2004, approximately 1,200 of the planned 6,000 new units were completed and a further 1,200 were under construction. Demolition of the 15-storey tower blocks and eight-storey 'slab' blocks had begun and both the civic centre and leisure centre on Ballymun's new 'Main Street' were open for business. Of the planned 6,000 new units, the split between social and private housing is approximately 50/50, with the voluntary sector providing about 10 per cent of the social housing. The total number of dwellings planned for the area as a whole is nearly 10,000, split between 40 per cent social housing to 60 per cent private housing. This is a huge shift from the pre-project ratio of 80 per cent social to 20 per cent private housing and also incorporates a significant increase in housing density. It is difficult to get clarity on the budget figures for a project of this size and complexity, however the housing element of the plan was estimated to cost 332 million in the Master Plan.

The progress report for 2003–2004 was upbeat about the increasing property values in the area and the attraction of private investment for the first time in decades. Unemployment was down and the number of childcare places was significantly increased with brand new neighbourhood facilities supporting crèches, job centres and other community services. With all the good news in the report however, a note of caution was sounded in the conclusion. 'The success reported in this document is at a crucial phase and needs commitment and bolstering to maintain momentum and ensure that the huge public investment is supplemented and enhanced by private investment and secured to make a solid framework for the future' (BRL 2005: 69). This suggests that management of the project was concerned that money (and government interest in the project) was running out. At the time of completing the case study, the project end date was 2010.

Republic of Ireland—Fatima Mansions: The Fatima Mansions project is located in the southwest section of Dublin City, relatively near to the city centre, consisting mainly of local authority constructed and managed flats. While the location is prime in terms of access to city-based amenities, jobs and transport systems, the area has a reputation for crime, drug-dealing and other anti-social behaviour that is one of the worst in the country. Originally consisting of 363 flats and 11 acres, Fatima Mansions represents a medium-sized project in Dublin and, at the end of the case study research in 2004, the project to regenerate the area was just getting underway, with about one third of the original 14 apartment blocks demolished, residents moved out and the redevelopment plan was approved and project managers were in place. While the project was originally conceived as a local authority one, in 2003 a decision was made to reconfigure the project as a public-private partnership (PPP) and to seek bidders to carry out the plans that had been agreed after protracted negotiations between residents, the local authority and elected officials.

In order to understand the context for the current regeneration project in Fatima Mansions it is helpful to sketch out some of the history of the area and the changes that impacted upon it. Following the initial construction of 14 four-storey flat complexes in 1951, the development 'housed a successful working-class community . . . forming a small part of the complex social fabric of the inner city with close ties to the industrial economic functions of the immediate area' (Punch, Redmond & Kelly 2007: 12). However, the early 1970s brought a severe recession, with many industries closing up or moving out of the city, leaving a concentration of low-skilled unemployed people in the area. The protracted recession and high levels of unemployment, along with an unravelling of the social fabric due to drugs, emigration and misguided government policies such as the 'surrender grants' of the 1980s left the area a virtual wasteland of boarded-up flats, drug-dealing and criminal gangs. The physical refurbishment of the flats by Dublin City Council in the late 1980s 'did nothing to halt the decay of the estate or improve other aspects of the quality of life' (Fahey 1999: 5).

In 1995, the local authority established the Fatima Task Force, made up of a number of community groups and statutory agencies, with the aim of tackling the socio-economic issues in the community. Around the same time another community-based 'uber-group'—Fatima Groups United—was formed, which had similar aims to the Fatima Task Force, but was made up of a wider set of community and voluntary groups and did not include the statutory representatives. Over time, Fatima Groups United (FGU) emerged as the representative 'voice' of the community and, in 2000, this group prepared a key document outlining the aims of the community for regeneration and a vision of how residents and other stakeholders could be included in the decision-making processes going forward. The document was titled *Eleven Acres, Ten Steps* and contained a list of ten strategic goals for the area. The goals had little to do with physical regeneration, but all had social and/or process elements that FGU felt were crucial to achieving a turnaround in the area. Many of these principles and aims were incorporated into the first 'Master Plan' for the project developed by the local authority in 2001, entitled *Regeneration/New Generation*, which marked the official beginning of the project.

During 2000, however, other changes were occurring that were to have significant impact on the current structure and aims of the project. The government passed the Planning and Development Act (2000) which made numerous changes to the legislation governing development, including a new provision allowing local authorities to reserve up to 20 per cent of all new developments for social and affordable housing. Though this was modified to the advantage of the private sector in an amendment in 2002, the change put developers on notice that the government was serious about increasing the output of social housing and that the private sector was going to have to contribute. Furthermore, the Act underpinned the shift towards mixed developments of social and private housing as a strategic direction in housing provision.

In addition, PPPs were included as an important element of the National Development Plan (NDP) 2000–2006 to speed up the provision of badly needed infrastructure and decrease demands on the Exchequer. The Department of Finance encouraged the various departments to increase their use of PPPs, with the effect that the Department of the Environment and Local Government created a special unit to identify likely projects that would benefit from this kind of structure. Under these circumstances, it is unsurprising that Dublin City Council decided to change to a PPP structure for the Fatima Mansions project in 2003, in spite of local opposition at the time.

Finally, the *Eleven Acres, Ten Steps* document recommended that a 'Fatima Regeneration Board' replace the 'Fatima Task Force' as the primary governance body for the project. This board was to comprise an equal number of community representatives (four) each from the Fatima Mansions estate and the surrounding Rialto area. This was seen as a crucial step in achieving better lines of communication and trust between residents of the two areas, as well as facilitating integrated decision-making. In addition, an equal number of representatives from the local political sphere and relevant local authority (two each) were on the board, with a chairman from outside this group to be selected by the board.

In early 2004, Moritz-Elliot, a joint venture between Moritz Holdings and P. Elliot Construction (Ltd), was selected to complete the project, with the local authority playing more of a facilitative role, rather than an active implementation role going forward. In the course of this shift to private sector implementation responsibility, some of the original plans were changed. The mix of public and private housing shifted significantly from a 50/50 split between social and private/affordable in 2001 to a 25/75 split in 2004. Furthermore, the planned density of the area was increased from 500 to 600 dwellings. The overall effect of this current plan sees the decrease by 60 per cent the number of social housing dwellings in the area (from 363 to 150) and the addition of a large number of private and affordable dwellings (360 private and 70 affordable). It is important to note, however, that in 2000, when the first plans for regeneration were being developed, just 255 of the 363 social housing flats were occupied. By August 2004, only 150 units remained occupied, as residents had already begun to move to other local authority dwellings to facilitate the first phases of demolition. The community-based Fatima Regeneration Board (FRB) was consulted as part of the changeover process and agreed to the changes after several community amenities were added.

Republic of Ireland—Hardwicke Street: The Hardwicke Street project is the smallest of the three urban regeneration developments studied in Dublin encompassing 11 blocks along the street and 210 flats. It is also the least complicated of the three in terms of the number of key decision-makers and the planning process and is a completed project in this study. Hardwicke Street is a significant point of reference in the North East Inner City Area of Dublin and all the buildings face Temple Street Church. The area was first developed in its modern form in 1957 with a row of houses that each had a view of the church. However, in the 1970s the street became a 'rat-run' for speeding cars, and the open area was used for stealing and dumping of cars and other anti-social and criminal activity. The area became rather a no-go area, with high levels of drugs, in the 1980s. After many years of the residents and the local authority trying to effect change incrementally, in the late 1990s it became clear that the entire area needed to be redeveloped as a matter of urgency.

The decision to include the area in the area regeneration programme was made by Dublin Corporation in 1997, however it was not until 1999 that initial consultations were made with the community and the budget approval for regeneration achieved. Subsequently, Dublin Corporation went through a significant reorganization, including its rebranding as Dublin City Council and the localization of housing management into four[14] regional management areas in 2000. Furthermore, a number of programmes and networks were being developed at the time, all focused on regeneration and all competing for attention in the area. These included the Inner City Organizations Network, the North West Inner City Network and the RAPID[15] programme. In 2001, a number of these networks, community groups and programme representatives came together and agreed with Dublin City Council that a study of the needs of the Hardwicke Street area was required to ensure that the regeneration plan took a holistic approach to the social, economic and structural issues that existed. A research task group was formed to oversee the 'needs analysis' activity, and included representatives from the various community networks, the RAPID programme, Dublin City Council and Hardwicke Street residents. Many of the recommendations that arose out of this research focused on social supports and community development and these were fed back for follow up to the local area office of Dublin City Council.

The physical regeneration project began in 2002, with Dublin City Council reviewing seven tenders for the job, as specified by the Council's Deputy City Architect, based on consultations up until that point. In that same year, the placement of an experienced and skilled housing officer in the North East Inner City office with responsibility for the Hardwicke Street project was seen as a contributing factor to building momentum for the project. The objectives of the development were to improve the area, examining space, facilities and access, and to 'design out' features that had contributed to anti-social behaviour while improving security and developing a sense of 'normalized' space. This involved changes to the layout of the area, changes to security and some social changes, including wider service provision. The issues relating to service provision were to be addressed by the local housing office, while contracts were signed with Foreman Construction (Ireland) Ltd to carry out the project for a budget of 9.5 million. This relatively large budget met with little resistance due to the fact that Hardwicke Street had long been on the financial 'books' of Dublin City Council and the Department of the Environment and was a high profile regeneration target. Drug-related crime and the murder of a local resident by vigilantes had lead to the original inclusion of Hardwicke Street in the Area Regeneration Programme budget in the late 1990s and the visibility of the project was such that the President of Ireland had visited the local tenants' group in 1998.

From 2002 to the final completion in May 2005,[16] there were few complications and the project proceeded much as planned—though some unplanned features were added at the request of tenants and some infrastructure difficulties arose. The architect hired by Dublin City Council to oversee the project was responsible for ensuring that the contractors delivered on target, and the local housing manager was responsible for liaising with residents and communicating any concerns or new requirements to the development team (consisting of the contractors, architect and the assistant city manager with responsibility for housing). In 2003, the community centre was opened with great fanfare with a ceremony and included a performance by the band of An Garda Síochána. The final development cost for renewal of 210 flats, a community centre and improvement to public areas and security came to €13.2 million—or approximately 40 per cent more than originally budgeted.

Healthcare Information Systems Projects

Northern Ireland–Theatre Management System (TMS): This project officially began at the end of 2004, but had been simmering for several years before that time. The project upon which the case data was based was aimed at developing a computer-based management system for operating theatre scheduling and management in Belfast City Hospital, but with future roll-outs planned across Northern Ireland's acute hospital population. The objectives of the system were to improve administrative efficiency and utilization of theatres and to produce management data relating to procedures performed, costs and inventory. Belfast City Hospital (BCH) is one of the larger hospitals in Northern Ireland with nine operating theatres and a full range of clinical procedures available on the premises. BCH had no theatre management system to speak of prior to the proposal to build TMS. Media and political attention spotlighting high numbers of patients on hospital waiting lists, and the Northern Ireland Accounting Office report that almost 40 per cent of available theatre capacity in Northern Ireland was not being used because of 'scheduling difficulties', provided the impetus to build the system.

In spite of the clear need for such a system, the project had a protracted start, both in terms of gaining approval to proceed and in finding and retaining an Information & Communications Technology (ICT) project manager. The difficulties were experienced at both the initial project proposal stage (it took over two years to get approval) and at the specification stage (it took a further two years to develop and gain approval for the detailed specifications). The delays were blamed on environmental uncertainty in the healthcare system overall—largely due to wider difficulties related to the devolution, and subsequent suspension, of the Northern Ireland regional government, the broadening of the scope of the project from a single hospital to all acute hospitals in Northern Ireland and the project management difficulties. Nevertheless, the project finally got underway in late 2006 with a bespoke system developed by Hewlett Packard, with TMS expected to be rolled-out in Belfast City Hospital's theatres as the first (pilot) site in late 2007. The project is considered to be one of several dozen 'strategic' projects in the Northern Ireland's Healthcare ICT Strategy.

Northern Ireland–Regional Acquired Brain Injury Unit ICT (RABIU): Like TMS, this project began in 2004, but was faster in its start-up phases and so was being implemented and staff were being trained by mid-2007. The system was designed to provide administrative functionality for all aspects of the new facility and services, which was developed to provide both inpatient and outpatient treatment for people with acquired brain injuries in Northern Ireland. Essentially, the development of the ICT project followed the granting of approval for a new facility to be built for this purpose, combining existing services from two separate healthcare organizations: inpatient services at Foster Green Hospital and outpatient patient therapy on Holywood Road, Belfast. Although the new facility was meant to serve all of the Northern Ireland population with the specific condition of acquired brain injury, it is relatively small by hospital standards with 25 inpatient beds, a range of therapy facilities and a pre-discharge 'assessment flat' for evaluating patients' capacity for managing at home.

The RABIU project had a relatively small budget of £150,000 and was, in reality, developed as an afterthought to the larger construction and fit-out budget for the new facility. In fact, the budget was approved well after the initial scoping of the project and so the project team had to cut back on their functional requirements. One of the key challenges of RABIU was in developing a system that could be used by administrators and clinical staff from two separate organizations, and much work was put into ensuring that the system addressed the requirements of both 'sides' while not increasing the data entry requirements. The project was developed on a bespoke basis by an outside vendor (Singularity) after existing systems in other similar facilities outside of Northern Ireland proved inadequate.

Northern Ireland–Electronic Prescribing and Eligibility System (EPES): This project was still in the design stages when the case was being written up, in spite of the fact that it had the earliest start date of all of the projects studied. Upon completion, the system is supposed to be rolled out to GPs and pharmacies across Northern Ireland and is aimed at improving efficiency and decreasing opportunities for fraud in the provision of and payments for prescription medicines. Funding was approved for the project in 1999 after an investigation revealed that the process of prescribing, filling and reimbursing costs for medicines in Northern Ireland was susceptible to various types of fraud. In a Public Accounts Committee inquiry it was shown that 95 per cent of recipients of prescriptions in Northern Ireland were claiming exemption from payment in 1996/1997, while the equivalent figure in England was 84 per cent and earlier studies suggested that only 67 per cent of the Northern Ireland population should have been eligible under the law. Furthermore, there were 1.74 million patients registered with GPs at the time while the entire population of Northern Ireland was just 1.66 million. The potential savings arising from the implementation of an automated prescribing and eligibility system were estimated at £4 million sterling per year—a considerable sum—and this did not include the process efficiencies that would accrue to GPs, pharmacists and patients.

However, in spite of the clear financial incentives to improve the controls and automation of the processes involved, the project took an extraordinarily long time to get underway. Concerns were raised about potential data protection violations and increased levels of staffing required in the Department of Work and Pensions to pursue the anticipated significant rise in allegations of fraud. The project was delayed for almost five years in order to investigate and resolve these issues, although the design tasks were marginally progressed. In 2004, the project began in earnest again. Due to the vast scope of the project and the number of stakeholders involved, not to mention the requirements of the project management methodology (PRINCE2) mandated by UK Government, detailed specifications took a long time to produce and agree, but finally, in 2006 Hewlett Packard (HP) was awarded a five-year contract worth £6.8 million sterling to develop and implement the system. By this time, however, the government's contract with community pharmacists in Northern Ireland was due for renewal. The EPES system became a bone of contention between the parties, and this issue was not resolved by the time of the case research. Furthermore, with the (re-)devolution of power to the regional (Northern Ireland) government in 2007, a campaign was launched to eliminate prescription charges in Northern Ireland completely and this has been endorsed by all of the main political parties. If this were to become law, the whole basis for the project disappears, leaving only the large contract with HP to sort out.

Republic of Ireland– Order Communication System (OCS): This project is located in Tallaght Hospital in South Dublin and its purpose is to facilitate communications among several departments in the hospital, with the first phase of the project focused on managing laboratory tests, ordered by consultants and conducted by phlebotomists and lab technicians. The genesis of the project was in the late 1960s with the plan to combine three existing inner city hospitals with inadequate facilities (Adelaide, Meath and the National Children's Hospital) into one large modern hospital on the outskirts of Dublin in the relatively new satellite town of Tallaght. Each hospital had its own departments and own way(s) of doing things and so bringing them together under one roof was not only a mammoth organizational task, but also a significant a political and architectural challenge. Established in the mid-1990s, Tallaght Hospital was the most complex healthcare project ever undertaken by the state up to that point. The original IT strategy for the hospital (developed by Ernst & Young in 1995) envisaged a fully integrated technical platform that would provide a shared database across all departments and allow communications among departmental systems via this database and associated communications software.

However, the original IT strategy had to be scrapped when it was found to be too difficult, both operationally (from a change management perspective) and technically, and so a more limited first phase was pursued which would facilitate communications among patient care departments and the clinical laboratory. Since nearly all departments interacted with the clinical laboratory in some way, this was seen as providing a good basis on which to build more comprehensive communications functionality across all departments. Furthermore, there were clear efficiency gains to be made from automating the process of ordering lab tests given the highly manual and error-prone process that was in place at the time. The project was begun in 1998, around the time that the hospital opened, and the first types of lab tests addressed were blood tests, as these were a large part of the lab's work. The first phase of the roll-out (2000) allowed clinicians to review the results of lab tests online rather than waiting for paper files to be delivered to the wards. The second phase replaced the manual ordering process with automated scanners and the online ordering and tracking of blood tests. The project was viewed as a success and cost in the region of 500,000. In fact, the efficiencies achieved inspired a spin-off project to examine if lab tests for outpatients, ordered by local GPs, could also be automated and results made available remotely. However, the original IS strategy of connecting all departments in the hospital via a communications system had yet to be realized by the time this research case was written.

Republic of Ireland–HealthLink: This project began roughly around the same time as the OCS project discussed above, as a pilot project in the Mater Hospital in North Dublin aimed at decreasing the cost and time involved in posting patient information to GPs by sending the information via telephone lines. In order to ensure security of patient data sent over the phone lines, specially made modems were purchased by 12 GP practices identified by the Mater Hospital to take part in the pilot. The modems were linked to computers in the GP practices to receive encrypted data, decrypt it and to display patient data generated by administrators and clinicians in the Mater Hospital. At the time, there was no Internet capability in Ireland and the technology used was simple electronic messaging. The pilot was deemed to be so beneficial in terms of time and cost savings that a national roll-out of the system was approved by the Department of Health in 1997.

Implementation was enhanced as well as complicated by several other concurrent developments. The first of these was General Practitioner Information Technology (GPIT), a national project begun in 1997 to improve the knowledge and use of IT among GPs in Ireland, which became linked with the expansion of the Mater Hospital pilot. The second was the rapid improvement and spread of communications technology, including, but not limited to, the roll-out of the Internet in Ireland. The modems and bespoke software to receive and display the data quickly became obsolete and overly expensive to maintain and the functionality was limited, given the improvement in GP office software that was being made available through the GPIT programme. In 2002, the newly formed Health Board Executive (HeBE) decided to set up a project to define a national messaging standard, HL7,[17] for health-related information. By this time there were almost 50 GP practices linked into the Mater Hospital which were not compliant with the proposed standard and, given that this was seen as a prototype for all healthcare information exchanges between hospitals and GP practices, it was considered strategic to convert to this standard. Since this was a major undertaking involving the redesign of the entire system, it was also seen as a good opportunity to 'migrate' the system to web technology which would make it cheaper to install and maintain as well as more easy to adapt to current and future GP and hospital IT applications. By 2004 over 200 GPs were using the system and several more Dublin hospitals had also linked into the system. However, there were still difficulties getting other regional hospitals to participate, as this had to be approved by the various Health Boards around the country and financial, as well as organizational constraints slowed progress significantly. As of May 2008, 19 of approximately 70 public and private hospitals, and over 1,200 of an estimated total of 2,500 GPs in the Irish Republic were using HealthLink.

Republic of Ireland–Electronic Health Record (EHR): This case is unusual in that while various national Healthcare IS strategy documents[18] state that a national standard for the EHR should be developed as part of an overall health information systems strategy, there is no overarching project aimed at creating the definitive EHR in the Republic of Ireland. This is also a strategic ICT priority in Northern Ireland, but it is being pursued there as a specific project under the overall Health ICT strategy. What is interesting about this case is that the definition and implementation of a national standard for patient information in the Irish Republic is emerging rather more organically and so was a particularly interesting, though slippery, case to examine for the purpose of the research.

The messaging protocol (HL7) mentioned in the HealthLink project is a significant step forward in the journey towards a national EHR standard. However, this protocol facilitates any number of different types and formats for an EHR, but it does not mandate that any particular type of data be included. Furthermore, the data elements and protocols established for the HealthLink project are targeted at a relatively limited set of information requirements compared to the broad spectrum of data that would be encompassed in an EHR standard. Complicating the picture in Ireland is the fact that a lot of work is being done on Europe-wide standards for the exchange of patient health data, the progress of which is reported annually at EU e-Health conferences among the Ministers of EU states convened since 2003. At the first of these, the EU Ministers declared their support for and commitment to *interoperability* standards among healthcare providers, which not only requires agreement around an EHR standard, but will also require some standardization at the level of software applications. Should standards be agreed at this level, healthcare information systems in Ireland would need to comply, requiring significant re-engineering to existing system along the lines of the comprehensive re-write of HealthLink in 2003.

Working from the opposite direction, IS software/hardware firms are competing to establish the 'gold standard' for various segments in the health industry, and the rapid pace at which both IT and health science evolve makes it difficult to anticipate which among the various competing standards will win out in the end. However, the consolidation of power over decision-making for healthcare IT in the recently established Health Services Executive (HSE) may prove to be a tipping point in the unfolding of the EHR project as control of existing systems, ICT infrastructure, strategic development and change management in healthcare IT should enable comprehensive projects to move forward at a greater pace.

Finally, the data protection issues that bedevilled the initial stages of the EPES system in Northern Ireland were dwarfed by those associated with the EHR implementation, as there are few examples of information that is more personal and more sensitive that an individual's health record. A project has been initiated under the 2004 health information strategy (Department of Health and Children 2004) to address the need for a unique identifier for each individual's health information which requires that legislation is passed, numbers allocated and IT systems across the health modified to accommodate this new identifier and to incorporate the required data security and access functionality. This is a tall order indeed, but one that will provide another link in the chain of events that may eventually lead to a national electronic health record.

2   Urban Regeneration in Ireland

INTRODUCTION

This chapter describes urban regeneration (UR) in Ireland as a system, applying the basic framework outlined in Chapter 1. The next chapter will follow the same outline, but will focus on IS in healthcare settings. In Chapter 1, six elements of a complex adaptive systems (CAS) were defined: system, agents, environmental rules, environmental factors, processes and outcomes. Rules and factors were further categorized as those outside the system—i.e., were part of the exogenous environment, and those created as a result of agent perceptions, actions and interactions over time—i.e., the endogenous environment.

Also in Chapter 1, the basic facts relating to urban regeneration in Ireland were described, including a summary of the socio-economic and political features of Ireland that appeared to be relevant in relation to both urban regeneration and healthcare, along with an overview of the cases on which the subsequent analyses are based. This chapter will use the information provided in Chapter 1 as the basic threads from which the tapestry of urban regeneration projects as 'systems' may be woven, i.e. to establish the boundaries of the systems studied and to identify the environmental elements (rules and factors) of urban regeneration in Ireland. In addition, material from the case studies will be used to support the definition of the remaining systems elements, i.e., agents, processes and outcomes (see Figure 1.2).

Demonstrating how the case studies may be interpreted as systems provides the foundation for any future claims of the relevance for CAS theory to public management, as it is necessary to show that the phenomenon studied may be understood as a system. The analysis will be repeated for healthcare information systems development in the next chapter—exploring how the same systems framework may be applied at a quite different level of organizational analysis, with the intention of supporting later claims that the analysis has relevance across various levels of public management phenomena. Chapters 2 and 3 are organized around the basic systems elements and both conclude with a summary of the key systems characteristics of the public administration activities studied.

URBAN REGENERATION SYSTEMS

In Chapter 1, the approach to selecting urban regeneration systems for the study was described in some detail (see *Setting the Stage for a CAS Analysis*). The main idea was to examine a number of projects that shared basic characteristics of context and purpose, but that were in different stages of development and involved different numbers and types of actors. The context consisted of the two largest cities in divided Ireland, over the period from 2004–2006, and the purpose of the projects was the improvement in the living conditions of residents in a particular geographic area, with an emphasis on housing as well as socio-economic improvements. It is worth noting that, while the projects shared a common overall context and purpose, the specific boundaries delineating the systems from their particular environments shifted over time. For example, the geographic boundaries of the projects themselves were established (and modified) over the course of each project—a system dynamic that is the focus of Chapter 5—as were the level and type of participation by agents and the specific results (outcomes, outputs and processes) to be achieved. Furthermore, the exogenous environment was incorporated to varying degrees into agents' perceptions of the endogenous environment in each project. These latter features are described in detail in this chapter.

In both jurisdictions three projects were chosen, each in different stages of development roughly corresponding to beginning, middle and end. In addition, projects differed in terms of the amount of housing and other physical or social services to be provided and the number and type of actors involved. The projects studied are shown in Table 2.1, classified by each of the three variables indicated.

ENVIRONMENTAL FACTORS AFFECTING
URBAN REGENERATION

As discussed in Chapter 1, the system environment is made up of factors and rules that influence decision-making by agents within the system. Factors may be categorized as a range of economic, demographic, political, relational and technological characteristics of the people and organizations located in the geographic area before and during the period in which an exercise in public management takes place. In some cases, the manifestation or 'value' of a factor at a particular place and time may constitute an important initial condition affecting outcomes, but this is generally only perceived in retrospect and often as part of an exercise in justification or approbation during subsequent evaluations. The extent to which factors appeared to play a key role as initial conditions in the urban regeneration projects studied will be highlighted in Chapter 4, and the topic will be taken up again in the second

Table 2.1   Projects Studied and Their Characteristics—Urban Regeneration

Urban Regeneration			
	Size	Stage	Complexity
Republic of Ireland: Dublin			
Ballymun	Large	Middle	High
Fatima Mansions	Medium/Large	Beginning	Medium
Hardwicke Street	Small	End	Low
Northern Ireland: Belfast			
Clonard/*Cluain Mór*	Large	End	Medium
Connswater	Medium	Middle	Low
Roden Street/Greater Village	Small	Beginning	High

half of this book as part of the focus on the CAS dynamics in public management. In this chapter, however, we will simply highlight which factors were identified by agents, as well as by researchers, as having influenced decision-making and outcomes within the projects studied.

In relation to urban regeneration in Ireland, the relevant *exogenous* factors may be seen in the history and politics of the two jurisdictions, as well as in their economic performance prior to and during the period of the study. In addition, it became clear over the course of the research that agents' characteristics that pre-date the system were also relevant factors driving decision-making. Interestingly, agent-based factors tend to transform quickly into *endogenous* factors, as they are manifest only in so far as the relevant organizations choose, or are compelled, to participate in a particular project and to interact with other agents. It is through the agents' interaction, arising from their participation in the various processes of the system, that the influence of these factors becomes clear, i.e. their power in relation to other agents, their reputation for trustworthiness and delivering on commitments and their capability to achieve particular outcomes or influence specific processes. However, factors relating to the social, economic and political contexts of the urban regeneration projects tended to persist in the perception of agents as *exogenous* factors, in spite of the fact that these factors were targeted for change through the actions of agents within the system. For example, segregation and poverty were seen as key exogenous factors driving the establishment of urban regeneration projects, but were nevertheless rarely seen as arising directly from the actions of agents within the project itself.

Drawing on the description of the environmental context(s) in the Republic of Ireland and Northern Ireland in Chapter 1, along with data from the six urban regeneration cases, the key exogenous factors relevant to decision-making in the urban regeneration projects are described below.

Exogenous Factors in the Urban Regeneration Environment

Social/demographic factors are those relating to the characteristics of citizens– e.g. age, race, religion, etc.—as well as to the nature of the relationship among different groups in society. In Northern Ireland, the relevant factors in this category were the existence of a divided society along religious, political and spatial lines and the declining Protestant population in Belfast and Derry in contrast to an increasing Catholic population. In the Republic of Ireland, the main social/demographic factors were an increasing population overall with a significant influx of European and non-European immigrants.

Economic factors have to do with employment opportunities and overall growth in output and personal/government wealth. In Northern Ireland, during the period studied, there was relatively weak growth—and what growth did occur was based on large public sector subsidy. Some indications of increased private sector investment in Northern Ireland were observed following the 'Good Friday Agreement' in 1998. In the Republic of Ireland, there were very high levels of economic growth during the mid- to late-1990s—a period that was referred to as the 'Celtic Tiger'—tapering off after 2002. The growth in output, employment and wealth was attributed to both government and EU investment as well as to the influx of multi-national firms, the 'open' economy of the Republic of Ireland and the impact of growth in the global economy.

Political factors are those that relate to the governance structures of the jurisdiction as well as to the distribution and use of power among different parties/groups. In Northern Ireland, the period in which the cases occurred was one of turmoil in government, with the devolved governance structures (the Executive and Assembly) suspended between 2002 and 2007. A review of public administration was initiated at the end of the period, increasing policy uncertainty for the public and private sectors alike, and many important public bodies were not elected but instead run by appointed boards. The political divisions between Protestant/Unionist/Loyalist (PUL) and Catholic/Nationalist/Republican (CNR) parties were deeply ingrained and the political legacy of the 'Troubles' is still evident in the period, with local councils having very little influence and a mindset of having to appease both sides with the provision of separate, but equal, public services. In the Republic of Ireland, the period was characterized by stability in government and control by a centre-right coalition. European policy was highly influential and local councils were steadily increasing their influence over area-based policies. The politics of 'partnership' played a significant role in urban regeneration policy and implementation.

Values and ideology as expressed by those responsible for public policy and implementation also appeared as key factors in the cases studied. In both Northern Ireland and the Irish Republic, social exclusion and poverty were seen as important issues, which could be addressed through physical, social and economic regeneration as well as through social housing programmes. Community involvement was perceived as important and was promoted in both jurisdictions, but was expressed differently on the ground, with the political divisions having a more prominent role in community activism in Northern Ireland than in the Irish Republic. The role of the private sector in supporting and facilitating social aims was more prominent in the Republic of Ireland than in Northern Ireland.

Environmental/physical factors include the nature of the landscape (both natural and built) and the quality and sustainability of the physical environment. In Northern Ireland, 'place' has a meaning and history that is tied up with the political and social divisions highlighted above. Physical divisions between communities are widely understood and in some cases clearly marked with 'peace walls', murals and other human artefacts. The built environment in all of the areas marked for regeneration was seen as decaying and there were local and national attempts to revitalize city centres and attract tourists. In the Republic of Ireland, the areas marked for regeneration were also considered to be physically decaying and in need of significant improvement both in terms of basic construction and in design approach.

Technological factors include planning, construction and design capabilities and norms, however these were rarely mentioned by interviewees as having a significant impact on outcomes over the period studied. They are included here largely to highlight the difference between the policy domains of urban regeneration and healthcare information systems. In the latter case, technology was far more influential, as will be discussed in Chapter 3. The only example of technological factors playing a role in urban regeneration was in the Republic of Ireland, where the planning approach was affected by changing views on urban design and density, as well as by a shift from a local *ad hoc* approach to national development planning.

Legal factors refer to the range of laws that affect individual and/or corporate actions, e.g., legislation relating to employment, competition, consumer, health and safety, etc. As was the case for technological factors, there was little mention of legal factors affecting decision-making or outcomes in the case studies. This is not to say that legal requirements were not observed or important, rather that they were simply not seen as key drivers of decision-making.

The factors described above are consistent with what are considered *contextual* factors in policy as well as in strategy literature, and as such are generally seen as independent features of the environment, which affect policy or strategy outcomes. In strategy literature, these are referred to as 'PESTEL' factors—an acronym that encompasses six of the factors discussed above. However, these were not the only factors mentioned by interviewees as affecting outcomes, and values/ideology have been included above for this reason. As noted earlier, characteristics of agents that pre-dated the establishment of an urban regeneration project were also perceived as affecting project processes and outcomes. These factors appear in the strategy literature as being part of the 'internal' organizational environment to be taken into account when developing business strategy, but are rarely included in public policy literature, aside from policy network studies. The research suggests that policy-makers would do well to consider explicitly the organizational features of participants in public sector activities and their potential impact on policy outcomes. We will refer to these types of exogenous factors as 'agent-based' to distinguish them from the other 'contextual' factors in the environment described above. Agent-based factors are described in more detail below.

Organizational capability refers to the knowledge, skill and productive capacity of potential participants (agents) as well as to the degree of interaction and communication among participants. In Northern Ireland, the Northern Ireland Housing Executive (NIHE) was perceived as highly capable and the single most appropriate entity for managing urban regeneration projects. Housing associations were seen as capable and efficient managers of social housing and there was a significant level of communication and coordination between the NIHE and housing associations pre-dating the cases studied. In addition, in the 1990s, responsibility for the development of all new social housing was shifted from the NIHE to housing associations. In the Republic of Ireland, local authorities were perceived as being the appropriate overseers of urban regeneration, but not necessarily as being efficient or very effective at delivering on project objectives. Views on the capability of housing associations were also mixed, with some seeing them as better managers of social housing than local authorities, but unable to deliver large-scale projects. In the Republic of Ireland, the private sector was perceived as being the most 'capable' of the various participants in terms of efficiency and ability to deliver on large projects—but there was considerable doubt as to the incentives for private firms to deliver on social objectives. In both jurisdictions, there was a perceived lack of integration across various bodies involved in urban regeneration policy and implementation.

Reputational factors refer to the way various participants are perceived not only in terms of their capability, but also in terms of their ethics and manner of interacting with other agents. In Northern Ireland, the NIHE had a reputation for being effective as well as for even-handedness in dealing with the two communities and for an ability to manage alongside the continuing influence of paramilitary groups. Both the NIHE and the housing associations were generally considered to be trustworthy partners. In the Republic of Ireland, tenants often perceived local authorities as being untrustworthy, but the private sector was seen as being even less preferable as partners in urban regeneration projects. There was also a degree of suspicion between local authorities and the private sector relating to motives and capabilities. Consistent with their perceived capability, housing associations in the Republic of Ireland were not seen as key players in urban regeneration.

Power differentials among participants refers to the ability of one agent to influence the actions of another—a characteristic that is latent until agents interact and/or are dependent upon one another to achieve their objectives. In Northern Ireland, there were strong ties within both the Protestant and Catholic local communities, enabling some influence over the NIHE and housing associations, but the two communities were in an ongoing standoff with each other over resource allocation. The NIHE was the central arbiter of urban regeneration decision-making and, as such, was the most powerful player in the cases. There were some references in the case studies to power struggles among different government departments affecting project processes and funding. In the Republic of Ireland, local communities were relatively weak compared to local authorities. Housing associations had very little power and the private sector had varying degrees of success in its ability to shape the actions of local authorities—and only then if the local authority was encouraged, or forced, by the Department of Finance to involve private firms. The two main Departments (Finance and Environment) involved in setting urban regeneration policy and programmes were highly influential and were observed to intervene directly in urban regeneration projects in some cases.

The extent to which agents perceived one or more of the exogenous factors as relevant to their decision-making is noted in Table 2.2. This is followed by a discussion of those factors deemed to be important by agents participating in the projects. Once a factor from the environment is considered important to the decision-making of an agent within the system, it becomes relevant as a feature of the system, as it is now part of the agent's schema and may also be a targeted outcome. Hence, the selection of exogenous factors as relevant to the decision-making of agents within a given system must be marked by a change in how we classify them—i.e., they become 'endogenous'. As noted above, *endogenous contextual* factors are rarely seen as factors that change significantly as a consequence of agent involvement in the system, in spite of the fact that they are often targets of urban regeneration. *Endogenous agent-based* factors, however, can be perceived as changing dramatically over the course of a project and, indeed, the desire to change one or more of these factors may have been part of the reason for participation by a particular agent in the first place. Also interesting, but not unexpected, was the tendency for different types of agents to assess the importance of factors in their decision-making differently—an observation that is mentioned in Table 2.2 and highlighted later in Figure 2.1.

Endogenous Contextual Factors

For public and non-profit agents, the main factors believed by them to affect decisions were closely related to the indicators used to identify the

Table 2.2 Endogenous Factors Perceived as Relevant to Agent Decision-Making —Urban Regeneration

Contextual Factors	Relevant to Agents?	Nature of Relevance
Social/ demo- graphic	*Some*	Factors of concern to public/non-profit agents—particularly the issues of social divisions being exacerbated by poor quality housing and/or environment (incorporating physical or environmental issues)
Economic	*Some*	Housing demand of general interest, but potential profit and business opportunities of primary concern to private firms
Political	*Some*	Public sector (civil service and local authorities) most influenced by political considerations, institutional structures generally understood as 'political' considerations
Values/ ideology	*Some (NI)*	Largely an expressed consideration in Northern Ireland, although commitment to community benefit generally observed across public/non-profits in both jurisdictions
Physical/ environ- mental	*All*	Location and state of physical infrastructure of relevance to all agents, but generally linked to other factors in terms of its influence on decision-making
Technology	*None*	No mention of technological factors as constraints or enablers of decision-making
Legal	*None*	No mention of legal factors as constraints or enablers of decision-making
Agent-based Factors	**Relevant to Agents?**	**Nature of Relevance**
Power differen- tials	*All*	Power differentials of significant concern to community agents, but maintaining 'control' also cited as important consideration for public sector. Private sector and non-profits tend to cite their lack of power as a key concern. Influence of sectarian groups of concern in the North, while some concern expressed in the Republic over the influence of criminal 'gangs'.
Reputation/ relationship between agents	*All*	Important across all agent types: Maintaining NIHE's reputation for 'even-handedness' seen as critical. Whereas competency/experience a major issue in the Republic. Community and/or sectarian affiliations mentioned in the North. Local authorities pursue relationships (or not) with a range of public sector agencies and community organisations. Private sector sees relationships with public sector and other private firms as key.
Organi- zational capability	*All*	Of importance to all, but most importance to private sector and of second highest importance to non-profit agents: Internal capability of significant importance to private sector, participation in 'public sector' projects seen as higher risk than private market.

need for action in the first place, i.e., segregation, unemployment, housing dereliction, poverty etc. However, the public agencies also identified political factors and legislation as drivers for action, while the non-profits considered these well down the list of important factors. Political factors, other than legislation, took the form of elected representatives or interest groups having an interest in the specific outcomes/outputs and intervening to try to influence decisions by agents to achieve these outcomes. Examples ranged from the far-reaching– the then Minister for Housing and Urban Regeneration in the Irish Republic intervening to fundamentally change the scale and scope of the Ballymun project– to the relatively minor– the NIHE changing the priorities of its regeneration plan in an area because a Member of Parliament expressed appreciation for a building during a walkabout of the area.

For private sector agents, salient exogenous factors were largely economic, such as house prices, tax incentives or disincentives and the economic outlook, particularly in so far as they affected profit opportunities. To the extent that they affected profit, private sector agents were also concerned about demographic factors, crime levels and projected population growth or decline. Social and political factors played a minor role for these agents. It should be noted here that policy—discussed in more detail in the next section on 'rules'—could and did affect perceptions of the economic and/or political factors influencing decision-making. In this, we may observe the overlapping nature of factors and rules and the difficulty in separating these elements of the 'environment'.

A major difference between the two jurisdictions was the degree to which sectarianism and mistrust of government in the community in Northern Ireland influenced decisions, as compared to the Irish Republic. Individuals representing Northern Ireland agents gave examples of decisions that were made largely due to these factors, ranging from which areas would be included in NIHE plans, to the design of buildings and walkways. It is difficult to categorize these factors as they could be considered social, political and even ideological features of the environment. Whatever their type, their impact was considerable in Northern Ireland. On the impact of technological factors, there was little to be found in either jurisdiction.

Endogenous Agent-Based Factors

Staff and organizational capability were perceived to be relevant factors for all agents—although to varying degrees. For the private sector, capability was the most important factor in decision-making (assuming basic profit thresholds had been met), while for the non-profit sector, capability was less important than social factors. For the public sector, capability was even less important, running a distant third behind social and policy factors in the Republic of Ireland and not in the top three in Northern Ireland. This lower ranking of capability stands in direct contrast to the relatively strong institutional position of the public sector agencies, i.e. their central position in determining the scale, timing and budget constraints for urban regeneration projects within their geographical remit. This may indicate that having the power to influence processes and rules may substitute for capability in so far as strategic decision-making is concerned. Figure 2.1 shows the overlap of the three top factors (social issues, reputation/networks, organizational capacity) influencing decision-making as reported by public sector, private sector and non-profit sector agents via the survey conducted for this research.

These different perspectives on the importance of agent capability may have contributed to the frustration expressed by private developers/build-ers interviewed concerning the difficulties in accomplishing joint objectives with the other two agent types. If capability doesn't feature in an organiza-tion's decision to commit to outcomes, then it may enter into agreements without knowing whether it has the necessary capabilities to fulfil its com-mitments. On the other hand, housing associations and government agen-cies find little common ground with developers/builders who need 'only' to worry about profit and not to address social or political objectives.

In contrast to the differences among agents' perceptions of contextual and agent capability factors, there was a surprising consensus on the impor-tance of reputation amongst all agents. Reputation came third in impor-tance for five of the six agent types surveyed and referred to how the agent was perceived in terms of trustworthiness and capability. For the NIHE, it also referred to its reputation for even-handedness in the allocation of social housing across the Catholic and Protestant communities. The only agents that did not consider reputation in the top three factors influencing decision-making were local authorities in the Republic of Ireland. How-ever, network relationships were amongst the top three factors for these agents and it might be that there are similarities in how local authorities in the Republic of Ireland perceive relationships to how the NIHE in North-ern Ireland perceives reputation.

In conclusion, while there was little common ground among different types of organizational agents in terms of the importance of various *con-textual* factors in decision-making, there is quite a significant overlap in agents' consideration of *agent-based* factors, particularly those having to do with agent interactions such as capability, reputation and relationships. In addition, the capability of agents to engage in activities and to achieve outcomes is clearly an important factor in decision-making, but one that institutional power may act as a substitute for in the case of the public sec-tor's decision-making. Finally, as reported in Rhodes and Murray (2007), the factors displayed in Figure 2.1 appear to align along a continuum of social versus individual accountability, with public sector agents attend-ing to factors that are of general societal interest, private sector agents emphasizing factors of immediate interest to them and non-profits falling somewhere in between. This was a satisfyingly unsurprising finding that prepares the way for more interesting findings reported later.

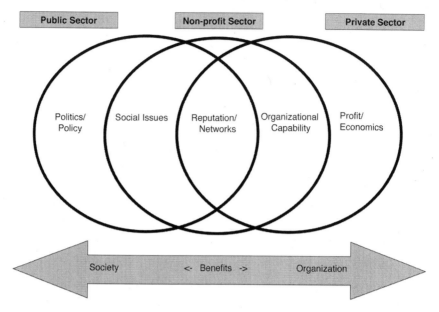

Figure 2.1 Decision factors of urban regeneration agents.

URBAN REGENERATION RULES

We continue the discussion of the exogenous and endogenous environment(s) of urban regeneration with a discussion of the *rules* governing the systems studied. As noted in the previous section, it can be difficult to separate factors from rules as they may overlap as well as influence one another, but it is, nevertheless, important to keep straight in one's mind the difference between them. A 'factor' is a characteristic or state of a physical or conceptual entity or entities, while a 'rule' is the perception of a cause/effect relationship between two or more states of physical or conceptual entities. The level of demand for housing in a particular area is a *factor* of the environment, while the relationship between housing demand and population growth is a *rule*.

As noted in Chapter 1, rules that appear to be of importance in public management systems are those relating to agent participation, system processes, payoffs and time/place. Establishing such rules is the main focus of policy and legislation relating to both urban regeneration and healthcare information systems and so any discussion of rules must begin with the relevant policy and legislation. This section begins with a summary of urban regeneration policy, followed by a brief discussion of the public management decision-making and accountability frameworks operating in each jurisdiction. This information may be seen as the exogenous rule environment of the specific urban regeneration projects studied and provides the basic material for the discussion of the endogenous rules described or observed in the cases themselves. A summary of the endogenous rules that appeared to operate in one or more cases—whether activated from the exogenous policy/practice environment or created internally through the interaction of agents over time—is provided at the end of this section.

Policy and Practice in Urban Regeneration

Republic of Ireland

Although the lack of a comprehensive urban regeneration strategy in the Irish Republic has been acknowledged (Shine and Norris 2006), the overall objective for urban regeneration may be found on the web site of the Department of the Environment, Heritage and Local Government (DoEHLG):

> The aim for regeneration projects is to build sustainable communities through a combination of social, educational and economic initiatives and also by rejuvenating the built environment by a mixture of demolition, construction and refurbishment of dwellings having regard to urban design guidelines.
>
> (www.environ.ie)[2]

A definition of sustainability, however, is elusive in Irish policy documents and it is in the description of the types of initiatives to be employed, rather than the objectives, that we may find the key rule-establishing elements of policy. The first urban regeneration initiatives in the Irish Republic were the Urban Renewal Scheme (URS), supplemented by the Remedial Works Scheme (RWS) for social housing; the early EU Poverty programmes and Area Partnerships; and by government and local authority direct funding. In this mix of funding schemes, we can see two fundamental aspects of the rule environment for urban regeneration in Ireland. The first of these is the myriad opportunities for agents involved in urban regeneration to access funding, and the second is the budget-driven approach (payoff rule) of urban regeneration policy. Furthermore, in the evolution of UR policy in the Republic of Ireland, we can observe an orientation towards involving the private and community sectors as key players early on—which is not the case in Northern Ireland.

The first URS was formalized in the 1986 Finance Act. Its aim was to promote investment in both residential and commercial property development by the private sector in designated inner city areas through the provision of tax reliefs rather than by allocation of grant funding. Between 1985 and 1996 over 100 areas were designated, in 35 urban centres (KPMG 1996). Designation included the Temple Bar and Custom House Docks areas, each of which was the subject of far larger regeneration programmes based on economic development rather than on social housing. Parallel to the URS, from 1985 onwards, the RWS provided funds directly to local authorities to refurbish social housing and to supplement local authorities' 'differential rents' income (which on its own was insufficient to maintain properties long-term).

While 'tax related incentives for development and occupation of property dominated the early policy approach' (Williams 2006: 546), a move towards a more integrated approach was made in response to a review of the URS in 1996 (KPMG 1996). After this report, local authorities applying for eligibility for another round of the URS were invited to draw up integrated area plans including community consultation and 49 areas were selected. Although the URS itself remained a tax relief measure, integrated area plans required the integration of private sector development with other funding programmes, thus making it possible to include areas with high levels of social housing. At the same time, RWS guidance was updated to emphasize that refurbishment schemes should take into account social and economic issues, through multi-agency working (DoEHLG 1999).

During the period of the research, a small number of other programmes was introduced, including Urban and Village Renewal, which provided public funding rather than tax reliefs under the 2000–2006 National Development Plan[3]; and the Revitalising Areas through Planning, Investment and Development (RAPID), a targeted regeneration programme for urban areas and small towns. 45 areas were selected with the help of deprivation indicators; however, very little new funding was available. Rather, the intention was to coordinate and prioritize existing sources of funding more effectively (Fitzpatrick Associates 2006). Finally, the large-scale regeneration of several areas in Dublin, i.e., Temple Bar, Ballymun and Dublin Docklands, made use of a variety of funding sources and tax reliefs.

By the turn of the century, urban regeneration in the Republic of Ireland was more integrated at the local level than previously, but still dependent upon a mix of funding sources and tax reliefs which needed to be drawn together locally into coherent programmes. This fragmentation was reflected in lines of accountability through three government departments, within the overall context of the National Development Plan and the social partnership agreements as coordinated by the Department of the *Taoiseach*.

Figure 2.2 provides details of decision-making and accountability. Programmes based on physical regeneration were accountable to the DoEHLG, which was also responsible for social housing expenditure and policy, and planning policy. Most programmes were administered by local councils, some by implementing agencies, which were connected to councils' City and County Development Boards (CCDBs). The CCDBs had responsibility for drawing up ten-year strategic plans for their areas, to include tackling social exclusion and promoting economic and cultural development. Programmes concerned mainly with social and economic regeneration were responsible to the Department of Community, Rural and Gaeltacht Affairs (DoCRGA), through the implementing body Pobal.[4] EU programmes were accountable through the all-Ireland Special EU Programmes Body to the Department of Finance.[5]

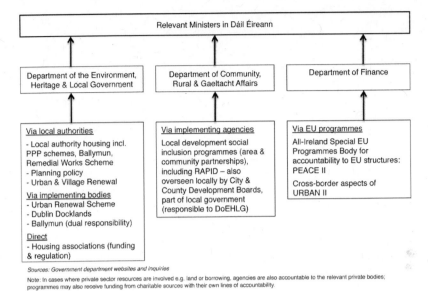

Figure 2.2 Structures for the administration of urban regeneration and related programmes in the Republic of Ireland.

Northern Ireland

During the period of the research, there existed an overarching policy framework for urban (and rural) renewal in Northern Ireland. *Northern Ireland's Strategy for Neighbourhood Renewal* was launched in 2003 and stated that:

Neighbourhood Renewal will help to close the gap between the quality of life for people in the most deprived neighbourhoods and the quality of life for the rest of society by pursuing two over-arching goals:

> To ensure that the people living in the most deprived neighbourhoods have access to the best possible services and to the opportunities which make for a better quality of life and prospects for themselves and their families; and
>
> To improve the environment and image of our most deprived neighbourhoods so that they become attractive places to live and invest in.
>
> (Department of Social Development 2003: 21)

Urban regeneration also sought to tackle community divisions, stating that 'integration of communities must be encouraged and segregation discouraged' (Department for Social Development (DSD) 2003: 5) and 'communities which have suffered the worst impact of the 'Troubles', must not lose out on the social and economic benefits that the "peace dividend" has brought for many of our citizens' (DSD 2003: 2).

However, this strategy was a quite recent development during the period of study and the majority of the projects selected had not been initiated under this programme. In fact, there was no mention of this strategy in any of our interviews as being central to decision-making, although references to similar objectives were made. Therefore, the general planning context remained important, as set out in Northern Ireland's Regional Development Strategy, *Shaping Our Future*:

> . . . promoting a sustained urban renaissance based on maintaining compact cities and towns, and creating high quality urban environments with improved urban transport systems, and green spaces, thus underpinning their strategic role as hubs of economic activity, employment and services, and providing more attractive towns in which to live
>
> (DSD 2001: vii)

Urban regeneration policy in Northern Ireland began with the Belfast Areas of Need programme in the 1970s (McCready 2001) and *Making Belfast Work* from 1988 (Birrell 1994). Both focused on social and community development, as did other early *ad hoc* schemes for various cities and towns in the province. At the same time, the NIHE undertook various area-based renewal schemes with the aim of improving housing quality, following the findings of the first House Condition Survey in 1974 that almost one in five homes were unfit for occupation (Murie 2001). In 1989, Belfast's Laganside waterfront redevelopment, incorporating entertainment and conference facilities along with luxury apartments, was unique in Northern Ireland (Greer 2001).

The most important tranches of EU funding for Northern Ireland were the PEACE programmes, officially known as the Special Support Programme for Peace and Reconciliation (EUSSPPR). The network of district partnerships set up to implement the first phase, PEACE I, became local strategy partnerships for PEACE II from 2000–2006, thus firmly establishing the principle of working in partnership. From 2000 onwards, the NIHE supplemented its programme of urban renewal with more widely-based housing strategies in parts of Belfast and in Derry, connecting housing redevelopment with a wider regeneration agenda, including multi-agency working and community consultation. Areas not covered by the housing strategies, but requiring significant redevelopment work, were also targeted through a housing market profile and economic appraisal; this was the route to redevelopment for the Northern Ireland case studies in this research.

By the time the Neighbourhood Renewal Strategy (NRS) was launched in 2003, a substantial network of regeneration projects and programmes was already in place, particularly in Belfast. The NRS adopted a comprehensive regeneration model as used in England, Scotland and Wales, consisting of the selection of priority areas through use of deprivation indicators, the formation of local partnership bodies and the production of a local area plan to improve social and economic conditions (DSD 2003). Responsibility for housing remained with the NIHE and with housing associations.

Various *ad hoc* programmes supplemented those described above. These included programmes to regenerate iconic sites in various cities (e.g. Crumlin Road Gaol and Girdwood barracks in North Belfast; Ebrington Barracks in the City of Derry/Londonderry; and the 'Titanic Quarter' regeneration in Belfast). A programme with a more social, as opposed to cultural-economic, emphasis was the 'Renewing Communities' pilot programme to improve social cohesion in working-class Protestant areas to address the alienation of these communities from the state (DSD 2006).

Responsibility for urban regeneration and housing was shared by several departments of the Northern Ireland Executive and is described in Figure 2.3. Urban regeneration operated under the strategic framework of the Programme for Government, coordinated by the Office of the First Minister and Deputy First Minister (OFMDFM). However, the department with the most extensive remit for urban regeneration was the DSD, which was also the department responsible for housing policy and regulating the NIHE

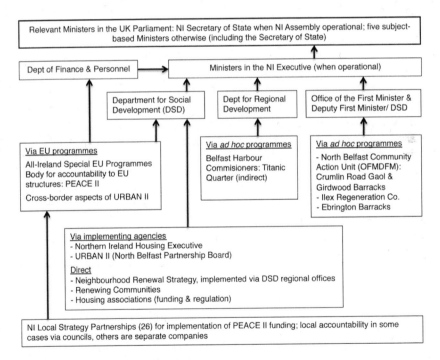

Figure 2.3 Structures for the administration of urban regeneration and related programmes in Northern Ireland.

and housing associations. The Neighbourhood Renewal Strategy was implemented via regional offices of DSD and the Renewing Communities implementation was also based at the DSD. The Northern Ireland Housing Executive reported to the DSD but, as is evident in the case studies, had a strategic role and significant autonomy. Other departments were directly or indirectly accountable for several programmes. As set out in Figure 2.4, local councils had little direct role in these programmes, which were all run by appointed boards.

Rules Applied in Urban Regeneration Projects

In both jurisdictions, urban regeneration was a multi-faceted approach to area-based improvements, usually targeted on areas in which physical, social and/or economic deprivation had been identified. The complexity of the problems to be addressed necessitated involvement of agents from the public, voluntary and community sectors, as well as providing opportunities for involvement from the private sector, particularly in the Republic of Ireland. The policy emphasis in both jurisdictions on community consultation and participation created an additional factor to be taken into account during policy development and implementation. The emphasis on tackling social exclusion was supplemented in Northern Ireland by the intention to address the damage done to communities during the 'Troubles'.

As was the case for decision-making factors, rules applied by agents in urban regeneration systems were only partly derived from the environment; rules were also established as part of the urban regeneration process itself. In some cases these rules were explicitly created as a result of agent interactions, such as rules relating to the payoffs for specific actions (in the form of contracts or incentives agreed to between the relevant participants), or process rules relating to which parties to include in various decision-making activities. In other cases, rules were not explicitly created by agents, but rather became operating norms adopted by agents over time as they sought to achieve their objectives in the context of a specific project. An example of this type of rule was the security and/or appeasement norms influencing agent behaviour in locations with significant paramilitary influence. Examples of agent, process, payoff and time/place rules operating in the cases are discussed below. How the different rules appeared (i.e., were they exogenously or endogenously created?) is also indicated.

Agent rules refer to those rules that govern which agents can or should participate in projects and what sort of role they will play, which were both exogenously established by legislation in the two jurisdictions studied as well as evolving over the course of the individual projects. In Northern Ireland, the NIHE was the responsible statutory entity for urban regeneration, while this role was legislatively established in the local authorities in the Republic of Ireland. Non-profit housing associations were given responsibility for all new social housing development in 1996 in Northern Ireland and around the same time, legislation in the Republic of Ireland required that area partnerships be in place before any new regeneration could be undertaken. During the projects themselves, roles for community groups and the private sector were established, and these, along with the specific role(s) of project specific agents, comprised the key endogenous agent rules.

Process rules refer to the types and order of actions and interactions that agents must undertake while participating in a given project. In Northern Ireland, urban regeneration is a relatively formalized process with a set of procedures that the NIHE must follow in a given order. In the Republic of Ireland, the process is much less formalized and largely left to the local authorities to manage. Having recognized the lack of formal process structure in the Irish Republic, there were still expectations as to how the various participants needed to work under the 'partnership' process and how local authorities could qualify as 'designated areas' under the tax legislation relating to urban regeneration. These exogenous rules and norms notwithstanding, the majority of process rules were established endogenously by project participants, notably by statutory agencies with overall responsibility for the projects. In fact, establishing process (and other) rules was a central focus of the activities in the beginning of projects, as will be discussed later in this chapter.

Payoff rules govern who benefits from, or pays for, the particular activities that will be undertaken. In Northern Ireland, the exogenous rules in this category had to do with the benefits to be gained by local residents in the form of payments to private residents or landlords to vacate their premises to make way for demolition, and the type and location of replacement housing for social renters. In the Republic of Ireland, these arrangements tended to be endogenous to a given project, while the exogenous rules related to tax incentives for private developers and/or investors to spur investment in a designated area. With respect to how much public money would be available to any given project, this was negotiated at the beginning (and often renegotiated subsequently) between the responsible statutory agency and the funding department(s) and, to a lesser extent, between community groups and various funding agencies including local authorities, government departments, EU funding bodies and a range of semi-state agencies with urban regeneration-related objectives. Contracts and budget negotiations occurred throughout the projects as endogenous payoff rule-setting activities, which formalized and specified the more general guidelines established at the beginning of projects.

Time/place rules are those that govern when and where a particular set of activities should take place. In Northern Ireland—and to a lesser extent in the Republic of Ireland—measures of area deprivation and housing quality establish the eligibility of an area for regeneration funding. In both jurisdictions, the responsible statutory agency could decide when to apply for these funds, and it is this decision that demarcates the beginning of a project. In addition, both jurisdictions have legislation that governs which areas are eligible for tax incentives for private investment—although these play a much more significant role in the Republic of Ireland. Like process rules, however, the majority of time/place rules are established during the projects themselves, with the clear definition of physical boundaries being a major milestone in project progress. Time– specifically the time required to complete elements of the projects—also becomes of greater importance as the project evolves, creating pressure on agents to complete tasks with or without meeting all of the desired objectives.

What was clear from the case studies was that rule activation or creation was a fundamental part of the system processes and might even be considered the main focus of interaction among agents—at least in the initializing processes. The process of *agreeing and approving solutions* was loaded with rule creation activities, including contract negotiations establishing payoffs and time/place rules and the activation of rules derived from the norms of participating agents such as architects, planners, local authorities, community representatives and construction firms. The process of *problem definition* was primarily aimed at selecting factors and rules from the environment that could be applied to the particular instance of urban regeneration in time and space. The process of *agent activation* included rule creation around the role and influence of existing agents as well as a rule challenging activity as new agents were created to change power differentials or respond to latent payoff opportunities in the environment. These processes are discussed in more detail later in this chapter.

One example of how existing rules in the environment were *selected* was how and when the responsible government authority chose to start an urban regeneration project. Qualifying for urban regeneration based on legislation and/or deprivation levels did not guarantee that urban regeneration would occur. It was up to the responsible government authority to put the project on its annual activity plan, to allocate funds and to signal to the community and other interested stakeholders that urban regeneration was to take place. While the start of all of the projects studied was highly influenced by political considerations, one of the main differences between the processes of regeneration in the two jurisdictions was how residents learned of the projects. Communities in Northern Ireland claimed to have been caught unawares by NIHE plans to regenerate their areas, while plans to regenerate in the Republic of Ireland were more often the subject of drawn-out discussions between the local authority and community representatives well before the project was launched.

An example of rule creation was the consolidation of resident interactions with other agents, often, but not always, through the creation a new community or project specific agent (PSA– see section on agents). In all cases in which they emerged, the PSA occupied a critical role in liaising with local residents to gather their views on regeneration and to facilitate consultation between community groups and other agents. Where no PSA existed, residents groups played this role– but with a more limited brief and less influence over decision-making by other agents. Furthermore, the PSAs acted not only to represent the views of the community, but also to facilitate collaboration amongst the agents responsible for implementing the agreed solution. Finally, PSAs could also influence the inclusion and exclusion of particular private and/or community sector agents in the project as a commissioning agent contracting with other agents for delivering particular elements of the project.

Another example of a rule arising from interactions among agents was the resolution of physical boundary issues, which established crucial place rules. Examples included the intense negotiations concerning a wall between Fatima Mansions and the adjoining neighbourhood in Dublin, which remained unresolved for many years. Only when this issue was resolved, and a residents' group representing residents on the other side of the wall was formed, did the project settle into a more stable progression. The creation of new access and exit roads for Ballymun was hotly debated and delayed the project. On Belfast's Roden Street, plans to relocate people across a road led to intense dissatisfaction among tenants and it was only when people were allowed to stay on 'their side' of the road that stakeholders could move on to other decision-making. In Clonard, implementation could not proceed until it was agreed among all stakeholders that an adjoining vacant property would be used permanently to relocate residents rather than for commercial development. Resolving physical boundary issues not only allowed the projects to progress, i.e., established an implementation rule, but also clarified the vision of the community and, in some cases, redefined the scope of the project overall.

In summary, rules were selected, modified and/or created during urban regeneration systems to a far greater extent than were factors in the environment. Rules from the environment that were selectively applied included legislative or policy rules establishing the conditions under which urban regeneration could occur, and professional practice rules that were applied to a greater or lesser extent in the development of solutions. Rules that were modified were largely those having to do with agents and payoffs. New agents were created or existing ones adapted to position themselves (or their constituents) more favourably vis-à-vis the evolving urban regeneration network and in so doing changed the interaction rules among all agents. Contracts and/or project 'master plans' were negotiated to clarify payoffs, as well as time/place features of the associated actions, that would result in profit for the private sector, improved quality of life for residents and political or social gain for the public/non-profit sectors. New rules related to how projects would be signalled to residents and other stakeholders, how interactions between residents and other agents would occur and in what order specific results would be achieved.

AGENTS IN URBAN REGENERATION

Across the six projects, the agents involved in urban regeneration were broadly similar and consisted of a range of organizations including area-based non-profit 'partnerships', developers/builders, residents' associations, non-profit housing associations, consultants and public sector agencies at different levels. However, while the private agents were identical, the public sector agents differed across the two jurisdictions (see Table 2.3).

This difference in the nature of the public sector agents reflects the impact of the differences in the systems environment(s)—specifically the history of a divided society and conflict between Catholics and Protestants in Northern Ireland. The NIHE is a 'non-departmental' public body, established by the Northern Ireland Housing Executive Act 1971. It was established after a period of protest and violence that marked the start of 'The Troubles' in Northern Ireland, and among its objectives was the elimination of the bias in favour of Protestant applicants in social housing development and allocation, which had been a feature of the local authority housing process. Effectively, the NIHE became a centralized implementation agent for the DSD when the DSD took over the social housing role from the Department of the Environment. In the Republic of Ireland, no such difficulties arose and the responsibility for social housing remained in the remit of the local authorities. The Department of the Environment, Heritage and Local Government continued in the role of providing policy guidance and funding for social housing, which it has had since the establishment of the Irish Republic.

This apparent decentralization in the public organizational infrastructure relating to urban regeneration and housing in the Republic of Ireland is somewhat challenged by the creation of the non-profit company Pobal.[6] Pobal was established in 1992 at the behest of the government to monitor the performance of a wide range of EU and Irish Government programmes, including social and community programmes undertaken as part of urban regeneration. In this, we may observe a tendency towards increasing central control in the system(s) of urban regeneration government across the two jurisdictions. However, neither Pobal, nor the Department of Community, Rural and Gaeltacht Affairs were mentioned by interviewees as having a significant role in the projects. This may have been due to the location of the projects in a major city with strong local councils.

The establishment of the NIHE in Northern Ireland represents a more extreme case of centralization, with wide-ranging impact on many of the systems elements, while Pobal in the Irish Republic is barely mentioned by any of the interviewees as impacting on decisions, in spite of its ubiquitous role as evaluator of performance by agents receiving public funding relating to urban regeneration and other socio-economic programmes.

The agents listed as 'private' sector in Table 2.3 are made up of a broad range of organizations, and are commonly thought of as coming from

Table 2.3   Agents in Urban Regeneration in Ireland

Agents	NI	ROI
Private Organizations		
Developers/Builders	✓	✓
Consultants (e.g., research/planning)	✓	✓
Housing associations	✓	✓
Housing associations	✓	✓
Area-based partnerships	✓	✓
Project specific organizations §	✓	✓
Professional services (e.g., legal, banking, estate agents, etc.)	-	✓
Public Organizations		
EU (structural fund programmes)	✓	✓
Govt: Dept of Finance	✓	✓
Govt: Dept of the Environment†	✓	✓
Govt: Dept for Social Development	✓	-
National housing authority (NIHE)	✓	-
Local development agencies	✓	-
Local (housing/planning) authority	-	✓
Performance monitoring (Pobal)∞	-	✓

˙In this study, community organizations include not only those that would normally be expected, e.g., sports clubs, parents organizations, women's centres, etc., but also various paramilitary organizations that have influence in the areas being regenerated.

§These organizations tend to have significant involvement by public sector representatives and, in some cases, may even be owned by a government entity. However, they are technically (legally) still private organizations with the ability to make decisions and take action that may prove challenging to the public sector agency responsible for the project overall.

†Note that this is the Department of the Environment, Heritage and Local Government in the Republic of Ireland and it is this department that has core authority over urban regeneration projects. The Department of the Environment in Northern Ireland has a role in urban regeneration only to the extent that it is the organizational 'home' of the planning service.

∞While technically a private legal entity, Pobal was established with a specific brief to evaluate performance of public and private sector agents who receive funding from either or both the EU and government departments in the Republic of Ireland. In effect it is an independent evaluator working on behalf of the public sector.

very different sectors of society. What they have in common, however, is that they are 'independent' agents in the system, i.e., they are not bound by legislative rules or government policy, they are able to decide whether or not to participate in projects (except in the case of the PSAs) and their ongoing existence depends upon their ability to attract and/or generate sufficient resources to pursue their objectives as a coherent entity. As we shall see later in the sections on processes and factors and rules, this characteristic of independence had implications for how agents interact and how they understand the environment and define the problem(s) to be solved.

Having noted the similarities, the differences between agents are still quite apparent. The builders and developers, along with the professional service firms and many of the research/planning consultants, make up the 'for-profit' contingent of agents in the system, i.e., those agents whose principal objective for participating in the projects is to make a profit. The residents' associations and community organizations are generally associated with the 'community' sector and their activities are aimed at improving the quality of life of the residents in the area being regenerated—although some community organizations may be involved in more than one area regeneration project. Also, there may be more pathological aspects of community activity in that some community organizations acting in the interests of a subset of citizens may damage the quality of life for others, for example, paramilitary organizations in Northern Ireland. The housing associations involved in these projects tended to operate at a national level and are generally considered to be part of the voluntary or non-profit sector. While they engage in activities similar to those of the builders and developers, their purpose(s) are more closely associated with those of the community and/or public sectors and they tend to draw upon a significant level of voluntary resources. Finally, the area-partnerships, PSAs and performance monitoring agencies, were all tightly connected to the public sector, via legal ownership and/or links to policy objectives. These are private non-profit agencies in a technical sense, but were funded and heavily influenced by government.

One of the more interesting findings of the research was that, while the majority of agents pre-existed the start of an urban regeneration project, a significant number of agents came into being during these projects. Of particular interest were the PSAs, which were composed of representatives of other participating agents and acted as a form of 'super-agent' with a focus on systemic levels of interaction and outcomes. Furthermore, these agents were often catalysts for the creation of other new agents, such as community organizations or small private firms, as well as being influential in the other aspects of the system such as new rules, which will be discussed later. The genesis and characteristics of the PSAs are worthy of detailed exploration due to their critical systemic roles and contribution to the complex adaptive systems dynamics described in the second half of this book.

In Ballymun, Dublin, the local authority (Dublin City Council) involved in the project created and owned a project specific agent, Ballymun Regeneration Ltd (BRL), to which it granted overall strategic and implementation authority across all aspects of the project. Although the board of BRL consisted of community representatives, local politicians, private sector representatives and local authority executives, the ultimate control of the agent, and of the project, remained in the hands of the local authority. BRL was in a position of power with respect to the private, non-profit and community sectors, having responsibility and authority for the coordination and purchasing of all services required to achieve the goals of the project. As such, BRL operated as a 'super-agent', managing a network of implementing agents all of which reported into it, but which also had to coordinate with each other to achieve complex outcomes.

A very different position (and genesis) was observed for the Greater Village Regeneration Trust (GVRT) in the Roden Street/Greater Village Area project in Belfast. This organization was founded by political and community representatives and did not have any members from the relevant government agency—the NIHE– on its board, although the NIHE did provide half funding for one employee of the organization. While the NIHE was supportive of the GVRT's establishment as a 'legitimate' representative of the community, it is questionable as to whether or not the NIHE considered the role of the GVRT to be central to its own urban regeneration objectives. While the GVRT was called upon to represent the views of residents to the NIHE, it had little direct influence over problem definition, solution or implementation. The GVRT's link to politicians in the area strengthened its position in negotiations with the NIHE, and fostered strong relationships with board members of the NIHE and other influential government agencies in the South Belfast city area. This enabled the GVRT to operate as an influential network node and pursue joint outcomes with other agents, including the NIHE, consistent with its own area-wide objectives.

Finally, the creation of the Fatima Regeneration Board (FRB) as a PSA for the Fatima Mansions urban regeneration project was agreed to by Dublin City Council at the behest of a coalition of community groups in the area after plans by the local authority for regeneration of the area were rejected by the community. The FRB included representation from public, private and community organizations and had an independent chairperson agreed on by all stakeholders. While the Dublin City Council did not devolve strategic and implementation authority to the FRB, it nevertheless played a central role in helping to define the problems of Fatima Mansions and in developing and agreeing solutions. Underlining the FRB's lack of implementation authority, mid-way through the project implementation authority was turned over to a public-private partnership run by a privately held joint venture company. During implementation, the FRB functioned more like a network hub, having relationships with all major stakeholders and being at the centre of decisions to act, if not at the centre of acting on those decisions.

PROCESSES IN URBAN REGENERATION

In identifying the main processes of the system, the focus was on those processes that involved significant interaction of agents as opposed to every activity undertaken by agents. This is because, as discussed in Chapter 1, interactions are considered to be a key driver of complex systems behaviour and, specifically, of non-linear outcomes. Processes are defined as a sequence of related actions and interactions that, taken together, are directed at achieving result(s). As we shall see in the discussion below, however, the sequencing of processes is rarely as linear as this definition would imply.

The processes of urban regeneration in the projects studied, though different in the detail of particular actions, appeared to follow a basic pattern of organizational activities. The four processes identified were identifying the problem(s), activating agents, agreeing on and approving the solution and implementing in the context of the approved/agreed solution. The first three processes did not always occur in the order listed. For example, sometimes the approval of elements of a solution occurred prior to the other two, and in many cases processes occurred in parallel. Furthermore, these first three processes exhibited significant interaction among agents, even if they were 'forced' to interact, while the fourth process of implementation was generally pursued by some agents engaging in minimal interaction with others. Nevertheless, across the broad range of agents involved in implementation, a significant amount of interaction did occur, particularly in the presence of a PSA. Each of the processes is discussed in greater detail in this section.

Identifying the Problem

Earlier in this chapter, the factors contributing to the initiation of urban regeneration projects were identified, involving housing quality and social and economic deprivation indicators, along with legislation that established some of the rules for why, when, where and how urban regeneration should occur. In addition, within the boundaries of each urban regeneration project, specific issues were taken up and/or goals established amongst agents or defined by fiat of the central government agency. These issues and/or goals generally took the form of specific environmental factors to be addressed along with outcome, output or process goals—to be discussed in greater detail in the section on outcomes in this chapter. The legislative activity of establishing the rules for urban regeneration, in combination with specification of the goals to be achieved for a given project, made up the overall process of 'identifying the problem'. One is immediately struck by the difficulties this poses for maintaining clear boundaries between the system and its environment. In fact, a fuzzy distinction between system and environment is evident in each of the basic elements of the system. As discussed in Midgley (2000), identifying the boundaries between a social system and its environment is fraught with difficulty, and poorly understood or deeply contested boundaries are all too often the cause of ongoing disputes among agents, unanticipated results or poor performance overall.

Several of the interviewees spoke of the process of problem identification as being at two different 'levels' of policy formulation– national and local—rather than seeing them as being outside or inside the system. For example, one local authority manager spoke of a shift in the Department of Finance's perspective on funding having a major impact on what the local authority could achieve, while an interviewee from the private sector suggested that interventions in the project from national government were 'required to get the project on track'. This perspective is somewhat difficult to reconcile with the Northern Ireland structure with one government agency (the NIHE) responsible for urban regeneration across the state—but nevertheless the perception remains that there are tensions as well as synergies between the government agents involved in problem definition across the boundaries of the system. This observation will be explored in more detail in Chapter 8.

Finally, we may make two observations about agent participation in the 'problem identification' process. The first is that external consultants were regularly engaged to conduct research into the particulars of the problem in the targeted area, both prior to the project start-up and during the course of the project. Consultants included econometric consulting firms, non-profit urban research organizations and academics specializing in social and/or urban research. Interestingly, interviewees from each of the projects in the Irish Republic mentioned the use of research consultants, but consultants were mentioned in only one project in Northern Ireland, which may indicate the existence of a normative rule for consultancy use in the Republic of Ireland. The second observation is that in cases where there was strong community representation in the problem definition process, the problem definition was expanded from that initially defined by the responsible government agency. This occurred in the Ballymun, Fatima Mansions and Roden Street projects. The involvement and impact of community groups across all projects is discussed in more detail in Chapter 6.

Activating Agents

In all projects there was evidence of the creation of new agents of various types with objectives related to the regeneration—or more generally 'improving'—of the targeted area. These ranged from local community groups forming to deal with a crisis in childcare or rumours of redevelopment, to the incorporation of semi-state bodies to address every aspect of regeneration. In three of the six projects, local community groups were well established prior to the initiation of the project. In the other three, community groups were established in response to plans, or rumours of plans, for regeneration by the statutory body responsible for the area. In those projects in which the community already had an established entity to represent its interests, not only did the problem definition expand, but the projects were larger, in terms of number of dwellings delivered and in the range and complexity of the project implemented.

While most public, community, private and non-governmental organizations (NGO) organizations were generally in existence prior to the start-up of a project, the initiation of even a relatively small project had a crystallizing effect in the area. Community organizations became focused on the regeneration project and some restructured to better position themselves vis-à-vis the emerging governance structures in the project. Examples were found in both jurisdictions, including Fatima Mansions, Ballymun, Roden Street and Connswater. In addition, community organizations, non-profits and private sector firms were created specifically to exploit funding incentives that were made available by the government to achieve specific outcomes. In both jurisdictions, the existence of national and EU funding for urban regeneration and community initiatives played a significant role in the start-up and ongoing activities of community groups, as well as making additional funding available to statutory bodies. These included the RAPID programme, Urban Renewal Acts (1986–1998) and the *National Development Plan 1999–2006* in the Republic of Ireland; and *Making Belfast Work*, the Belfast Partnership programme and Peace I/II in Northern Ireland. What is suggested by these findings is that 'active collaboration' in a jurisdiction (Agronoff and McGuire 2004) is often linked with the formation of new organizations as well as the reorientation of the purpose and/or activities of existing organizations.

Agreeing/Approving Solutions

This process sometimes overlapped with the process of 'identifying the problem', but was nonetheless different in the types of activities undertaken, the results achieved and the agents involved. In addition, it was during this process that the governance structures for involving non-governmental agencies and, in particular, community groups, were decided. In this process, professional planners and architects were generally hired to propose alternatives for physical regeneration that were then debated among participating agents. The influence of these agents was significant as they defined the range of alternative solutions to be considered. However, in two of the projects, alternatives suggested by the contracted professionals (paid for by the statutory agency) were deemed insufficient and the community-based agents countered with additional alternative solutions of their own.

The interactions among agents to come to agreement around solutions varied widely depending upon the agent types. The private sector tended to engage with the public sector agency overseeing the project via contracts or 'approvals' in the case of the non-profit agents. The interaction between the public agency responsible and various members of the community was significantly more complicated and, in the projects we studied, was organized in one of four ways:

Through individual tenants. In Hardwicke Street, Dublin, there was no tenants' association, but regular consultation meetings were held and individual tenants were involved in a research project to consult on the redevelopment, a situation that seemed to work well.

Through a tenants' or residents' association. In Clonard/*Cluain Mór* and in Connswater, both in Belfast, residents' associations were founded in response to rumours of redevelopment. The Connswater group, (Mersey Street Residents' Association (MARA)) took longer to establish itself, but eventually both groups established good relationships with the implementing agencies. In both cases, it was assumed that the groups would continue after the end of the regeneration work.

Through an advocacy body which coordinated residents' views from several groups. Ballymun and Fatima Mansions, both in Dublin, had more complex structures of community representation. Ballymun's resident involvement structure included an advocacy organization, the Ballymun Neighbourhood Council (BNC), previously the Ballymun Housing Task Force (BHTF), which liaised with BRL and with Dublin City Council as the main social landlord, collecting residents' views through five neighbourhood forums (the BNC Board had wider membership). The relationship between BRL and both the BHTF and the BNC was difficult for much of the regeneration period (Boyle 2005, Muir 2004). Residents of Fatima Mansions were organized via the advocacy body, Fatima Groups United (FGU), as well as participating in a separate Fatima Task Force, which had a wider membership, including groups and agencies from the statutory, voluntary and community sectors, along with politicians. The Task Force was replaced by the FRB in 2001. Although the working relationship between residents and Dublin City Council was poor between 1998–2000, it subsequently improved.

Through an organization that represented residents' interests as part of a wider remit. In the remaining case study, Roden Street in Belfast, community representation was part of a wider range of regeneration responsibilities undertaken by the GVRT.[7] The GVRT convened a Housing Focus Group from 2004 to assist with consultation on the Roden Street project, and a Community Sustainability Officer was employed to assist with the Roden Street redevelopment. The GVRT's working relationship with the NIHE involved a great deal of conflict, although communication with the housing association was better.

In addition to the above activities for coming to agreement, this process was vulnerable to political input. Examples of this included the political decisions to expand dramatically the scope of the Ballymun project, to change the Fatima Mansions project to a PPP and to have social housing built and managed by Housing Associations in Clonard. In fact, several of the 'bifurcation points' to be discussed in the second half of this book arose through the intervention of politicians.

Finally, agreement on a solution between private and public agents involved in negotiation did not lead directly to action by the appropriate agents. *Agreement* was something that was achieved between the community and the statutory agency (or semi-state body) leading the project, while *approval* was something that only local and/or national statutory agencies could provide. In both jurisdictions, planning permission was required to pursue specific physical changes to the area. This was somewhat less complicated in the Republic of Ireland because the planning authority was the local authority, while it is a separate state level entity in Northern Ireland. The Planning Service in Northern Ireland is a state level 'executive' function under the Department of the Environment. Prior to the reform of Northern Ireland's local government in the early 1970s, planning was a function of the local authorities, however it was centralized along with many of the functions of the local authorities after the Macrory Report of 1970. Prior to planning approval, however, another approval was required in both jurisdictions. In the case of Northern Ireland a 'vesting order' was required from the DSD prior to any regeneration project getting underway. In the Irish Republic, local authorities required specific funding approval for any major regeneration projects from the Department of the Environment, Heritage and Local Government. In four of the six projects (two in each jurisdiction), this 'interim' level of approval was sought by the statutory agency involved, prior to any consultation processes with community-based agents. This suggests that while there may have been significant negotiation of the details of an urban regeneration project, in practice key constraints were in place before negotiations even started.

Implementing the Agreed Solution

The implementation processes observed were more varied than the start-up processes of problem definition, activating agents and solution generation. This may be explained by the varying size, complexity and range of organizational involvement, and the status of the projects chosen. Nonetheless, there were still some patterns that may be of general interest and thus appropriate to this analysis. The first of these was mentioned earlier and relates to the decline in interaction among agents; the second is the impact of the passage of time on the decision-making of agents.

During implementation, interaction between all agents decreased, with each organization pursuing its separate objectives under the umbrella of the overall project design. Having achieved approval for proposed solutions (whether agreed amongst all participants or not), the agents with responsibility for implementation pursued their objectives without the high level of interaction present in the initial stages. While some agents produced progress reports and held meetings together, these appeared to be perfunctory interactions such as reporting on key checkpoints and fulfilling formal communications requirements. This is not to say that important decisions affecting key outputs and outcomes were not made, but these tended to be made without high profile consultations between stakeholders. In some cases this resulted in dissatisfaction among residents, as they were generally the ones being excluded from the consultations, but in several projects a local project office was established on or near the project site, staffed by the implementation organization and, in some cases, with space for community representatives. In such cases, interviewees suggested that the physical presence of project staff facilitated implementation, by providing an informal channel of communication between residents and the implementation team and an early warning system of potential physical or social issues arising as the project progressed. It is not possible to say if the establishment of these local project offices had a measurable impact on the projects, but interviewees invariably saw them as positive elements contributing to overall project success.

The second pattern observed was that the passing of time had more impact on implementation than in the initiation activities. Figure 2.4 provides an indication of the time required for each of the six projects with the darker bars representing the time up to agreed/approved solution and the lighter bars representing implementation timescale.

As the projects progressed, time became an important 'outcome' that influenced decision-making. Almost all interviewees had something to say about the time required to accomplish goals or achieve milestones, and how the passage of time directly influenced decisions. The need to accomplish something by a certain date, or within a certain timeframe, appeared to drive decisions and, while not precisely a rule, the passing of time provided important feedback. For example, several of the private sector interviewees described decisions, in relation to project design and structural components, which had been made due to the amount of time that would be saved (or had already been 'wasted') by making a particular choice. Of course, 'time is money' in the private for-profit sector, but this also appeared to press on decisions made by agents in other sectors. Time became more of an imperative as it progressed and project objectives were not achieved. In some cases, the passing of time and the lack of goal achievement resulted in a revisiting of the agreed goals as participants realized that compromises would be required to progress towards any kind of outcome.

OUTCOMES OF URBAN REGENERATION

Outcomes in public management are generally taken to refer to aggregate measures of social and economic welfare in a particular area, such

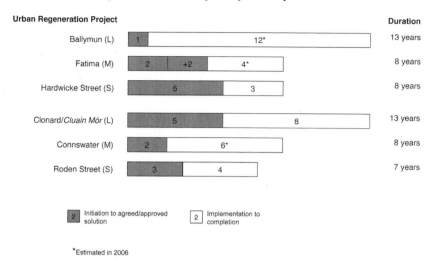

Figure 2.4 Urban regeneration project timelines.

as unemployment, educational attainment, income gaps, etc. that are the result of numerous (and generally not well understood) factors, agents and processes interacting over time (Pollitt and Bouckaert 2004). More often than not, outcomes cannot be attributed to a specific set of events or agents. Nevertheless, they can be powerful feedback mechanisms driving agent behaviour. A list of the types of outcomes referred to by interviewees and in documentation as driving agent decision-making in the projects studied is given in Table 2.4.

An example of an outcome driving agent behaviour in urban regeneration was the response, by Ballymun Regeneration Ltd, to the lack of tenant 'mix' in the new apartment blocks constructed as part of the regeneration plan. The objective for these apartments was to attract employed service workers who may have had low incomes, but who could improve the overall employment and income profile of the area. Instead, investors bought the apartments, and then rented them to unemployed people who qualified for rent subsidies. In order to discourage this activity, BRL lobbied for legislation to limit the number of people on rent subsidies who could rent in this area. In general, however, outcomes were not mentioned by interviewees as drivers of agent behaviour during a project; rather they were used to justify the initiation of a project and characterize the problem to be solved, but then were not referred to again until the end of the project, if at all. In fact, some outcomes acted more as initialization rules, in that regeneration would only be considered if a specified outcome measure dropped below, or rose above, a particular threshold.

The more relevant feedback loops during a project related to outputs and process goals. A clear distinction must be made between outcomes, outputs, process goals and other types of results arising from the system, as they are all relevant, but distinct, aspects of the feedback loop in the CAS framework. Outputs and process goals are understood by participants to contribute to the achievement of desired outcomes, but the links between outputs, processes and outcomes were never precisely defined. *Outputs* are tangible or intangible products that arise from the operation of the system itself. The system outputs agreed to by agents included the number of private dwellings versus social dwellings in the area, public amenities to be provided as part of the regeneration, employment targets for local residents, number and/or type of new businesses to be established in the area and the number and/or type of social services to be established in the area. Some of these outputs are within the remit of the central government agency. However private, non-profit and peripheral public agencies could be contracted by the central agencies to achieve certain outputs– the most obvious case being builders and/or housing associations providing new dwellings.

With respect to outputs, two exhibited interesting patterns that differed across the jurisdictions studied. These were the number of dwellings produced and the tenure type of the dwellings. In Northern Ireland, regeneration projects tended to result in a decrease in the number of dwellings in a particular area—in fact, one interviewee commented that the 'norm' was a decrease in dwellings of 50–60 per cent– while in the Irish Republic the opposite was the case. Interviewees and members of the advisory committee attributed this to differing environmental factors across the two jurisdictions. One factor was the density and/or age of housing, as Belfast had older and more closely packed housing stock than Dublin. A second was the relationship between demand and supply—while there was a significant shortage of housing in Dublin during the time of the research, demand was flat to slightly increasing in Belfast over the same period.

In terms of tenure, the mix remained relatively stable in projects in Northern Ireland or perhaps shifted slightly towards more social housing, while there was a definite shift from social housing to private housing in the Republic of Ireland. In the latter jurisdiction, projects were in areas with high percentages of social housing, and a mixed tenure approach to housing was seen by interviewees and policy experts as a mechanism to achieve social and economic integration. Those areas targeted for regeneration in Northern Ireland were already mixed tenure areas, with the majority of dwellings privately-owned or rented. Hence, it is unsurprising that the effect on tenures is different in the two jurisdictions as they began in different tenure states. However, it was a source of contention and media commentary in the Republic of Ireland that projects aimed at regeneration tended to result in less social housing, during a period in which demand for social housing was skyrocketing. The observed tenure trajectories in the two jurisdictions suggest that there may be some type of tenure 'equilibrium' dynamic in operation, as areas move towards a balance between the dominant tenure types in the society.

Process goals are activities, checkpoints or agent participation rates that are agreed to among participants (or in some cases established in legislation) that may become part of the 'rules of the game' (urban regeneration rules) as discussed in the previous section. Process goals address issues such as which agents are to be involved in which activities; the degree to which decisions should be by consensus, by vote or made by a particular agent; the level and periodicity of information-sharing among agents; and the time periods in the unfolding process at which goals achievement should be reviewed by stakeholders. Rules that relate to process goals are generally not explicitly stated, but are rather understood as giving license to agents to proceed with their course of action as long as they achieve whatever process goals (and outputs) are agreed. Output measures could also act as process rules, in that the achievement (or not) of outputs by a given agent or group of agents could be used to justify the cessation of activities or the transfer of responsibility from one agent to another. In projects in which a project specific agent was created, it was observed that process goals were more prevalent in these projects than in those with no PSA.

In addition to outcomes, outputs and process goals, interviewees also referred to *project-related targets* as important results of projects. In project management literature, outcomes and outputs are categorized as 'performance' measures of what the project is supposed to achieve. It is well established in the project management literature that the results of any project should include not only the 'performance' elements, but also the cost and amount of time required to achieve those performance outcomes (Meredith and Mantel 2006). While attention was paid to time and budgets, it was unusual for the costs related to the activities of all of the relevant actors in a given project to be accounted for in total. The main government actors managed costs that were within their remit, including funding other actors, so this proportion of the overall cost of a project is traceable. However, the costs of other actors such as residents' associations, area partnerships, builders/developers and any other community groups that engage with these agents to accomplish the performance elements of the project were generally not counted within the cost of the project. So an overall cost 'result' was difficult, or even impossible, to measure and did not feature in interviews and/or project documentation.

Time, or more specifically the elapsed amount of time, was a very visible measurement and nearly all interviewees had something to say about the time required to accomplish goals or achieve milestones, and about how the passage of time influenced decisions directly. The need to accomplish something by a certain date, or within a certain timeframe, had significant impact on decisions that were made by most of the actors studied. For some actors, particularly the private firms, time was directly related to cost and therefore these might be combined into a single variable. However, for others, primarily those in the public sector or community groups, time had more to do with perceptions of accomplishment, establishing/enhancing legitimacy or providing a reason for a particular decision. The passage of time contributed to an important feedback mechanism in the system that impacted on agency decision-making and structure (agent perceptions and

Table 2.4   Results for Urban Regeneration in Ireland

	Used as a Rule	Used as a Goal
Outcomes		
Tenure mix	-	✓
Unemployment figures	✓	✓
Income levels	✓	-
Number of new business start-ups	-	✓
Residential and commercial real estate values	-	✓
Educational attainment levels	✓	-
Crime statistics	✓	-
Number of jobs in local economy	-	✓
Health indicators	✓	-
Level of community involvement	✓	-
Outputs		
Number of dwellings (sometimes specified by size)	✓	✓
Housing quality indicators	-	-
Number of families/individuals relocated	-	✓
Number of childcare places	-	✓
Number of job training programmes/capacity	-	✓
Quality of (visual) physical environment	-	✓
Capacity for drug dependency treatment	-	✓
Number/type of new amenities in the area	-	✓
Number of new community organizations		✓
Process goals		
Who should be included in decision-making	✓	✓
Decision-making approach (e.g., consensus, vote, key checkpoints, etc.)	-	sometimes
Information creation/dissemination	sometimes	sometimes
Project-related targets		
Cost	sometimes	sometimes
Completion time	sometimes	✓

network positions). Table 2.4 provides a list of the each of the different types of systems results (including, but not limited to, outcomes) that acted as feedback elements in the projects, and how they were used, e.g. as a marker for goal-directed activity or, more forcefully, as a rule with associated incentives and penalties.

CONCLUSION: URBAN REGENERATION PROJECTS AS COMPLEX ADAPTIVE SYSTEMS

In this chapter the basic elements required to describe urban regeneration as an open organizational system have been defined. In particular, the details of the agents, processes, environment (factors and rules) and outcomes have been described, based on six cases of urban regeneration in Ireland. The presence of each of these elements, and the goal-directed nature of the actions by agents within the urban regeneration projects studied, supports the claim that these phenomena may be viewed as systems in that they fulfil the definition of a system as a 'mutually consistent ecology of parts, along with internal models and rules guiding them' (Caldart and Ricart 2004: 97). In so doing, we have laid the foundation for exploring whether or not urban regeneration represents a *complex adaptive* system, which requires not only that the necessary elements are identified, but also that the dynamics of complexity are also observed. This latter requirement is taken up in the second half of the book, following a similar exercise in systems analysis relating to the information systems projects in healthcare settings.

Figure 2.5 highlights the specific systems elements identified in urban regeneration in Ireland. As may be seen from the figure, a new 'box' has appeared, representing the presence of agents in the environment—which may or may not choose to enter the system over the course of the system's existence. This is an important feature of inter-organizational systems that is easily overlooked if one draws only from classic open system theory in developing a systems framework for public management. Its importance lies in its implications for the practicality of managing systems using management strategies that are designed for systems with less permeable/fuzzy boundaries (such as those of a single organization or a physical system). Furthermore, these systems may be perceived by agents as mechanisms for facilitating adaptation, i.e., that their participation in the system will result in improved (or possibly dis-improved) organizational capability, influence, reputation etc. This aspect of inter-organizational systems is relatively under-explored in recent literature on public administration and systems theory (e.g., recent special editions of *Public Administration Quarterly* (2005, 2008) and *Public Management Review* (2008)).

Figure 2.5 also indicates those elements of urban regeneration systems that are uniquely associated with the activities engaged in by agents as a function of their participation in the system. These appear in italics and

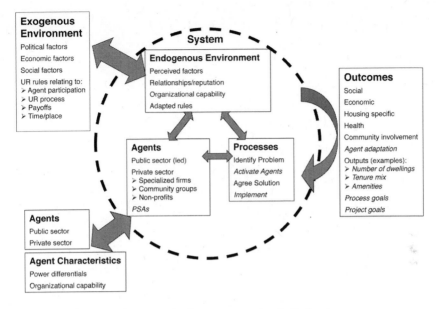

Figure 2.5   Systems elements of urban regeneration in Ireland.

include not only the project and process goals and outputs of agent activity within the system, but also the construction of the internal environment, the creation of PSAs, and the activation (and adaptation) of agents as a direct result of the opportunities and threats to stakeholders represented by the system. These, then, constitute the specific impact on society that a public service system of this type can make.

The identification of this set of elements supports the claim that these systems are not only *open* with respect to agents, rules and the ongoing response to and impact on factors in the environment, but are also *adaptive* systems, at least in so far as agents adapt to and seek to influence the adaptation of other agents. Furthermore, the creation and ongoing modification of the internal environment of the system suggests that the system as a whole adapts over time, not only due to inputs from the external environment, but also due to the interactions of agents within the system. In fact, the construction of this internal environment is an explicit activity engaged in by participating agents in the course of their involvement of the main processes identified. The observations that agents exist outside the system; that they may or may not decide to engage in interactions with other agents; that they construct an internal 'environment' via their interactions; and that they adapt over time to each other, to the rules of this internal environment as well as to changes in the endogenous environment, provides compelling evidence that these are *self-organizing* systems.

Beyond this important set of observations about the basic elements and self-organizing dynamics of these systems, there are a number of detailed observations from the projects that have potentially broader implications for public administration in general:

- No matter how inclusive or consultative the intentions of those involved in inter-organizational urban regeneration projects, they were largely controlled by the public sector entity with jurisdiction in the location/policy arena in which the project took place. Policy interventions such as consultative processes, PPPs and national or supranational programmes contributed to widening the range of agents involved and the breadth of their involvement, but the evidence suggests that the primary mover in these systems was still the relevant public sector agency (local authority in the Republic of Ireland, NIHE in Northern Ireland).
- Having acknowledged the above, in half of the projects studied, a PSA was created with a key role in facilitating agent interaction across all of the processes of the system and, in one case (Ballymun), the PSA became the dominant agent in relation to all other agents aside from the local authority. Each PSA invariably took on the role of liaising with the community affected by the project and in this way increased the participative activities in the system. PSAs had offices in the locale of the targeted regeneration area, and projects with PSAs appeared to have more community participation in the project processes of problem definition and solution agreement. PSAs also acted as incubators for the new or reinvigorated community-based agents. Another role of PSAs was to facilitate agreement between agents with different perceptions of decision factors. This increase in community participation, shared schemata between agents and agent activation did not come for 'free', however, as an increase in project scope and in the number of social/process goals was also observed in projects with PSAs.
- It was noted that the role of the passage of time as a feedback mechanism was apparent throughout the processes of urban regeneration and that its importance appeared to increase as the projects moved into their implementation phases. This feedback dynamic may contribute to the persistently observed disconnect between policy and implementation in public administration (Pressman and Wildavsky 1979, Rhodes R.A.W. 1988, Chapman 2002).
- Outcomes arising from previous urban regeneration projects, from other policy interventions or from historical developments play a role as 'factors' driving the establishment of new projects. However, these appear to decrease in importance as direct influencers of actions as new objectives are agreed amongst participants. These new factors take the form of outputs, process goals and project targets– all of which were relevant to agent decision-making in the form of feedback

loops. Performance management in the public sector, therefore, needs not only to be able to adapt over time to the changing nature of objectives, but also must adapt to the tendency for open systems to become gradually more closed as agents establish their own systems-specific set of feedback mechanisms to increase control, while at the same time decreasing the interaction with the external environment.

3 Healthcare Information Systems in Ireland

INTRODUCTION

In this chapter, as in the previous one, a domain of public administration is described using the systems framework described in Chapter 1. However, the domain of activity is radically different to that of urban regeneration. In this chapter we seek to demonstrate that the systems framework described in Chapter 1can be applied in quite different public administration contexts, with a particular objective of establishing the scalability of the framework in terms of organization level. The public management domain explored is information systems projects in healthcare settings. The healthcare information systems (HCIS) domain was selected to represent *intra*-organizational complex systems, in contrast to the *inter*-organizational systems represented by urban regeneration (UR) projects. Like urban regeneration, the HCIS projects involve multiple heterogeneous agents, but—as we shall see later—their heterogeneity springs from a different source. Also, exploring the healthcare setting allows us to take on a completely different set of policies and governance structures, not to mention different professional norms, to those operating in urban regeneration. Finally, the focus on information systems projects in healthcare contributes to the potential for different agent schemata operating within the system and also allows us to analyze a critical issue in healthcare, as well as in other social service areas, namely the efficient and effective use of information to provide public services.

As in the previous chapter, we demonstrate how the six cases studied may be interpreted as systems using the basic systems framework consisting of six elements. These elements are the system itself as defined by the boundaries between the system and its environment, the environmental factors that drive decision-making within the system, the environmental rules constraining agent decision-making, the agents acting and interacting within the system, the processes of action and interaction engaged in by the agents and the outcomes of agent activity within the system. The chapter will conclude with a summary of the systems characteristics for HCIS projects and a discussion of the key similarities and differences between elements found in this domain as compared to those in the urban regeneration domain.

HEALTHCARE INFORMATION SYSTEMS PROJECTS
AS PUBLIC MANAGEMENT SYSTEMS

In Chapter 1 the research strategy was explained, organized around the selection of projects in two different public management domains. The HCIS domain was chosen because it was significantly different from urban regeneration in terms of the organizational level at which the activity was undertaken and also in terms of the policies, professional norms and potential environmental factors that could affect the activity. In addition—as with the urban regeneration cases selected—the HCIS projects were chosen such that they represented activity in different jurisdictions, at different scales of activity and in different stages of completion. Table 3.1 shows how each of the projects studied mapped to the project variables used to select cases within each domain.

From the table it is clear that within the healthcare domain, care was taken to examine cases that covered a broad range of 'locations' on the topography of public management projects. It was hoped that this would allow researchers to identify the essential elements of these endeavours that persisted across contexts and time.

In analyzing the HCIS projects, it was observed that the boundaries between the 'regular' activity of the organization and the project activity were clearly delineated. Project activity was seen as different from the day-to-day work of the hospital or healthcare environment in which the project was being undertaken, and the participants often took on different roles as

Table 3.1   Projects Studied and Their Characteristics—HCIS

Healthcare Information Systems			
	Size	Stage	Complexity
Republic of Ireland: Dublin			
Electronic Health Record (EHR)	Large	Beginning	High
HealthLink	Medium/Large	Middle	Low
Order Communication System (OCS)	Small	End	Medium
Northern Ireland: Belfast			
Electronic Prescribing and Eligibility System (EPES)	Large	Beginning	High
Regional Acquired Brain Injury Unit (RABIU)	Medium	End	Low
Theatre Management System (TMS)	Small*	Middle	Medium

*Note that this case study followed the development of a pilot of the system in a single hospital. This was part of a much larger project to roll out theatre management systems across all acute hospitals in Northern Ireland.

project members than they had elsewhere in (or outside of) the organization. Even in the case of the information systems professionals– whether from inside or outside of the organization—while their role on a particular project was consistent with their overall work responsibilities, each project had its own requirements with respect to the role that the individual played. In one case, an individual hired by the hospital specifically to take on the role of project manager found himself unable to adjust to the demands and interactions among participants and left the project abruptly.

This relatively clear boundary with respect to how participants saw their project work as being distinct from other work differed from the observations in the urban regeneration projects. In that domain, the majority of participants understood their role on the project to be a facet of their main activity. The only exception to this was the local authorities in the Republic of Ireland for whom the UR projects were bounded activities outside of their main ones. The establishment of clear boundaries for HCIS projects is a theme that runs throughout this chapter. It is also worth noting that the elapsed time for these projects was, on average, significantly shorter than that observed in the urban regeneration projects. The median length of time for the HCIS projects was four years, while that for urban regeneration was eight.

ENVIRONMENTAL FACTORS AFFECTING HEALTHCARE INFORMATION SYSTEMS

The HCIS projects studied were active in roughly the same period and in the same locations as were the UR projects and so it might be assumed that, broadly speaking, their environments were the same. Nothing could be further from the truth, for, although the organizations and the individuals occupied the same space-time environment, the features of that environment relevant to the activities undertaken were vastly different. Of course, this might have been anticipated given the efforts to choose completely different public administration domains, but the extent to which it was the case was somewhat surprising.

To begin with, socio-economic factors—so prevalent in the decision-making for urban regeneration—were largely irrelevant in the HCIS projects. Interviewees never referred to community or individual wealth or social status as enablers or constraints of project objectives, nor as reasons to engage in the project in the first place. Nor was there an explicit recognition that the overall economic status of the jurisdictions had any bearing on the projects—in fact, in the relatively less well off Northern Ireland, HCIS projects were as large (and costly), or larger, than those undertaken in the Republic of Ireland. Addressing inequities in healthcare access—a central policy objective in both jurisdictions—was never mentioned. Addressing cost and/or efficiency objectives in relation to the provision of health services was a central objective of the projects but, except in the case of waiting times for procedures in hospital, there was very little impartial, consistent evidence from the 'outside' world that the cost or efficiency of existing services was comparatively poor. This is not to say that data regarding cost, throughput, capacity or time spent by healthcare professionals was not collected and analyzed—it was—but the data was unique to each project and regularly challenged by constituencies within the projects as questionable bases on which to invest significant funds.

History had little influence, except in Northern Ireland where sectarian divisions influenced which hospitals people would attend. Politics, however, played a significant role in terms of the effect of public sector reform initiatives and the institutional structures governing agreeing solutions and funding. In fact, all of the projects studied were promoted, to a greater or lesser degree, as being part of the reform or 'modernization' agenda for public service. In addition, all of the Northern Ireland projects and two of the three projects in the Republic of Ireland were affected by the political manoeuvring and institutional re-organizing among government departments, agencies and/or professional associations. The following section summarizes the basic features of the exogenous environment for HCIS projects, drawing on the environmental context(s) discussion in Chapter 1, along with data from the case studies.

Exogenous Factors in the HCIS Environment

As was the case in Chapter 2, the factors in the environment described below are grouped under PESTEL categories from policy and strategy literature along with categories relating to the specific characteristics of agents that pre-date the establishment of the systems studied.

Social/demographic factors are those that relate to the characteristics of citizens and, as noted above, these appeared to have little to do with decision-making or outcomes in our project. Having noted this, it was still the case that the divided society in Northern Ireland affected the location and number of public services provided, i.e., there were two hospitals in an area—one for Catholics and one for Protestants. In addition, migration into Northern Ireland cities and low level healthcare jobs created some tensions that were not observed in the Republic of Ireland. Nevertheless, the increasing population in the Irish Republic—some of which was due to increasing levels of inward migration– increased demand for healthcare across all services.

Economic factors, too, had little obvious affect on the projects—at least in so far as employment and gross domestic product (GDP) figures were concerned. It is the case that the relatively stagnant economy in Northern Ireland, coupled with the large public sector and public subsidies, may have put more pressure on hospitals in this jurisdiction to look for efficiencies from information & communication technology (ICT). Economic factors in the Republic of Ireland were exactly the reverse, with a rapidly expanding 'Celtic Tiger' growth (recently subsided) and huge increases in public funding for healthcare after years of neglect. A further difference between the two regions were the funding models in healthcare, with the National Health Service (NHS) model of broad public healthcare provision in Northern Ireland and a mix of public and private funding in the Republic.

Political factors did play a quite significant role, particularly in the north where political divisions were still very evident, and which had seen a period of turmoil in government. There were significant changes in both jurisdictions to institutional structures of public healthcare towards the consolidation of services. This created uncertainties that, in turn, caused delays, particularly in the north. Public sector reform initiatives were behind several of the Northern Ireland projects, and the underlying search for efficiencies in public service was evident in the justification processes for ICT projects across both jurisdictions.

Values/ideological factors as expressed in policy and by agents in strategies and plans played an important role in decision-making. The right to privacy is enshrined in legislation and in professional norms in healthcare and this had a significant impact on ICT design. Furthermore, access to healthcare is a fundamental right both in EU as well as local (UK/Republic of Ireland) policy with the effect that efficiencies must be found without resorting to the cutting back of citizen access. Standardization and efficiency are central values in ICT and in hospital management professions, and were reinforced by public sector reform, with some conflict observed between these objectives and 'patient-centred' healthcare. In both jurisdictions, aspirations for a more active role for patients and healthcare consumers were not reflected in the project designs or outcomes.

Technological factors were much more relevant to the HCIS projects than to the UR projects, and included significant improvements in communications technology and penetration into businesses, public sector organizations and households. The existence of an active ICT innovation sector in the Republic of Ireland may have contributed to this broad trend. The prevalence of 'best practice' standards in information systems development was influential in the processes of the Northern Ireland projects and both jurisdictions had evolving national ICT strategies in the healthcare area.

Physical/environmental factors played a relatively muted role in these projects although there was some evidence that the location of healthcare facilities could be controversial e.g. in the west of Ireland and in Belfast.

Legal factors were relevant in so far as they related to the right to privacy and the right to access healthcare services.

Functional capability factors are those that represent an agent's level of expertise or ability to represent a constituency in their role on the project. Agents, both within an organization and from the outside, were explicitly chosen (by the project sponsors) to participate based on their functional

Table 3.2   Endogenous Factors Perceived as Relevant to Agent Decision-Making
—HCIS

Contextual Factors	Relevant to Agents?	Nature of Relevance
Social/ demo- graphic	*None*	No reference in interviewees and only passing refer- ence in project documents to social factors driving decision--making. Having acknowledged this, there was clearly a legacy of the impact of a divided society in the provision of health services in Northern Ireland.
Economic	*Some*	Significant funding available to create HCIS from 2004 Strategies, and prior to that to increase effi- ciency and decrease waiting lists.
Political	*All*	Hospital management pressured to adopt HCIS as a route to efficiency and in fulfilment of public manage- ment reform agenda. Institutional changes affecting healthcare system overall.
Values/ ideology	*All*	Values expressed in healthcare policy, in the professional norms of participants and in ICT practices and policy all have significant influence and are the source of some conflict among agents.
Physical/ environ- mental	*Some*	ICT projects may be associated with new facilities.
Technology	*All*	Technological developments create perceived oppor- tunities and influence solutions proposed. Appears to be of greater significance in ROI.
Legal	*Some*	Legal requirements relating to Data Protection have an impact on project cost and progress—particularly in Northern Ireland.
Agent-based Factors	**Relevant to Agents?**	**Nature of Relevance**
Power differen- tials	*All*	Power differentials are of significant importance in decision-making and in the participation of agents. Clinicians in ROI and government agents in North- ern Ireland wield significant power in determining project objectives and processes.
Reputation/ relationship between agents	*All*	Reputation of limited importance—at least in so far as these are distinct from power relationships and functional capability—although reputation for ICT consultants an important factor. Relationships between agents seen as fairly important by all agents and very important between ICT agents and systems 'users'.
Functional Capacity (Organi- zational capability)	*All*	Of critical importance in relation to ICT and clini- cal agents. Less so to government and management agents, although the ability of an agent to represent an important stakeholder constituency was considered important by these agents.

capability. While functional capability is not precisely the same as the organizational capability category used in the discussion of the UR projects, they are sufficiently close both in meaning and importance to be considered together in the analysis presented later in Chapter 4.

Reputational/relationship factors appeared to be of less importance in these projects than in the UR projects, although these factors may have been subsumed under the functional capability category discussed above. It is difficult to believe that reputations and relationships played no role in decision-making, but the data in the cases provided no support for the hypothesis that they were important factors.

Power differentials among agents were quite relevant in the HCIS projects. In Northern Ireland, the government had significant power to influence hospital management and project decisions, while this influence was less obvious in the Republic of Ireland. In both jurisdictions, clinicians and clinical professional bodies had significant power in relation to management and ICT agents, and the boundaries between the various professions were clear. There were some indications of boundaries and tensions between centrally-run services and regional or local service centres/hospitals—as well as between healthcare professions and healthcare reform policy-makers. The relevance of various factors to agent decision-making is summarized in Table 3.2.

Endogenous Contextual Factors

Along with politics, the two contextual factors that appeared to have most influence in the decision-making of agents in HCIS projects were technological and value-driven. Technological factors were, broadly speaking, the ICT available at the time. The influence of technical advances and standards was most apparent in the Republic of Ireland, with all three projects having been tied to opportunities arising from new technologies and/or the achievement of a critical mass of technical capability across healthcare professionals. HealthLink is a good example of this, in which significant advances in communications technology (the Internet), computing (the personal computer), software (transmission protocols and GP office management packages) and increased computing skills in GP office staff all combined to facilitate the roll-out and success of the project. In the North, the main influence of the technological environment appeared to be related to incremental improvements in technology, but more importantly, was driven by professional values, methods and norms of ICT development and application. For example the 'PRINCE2'[1] development methodology was promoted as a best practice in UK public sector projects and its use required that projects' processes be conducted in precise ways. In both jurisdictions, a broad trend was the steady improvement in technology, both in clinical and managerial applications, which produced a steady stream of innovation opportunities across the healthcare sector, but also made managers cautious of committing to a particular ICT solution in the hope or fear that a better one would appear in the near future.

An example of the type of professional ICT value driving the Northern Ireland projects to a large extent, and those in the Republic of Ireland to a lesser extent, is that of 'standardization'. In the ICT world, standardization—of data, hardware, software and processes—is a highly sought-after objective in the design and development of information systems. Where standardization cannot be achieved, 'interoperability' is pursued, meaning that different elements of a system or technical infrastructure are designed to operate in conjunction with each other, albeit with some 'interfacing' technology present. It is taken as a given in this profession that a trajectory towards standardization and/or interoperability is to be desired. This underlying objective was cited by all of the technical interviewees, several of the non-technical interviewees, and in documents in the North. While standardization (and/or interoperability) was a value that also appeared in projects in the Republic of Ireland—notably in the Electronic Health Record (EHR) and HealthLink– it was more in the background of the these projects. Interestingly, in the Order Communication System (OCS) project there was an explicit recognition by the project team that standardization of ICT across the various clinical departments in the new hospital was not feasible, and so the design was modified to create a powerful translation engine that could pass information around to each of the departmental systems, thereby achieving inter-operability in lieu of standardization.

Professional values in the ICT world were not the only ones driving project decisions in HCIS. Healthcare professionals expressed a common value of individualization and professional discretion with respect to the treatment that patients receive. While not in direct conflict with the value of standardization of technology, there were clear conflicts within projects over the standardization of processes and/or practice associated with the roll-out of new technology. This was particularly noticeable in the Regional Acquired Brain Injury Unit (RABIU) and OCS projects in which different clinical and administrative constituencies resisted the standardization of their processes on the basis of concerns over the impact on patient care. Of course, there was also evidence that healthcare professionals, like most people, were resistant to any change that appeared to increase or change the nature of their work. Finally, the evidence in the Electronic Prescribing and Eligibility System (EPES) case suggests that the resistance to the proposed changes arising from the system was also driven by concerns around loss of income and influence.

At the intersection of the healthcare and ICT domains, there was also a strong concern with data protection and the individual patient's right to privacy. This was a major focus of EU legislation, and data protection legal issues were among the most difficult to sort out—delaying by years several of the projects, including EHR in the Republic and EPES in the North. Not surprisingly, the larger the scope of the system in terms of the coverage of healthcare providers and patients across the jurisdictions, the greater the issues surrounding data protection.

Endogenous Agent-Based Factors

As was the case in urban regeneration, the influence of agent-based factors was observed in the HCIS projects. Recall that these are characteristics of agents that pre-exist the establishment of the project and which have influence on the actions and interactions of agents during the project. The values associated with the various professions have already been discussed previously. Latent power relationships among agents were pervasive in their effect—including the relationships between the clinical staff and/or departments, between IT project managers and clinical staff, between internal ICT staff and ICT consultants and between government agency representatives and other members of the project teams or boards. Examples include Belfast's Theatre Management System (TMS), where the IT project manager left due to conflicts with clinicians, and the prioritization of the laboratory in the OCS project due to the relatively low power of the technicians in relation to the consultants. Major impacts were observed in the ongoing battle between government, IT consultants, GPs and pharmacists in the EPES system. The influence of hospital consultants/GPs in the majority of projects during project planning stages and the influence of IT consultants in the project justification stages also had significant impacts. Having noted these examples of specific power relationships influencing particular projects, it is the case that, overall, HCIS projects were driven by medical consultants in the Irish Republic, and by government or health management agents in the North. The expressions of power relationships were more obvious in the *intra*-organizational settings of HCIS than in the *inter*-organizational settings of urban regeneration– perhaps a function of levels of familiarity among agents in the intra-organizational setting, as well as of differing norms in both sectors. We will return to this point in the discussion of rules later in this chapter.

Agent capacity also drove decision-making in these projects, but the nature of capacity was somewhat different to that in urban regeneration. In HCIS, capacity had to do with the agent's functional capability—i.e., could they be relied upon to represent the interests and skills of the group they were associated with– and also with the agent's ability to contribute to a successful information systems project. This was most relevant in the case of the ICT professionals, particularly in the decisions to hire different types of consultants—and in the decisions of the consultants themselves in bidding for the work. Functional capability also played a role in the degree to which clinical and managerial project participants were included and/ or relied upon and their views taken into account. Functional capability featured in the EPES system, where the Department of Work and Pensions was unsure of its ability to process all of the potential instances of fraud that would be identified. It also featured in the HealthLink system, where only those GPs who could use PCs and modems could participate (at least in the early roll-out).

Interestingly, reputation, as a characteristic distinct from capability, did not appear as a factor in decision-making in these projects. However, relationships and institutional structures did play a role, in that the need to involve numerous government agency and/or stakeholder representatives in deciding functionality, implementation stages and targeted user groups meant that compromises needed to be reached and, more often than not, delays ensued.

Finally, there was much more emphasis on establishing the budget and business case parameters early on in the HCIS projects than in the urban regeneration projects. In particular, the expected patient and/or organizational gain arising from the system, and the cost of achieving these, were key decision outcomes that became factors which influenced subsequent decision-making by agents. The example of RABIU stands out as having a budget even before the project team knew what was required from the system. It is a feature of ICT systems to work to a budget—particularly if development is outsourced to ICT consultants. In essence, these elements of budget and organizational benefit may be grouped together as the *organizational gain* accruing to the hospital, other systems participants and/or the healthcare system as a whole, from the proposed system. Whatever the level of organization—whether a single hospital, or a government department representing all hospitals and health trusts—the belief that some organizational gain was to be achieved was at the core of many of the explicit decisions made. Later in this chapter in the section on processes, and again in the outcomes section, we will discuss how these imposed a kind of project boundary in terms of constraining decisions.

Although a formal survey of agents was not conducted (as there was for urban regeneration), it is still possible to highlight patterns of prioritization of factors across different agent types found in the cases. While this analysis anticipates the discussion of agent types later in the chapter, it is useful to conclude this discussion with a summary of which factors were important to which agent types—as was done in the chapter on urban regeneration.

Power relations were seen as important to agents of all types (but more prevalent in the Northern Ireland setting), while political considerations were largely confined to government and hospital management agents. Organizational gains—encompassing efficiency increases, cost decreases and increased capacity– were mentioned by healthcare management and clinical agents as being very important, while acknowledged as being important by the other agents. Organizational capability was important primarily to the ICT consultants and healthcare agents (with the notable exception of the Department of Work and Pensions in Northern Ireland).

All agents cited increasing and unmet demand for services as a key factor. Factors largely present only in the ICT domain had to do with policies aimed at universal access to communications and computing technology, and the constant jockeying by industry competitors and standards bodies to establish industry standards.

In addition, there was one 'factor' that emerged as important over the life of the system, which was largely a characteristic of the project itself. This was the potential for extending the system to other departments, hospitals or GP offices. We may term this characteristic of the project the 'roll-out potential' of the system and in several of the projects studied this characteristic influenced decisions made. Consistent with their emphasis on standardization, ICT agents were interested in enhancing the system to ensure that is was operational in multiple technical and organizational contexts, while government agents were interested in installing the system in multiple locations to gain economies of scale and improve efficiencies in communication among organizations.

Figure 3.1 applies the same diagrammatic representation to this analysis as was used in Chapter 2.

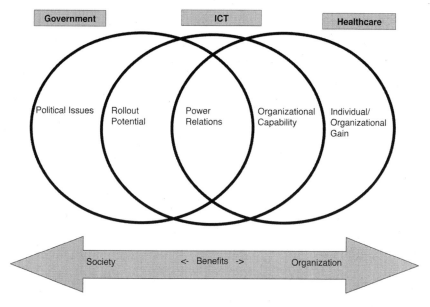

Figure 3.1 Decision factors of HCIS agents.

In some ways, the factors appeared to be similar to those mentioned in the urban regeneration cases. Political Issues and Organizational Capability can be mapped to nearly identical categories in urban regeneration, while Power Relations occupy the same central position in HCIS as Network Relationships do in urban regeneration. In addition, it could be argued that the Economics factor mentioned by private sector agents in urban regeneration is similar to the factor of Organizational Gain in the HCIS, in that each has to do with what value the agent can expect to realize from participation. The only factor that is quite different in the HCIS case is 'Roll-out potential', which appears to be connected to the ICT industry's emphasis on industry and system standards as well as their perception of what constitutes value in ICT. In urban regeneration, this spot in the diagram was occupied by 'social' factors, seen as drivers of decision-making in both public and non-profit agents, but more important to the non-profit sector agents. We return to this comparison between the two domains in Chapter 4.

HEALTHCARE INFORMATION SYSTEMS RULES

The discussion of the exogenous and endogenous environment(s) of HCIS continues with a discussion of the rules governing the projects studied. The relationship of factors and rules to the systems studied is dynamic and ongoing, as they help to shape the systems outcomes through direct, as well as complex, interactions with agent decision-making. As highlighted in the previous section, an example of a 'factor' in the HCIS environment is the capability and rate of change in ICT technology, while an example of a 'rule' in HCIS is the method by which individuals pay for healthcare—i.e. via public insurance in Northern Ireland and a combination of public and private sources in the Republic.

As noted in Chapter 1, rules that appear to be of importance in public management systems are those that relate to agent participation, system processes, payoffs and time/place. Establishing such rules is the main focus of policy and legislation relating to both urban regeneration and HCIS and so any discussion of rules must begin with the relevant policy and legislation. This requires that we look at two largely separate policy areas—healthcare and information systems. This analysis is followed by a brief discussion of the public management decision-making and accountability frameworks operating in healthcare in each jurisdiction, as the management of information systems is subsumed into the remit of the healthcare agencies and delivery points. A summary of the endogenous rules that appeared to operate in one or more cases (whether activated from the exogenous policy/practice environment or created internally through the interaction of agents over time) is provided at the end of this section.

Policy and Practice in Healthcare Information Systems in Ireland

Republic of Ireland

Two strategies around healthcare and information systems were published by the Irish Government during the period of the research: *Quality and Fairness: a health system for you* (Department of Health and Children 2001) and the *Health Information Strategy* (Department of Health and Children 2004). The 2001 strategy was largely aspirational, emphasizing patient empowerment:

> A health system that supports and empowers you, your family and community to achieve your full health potential . . . A health system that is there when you need it, that is fair, and that you can trust . . . A health system that encourages you to have your say, listens to you, and ensures that your views are taken into account.
>
> (Department of Health and Children (DoHC) 2001: 8)

The strategy also stated that: 'Information plays a central role in supporting strategic goals and in underpinning the principles of the Health Strategy. It must not be seen merely as an add-on' (DoHC 2001: 131–132).

The later *Health Information Strategy* developed the idea of information as an enabling resource, within the context of data protection rights:

> The vision of the Strategy is to ensure that all stakeholders, namely the general public, clients/patients, careers, health professionals, service staff, service managers, policy makers, Government, researchers and the media can readily access trustworthy information and can use it appropriately.
>
> (DoHC 2004: 7)

Striking a balance between efficient and effective use of information and the protection of personal rights, the four principles of the Strategy were to:

- Safeguard the privacy and confidentiality of personal health information
- Ensure that health information systems are efficient and effective
- Promote the optimal use of health information
- Ensure the high quality of health information

(DoHC 2004: 7)

The healthcare system in the Republic of Ireland is a mixed market, in which in-patient procedures are largely covered by public (or private) insurance, and capped charges are levied for hospital and general practitioner visits. Vulnerable groups receive free treatment under a medical card system. In 2003, tax-deductible private insurance cover was held by 50 per cent of the population (Layte *et al.* 2007), the advantage of which is quicker access to services either as 'private patients' in public hospitals or by accessing care in private hospitals. Issues of concern around health provision in the Irish Republic have included equity within a mixed provision system, the length of waiting lists and pressure on accident and emergency services (Downey-Ennis and Harrington 2002, Wiley 2005, Layte *et al.* 2007). During the economic boom of the 'Celtic tiger', per capita non-capital public expenditure on health services rose from 60 per cent of the EU average in 1990 to 101.8 per cent in 2002; and capital investment also increased significantly (Wiley 2005).

Key policy statements on health were issued in 1966, 1986, 1994 and 2001 with the latest one– *Quality and Fairness: a health system for you* (Department of Health and Children 2001)– mentioned above. In addition to the overarching objectives, the document also lists a number of more specific strategies covering cancer, children's health, public health, smoking policy, cardiovascular health, the health of adolescents, drugs strategy, palliative care and AIDS. In addition, commitments are made to: 'information on which to plan and organize the health system; investment in national health information systems as set out in the forthcoming National Health Information Strategy; and the development of electronic health record to enhance the quality and safety of care' (Department of Health and Children 2001: 94).

HCIS policy has been developed within the context of both healthcare policy and wider government policies on the use of information technology in public services. However, ICT policy development lagged behind implementation of several of the case study projects in this research, with the 2004 *Health Information Strategy* coming well after the initiation of all but the Electronic Health Record. Much of this approach was cross-referenced to the subsequent government-wide strategy *New Connections* (Department of the *Taoiseach* 2002), which recognized the importance of electronic patient records and a unique patient identification system. The 2007–2013 National Development Plan includes capital funding for ICT development in the health sector. The commitment to upholding data protection rights, along with improving health information, is discussed in relation to electronic health records in the consultation document for a new *Health Information Bill* (Department of Health and Children 2008).

Structures for the administration of healthcare in the Irish Republic changed radically during the course of this research. Much of the background for the case studies took place under the governance system established following the Health Act 1970, consisting of a Department of Health and eight regional health boards which 'became the main providers of health and personal social services through three core programmes: general hospitals, special hospitals and community care programmes' (Wiley 2005: 169).

The Health Act 2004 put in place a new system, as shown in Figure 3.2. The government department with responsibility for health policy development and service planning became the Department of Health and Children (DoHC). Health and community care services delivery was centralized under a new agency, the Health Service Executive (HSE), established in 2005, which took over the role of the health boards—although eight geographical groups remained for the administration of acute hospital services. The Health Information and Quality Authority (HIQA) was set up in 2007 to develop health information systems and to implement a programme of quality assurance. It had no responsibility for inspection of mental health services, which was carried out by a separate Mental Health Commission. All four agencies report to the Minister for Health and Children.

Responsibility for various aspects of HCIS is divided between the HSE, DoHC and HIQA. Delivery of information systems projects is the responsibility of the HSE's ICT Directorate (Ryan *et al.* 2007) whereas delivery of the *Health Information Strategy* (DoHC 2004) is the responsibility of the DoHC. In turn, the DoHC has connections with HIQA, whose

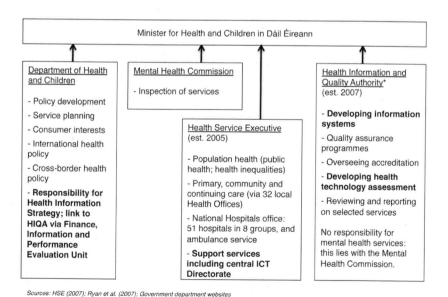

Figure 3.2   Structures for the administration of healthcare in the Republic of Ireland.

responsibilities include a number of information and technology functions and whose review function would include the effectiveness of information systems. The extent to which the Mental Health Commission involves itself in ICT projects is unclear, although Ryan *et al.* (2007) report their involvement in one ICT project.

Northern Ireland

Published by the Department of Health, Social Services and Public Safety (DHSSPS), Northern Ireland's contemporary health strategy, *A Healthier Future*, stated: 'Our overall aim is to improve the physical and mental health and social wellbeing of the people of Northern Ireland' (DHSSPS 2004: 8). Five strategic cross-cutting themes were identified: investing for health and wellbeing; involving people; teams which deliver; responsive and integrated services; improving quality.

As part of the responsive and integrated services theme, a significant commitment was made to the use of new technologies with numerous processes and outcomes to be improved through better use of ICT.

Following the commitment to ICT development in *A Healthier Future*, the Information and Communications Technology Strategy (DHSSPS 2005a), and its accompanying implementation paper (DHSSPS 2005b), were published, with specific sub-strategies aimed at achieving the objectives stated in the overall healthcare strategy. In the Information and Communications Technology Strategy, it is acknowledged that the two key themes of Electronic Care Records and Electronic Communications required significantly improved infrastructure. In addition, a cross-departmental Data Protection Review by the Department of Finance and Personnel (DFP) covering these projects, and others in HCIS, appears to have been prompted by data security incidents elsewhere in the UK (DFP 2008) and is part of the data protection context of HCIS in Northern Ireland.

Northern Ireland's healthcare system is run under the principles of the UK's NHS, and responsibility for local policy and administration is devolved to the Northern Ireland Assembly. The NHS in Northern Ireland was established in 1948, following the Health Services Act (NI) 1946. The system was restructured in 1974 around four health and social services boards, which became purchasers of services from health trusts in 1991 after the introduction of the internal market (Jordan *et al.* 2006). The aims of the internal market were to improve efficiency, accountability, planning and coordination, service quality, patient choice and equity of provision, through changing the culture to make it more businesslike; all claims that have been disputed to a lesser or greater extent. While budget allocation and management are based on an internal 'quasi' market, medical services are free to the consumer at point of use. A subsidized flat rate charge is made for prescribed medicines, although after the end of the research period an announcement was made that this would be abolished and prescription medicines would be free.

The coming of devolution and the Northern Ireland Assembly in 1999 provided the opportunity for Northern Ireland politicians to shape healthcare policy more actively than had been possible under direct rule.[2] Prior to the publication of Northern Ireland's 20-year comprehensive strategy *A Healthier Future*, one of the Assembly's first consultation processes and agreed strategies was the Public Health Strategy, *Investing for Health*, which focused on improving health and well being, and on reducing health inequalities, including tackling poverty (Campbell 2003, Jordan *et al.* 2006). Responsibility for implementation was given to Directors of Public Health within the health boards. A separate mental health strategy was also agreed in 2003.

There has also been a focus on service restructuring since 1999. In 2003, the report *Developing Better Services* proposed a rationalization and modernization of acute care hospitals (Campbell 2003), a set of proposals that proved particularly controversial in the less populated west of the province. At the same time, a waiting list initiative was proposed, which had implications for information systems, and a new staff contracts structure placed a greater emphasis on performance. A Regulation Quality and Improvement Authority was established in 2005,[3] the same year as the report of an independent review of health and social services, the Appleby Review. Appleby recommended improved performance management, information and incentives for staff, along with a better system of accountability (Jordan *et al.* 2006). At the same time, the Review of Public Administration was examining all aspects of public service delivery in Northern Ireland, and although the results were announced in 2005, implementation was just beginning by the end of the research period in 2007. The new, simplified Health and Personal Services Structure (HPSS) includes a strategic body, seven local commissioning groups, a smaller number of health trusts and a single patient council (DHSSPS 2007).

Although developed under the auspices of the NHS, the administrative structure in Northern Ireland is unique within the UK, with health and social services under the same administrative structure, the HPSS, rather than the NHS alone. In the rest of the UK, local councils are responsible for the administration of social services, while health is under the auspices of the NHS.

Structures for the administration of healthcare in Northern Ireland were reviewed during the research period of 2004–2007 but, as described above, implementation had only just begun, so details of the older system are provided here and in Figure 3.3. As in the Irish Republic, all bodies are run by appointed Boards, with the exception of the DHSSPS. which reports directly to the Minister for Health, Social Services and Public Safety, whether in the Assembly or at Westminster. The Minister is accountable through Assembly or Parliamentary Committee systems, the Northern Ireland Executive

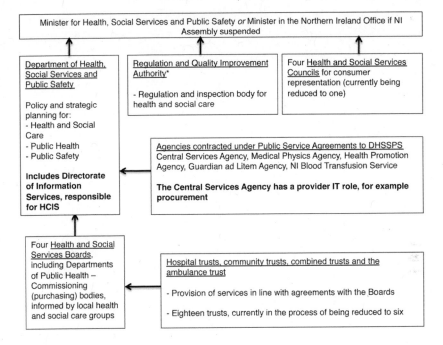

Figure 3.3   Structures for the administration of healthcare in Northern Ireland.

or the Westminster Cabinet, and the Northern Ireland Assembly or the House of Commons.

Figure 3.3 shows how the purchaser/provider split operates, with the regional Health and Social Services Boards contracting with Heath Trusts and reporting to the DHSSPS. Other agencies engage with the DHSSPS via Public Service Agreements, again a quasi-contractual and monitored situation. The Regulation and Quality Improvement Authority appears to be broadening its remit to include all hospital and social care services; and unlike in the Irish Republic, consumer representation is built into the system with the health and social services councils.

Rules Applied in HCIS Projects in Ireland

In both jurisdictions, healthcare was a mainstream service with a more integrated structure than urban regeneration. Structures were highly centralized, with little role for local councils or other local organizations, and restructuring was in the process of intensifying this centralization. The role of the market was important in different ways in each jurisdiction, with a mixed market including a strong private insurance component in the south, and quasi-market mechanisms in place between purchaser and provider in the North, which did not involve the patient/consumer in purchasing decisions. In Northern Ireland, consumer representation was built into the governing structures, but in the Republic of Ireland it was carried out by voluntary organizations; appointed members run all administrative health boards. Both systems included personal social services within their structures and both jurisdictions had policies for the development of HCIS, published in the same year, which emphasized both the importance of ICT to the development of high quality patient care, and the need to be continually aware of data protection and informed consent issues.

The exogenous rules arising from policy appeared to have had less impact on the decisions made in the HCIS projects than was the case in urban regeneration. Legislation and public sector strategy were less influential in HCIS than in urban regeneration, as the endogenous rules selected from the environment stemmed more from industry and professional norms. These were discussed briefly in the previous section on factors as linked to professional values in healthcare, management and ICT. The impact of these values on the rules operating within the projects was particularly noticeable in the rules applying to processes. It may be the case that intra-organizational systems are generally less affected by legislative rules than by rules that derive from the relevant sector's norms and the practices of the organization itself. Inter-organizational systems on the other hand, require that agents must engage directly with other organizations to establish some common basis for their interactions. Relevant legislation may provide or impose a convenient, and relatively objective, starting point for this purpose.

Nevertheless, it is still the case that the influence of policy and the institutional structures in each jurisdiction was observable in the projects. For example, the policies concerning value for money and public procurement arising from EU or national legislation influenced agent rules as well as processes and payoffs. Furthermore, the strategies in both Northern Ireland and the Irish Republic were occasionally referred to as contributing to the justification of a project overall or, more often, in the roll-out process.

As in the case of urban regeneration, rules were also created—explicitly or implicitly– as a result of agent interactions. The most obvious example of this was during the processes of 'project justification' and 'agree/approve solution' in which the basic cost and desired outcome parameters for the projects were agreed, and these then became boundaries within which other decisions could be made. Apart from these, however, it was difficult to identify any other rules that emerged as agents interacted in the projects over time. The pattern of progressive rule evolution observed in urban regeneration was not apparent in the HCIS cases and the projects seemed to move along their unfolding paths without the need for creating additional rules governing payoffs, agents, processes or time/place. Certainly there were progressively more specific or agreed understandings of what the system would do, who could or should use it and what it would cost to develop and operate, but this was all done within the cognitive and normative rules that the various agents brought with them from their industry sector and organizational positions. The one exception to this was the decision about extending the system (roll-out potential), which may (or may not) arise at any point in the project and the outcome of which had significant implications in subsequent actions and decisions. Examples of agent, process, payoff and time/place rules operating in the cases are discussed below. How the different rules appeared (i.e., were they exogenously or endogenously created?) is also indicated.

Agent rules were present in the environment both in terms of the healthcare funding models and the institutional governance structures in place. In Northern Ireland the central government was the primary mover and neither local agencies nor citizens/patients had much of a role—in spite of the fact that community involvement is an espoused objective. In the mixed-market model in the Republic of Ireland, the private sector and religious bodies were players in healthcare delivery and a significant ICT sector could be drawn on for consulting and technical expertise. As far as the endogenous agent rules observed, lead organizations were either self-appointed or charged with responsibility for developing system(s) by the relevant department. In Northern Ireland regional or national systems, project oversight bodies were established to be representative of stakeholders (although patients were largely ignored as a constituency). Specific individuals' participation was established within projects based largely on functional capability.

Process rules in the environment were largely derived from professional practices in ICT and healthcare. Best practice in UK ICT development methodology (promoted by Northern Ireland Government agencies), and project management, technical orientation, goals and process norms were deeply embedded in the management and ICT professions in both jurisdictions. Norms concerning independence, expertise and authority were equally deeply embedded in the clinical professions involved. The institutional structures were undergoing intense change, creating some uncertainty in decision-making processes and—in Northern Ireland—the institutional structure was strongly contract orientated. The professional norms of project management were highly influential in the process norms adopted within the projects. Endogenous rule-setting was a key focus during the beginning processes in the projects (initiation, justification and requirements definition), thereby creating the internal rule environment at the outset. In addition, the question of whether or not to proceed with a 'roll-out' of a pilot system to other organizations was an important process decision taken largely within the boundaries of the project—although by different agents in the two jurisdictions. In Northern Ireland, this decision was an executive one made by government agents participating in the project boards, while in the Republic of Ireland it was more organically decided by agents deciding whether or not to use the new system.

Payoff rules in the environment were less explicit than in the UR projects as the specific funding requirements and efficiency (or other) gains were established during the early processes of the projects themselves. Targeted funding was less common in these projects although the 'Spend to Save' programme identified in the EPES project is an example of this type of exogenous payoff rule. There appears to be some kind of status payoff for being involved in pilot projects in both jurisdictions and possibly some negative payoffs for not complying with agreed (endogenous) budget and timeframe rules. Mostly, however, the payoff rules were project specific (endogenous) and established in the initial processes of justification and agreeing solutions. These include the targeted organizational gain to be achieved, the money to be spent, and the specific stakeholders expected to benefit.

Time/place rules: There was little in the environment to influence the particular time and place in which projects will occur. An exception to this is the case in which a new (major) facility is planned and requires information system development. Technological developments can sometimes create opportunities, if not imperatives, to pursue HCIS. As was the case for other types of rules, time/place rules tend to be established via the interactions among agents within the project boundary. How much time would be required to deliver the agreed functionality and what organizations and/or functions within organizations should be affected were all decisions taken by project participants. The passing of time did play a role in decision-making as deadlines loomed, but budget 'rules' appeared to be more relevant in HCIS cases than in UR—where time was a more salient concern.

AGENTS IN HEALTHCARE INFORMATION SYSTEMS

As in urban regeneration, broad consistency was found across projects in terms of the agents involved. In particular, individuals filled each of the key project roles—generally in order to bring a particular functional skill or to represent a particular group of stakeholders in the project. For example, across all projects, there were people in the roles of project manager, ICT manager, user representative, hospital management, clinical sponsor and clinical users. These roles appeared throughout the projects studied and seemed to represent the standard internal groups brought together to achieve ICT-related organizational objectives.

Another common thread across the projects was the use of ICT consultants and solutions providers to provide expertise at various stages of projects. These brought expertise in relation to ICT strategy, developments in management and healthcare-specific ICT systems, expertise in project management and systems design, development platforms (i.e., the hardware and software required) and, in one case, a range of turn-key solutions for GPs. In this, the HCIS projects were similar to the urban regeneration projects in use of policy, planning, engineering and other technical consultants to assess requirements and identify solutions.

Where the projects differed was in the level of involvement by government departments and agencies. In Northern Ireland, no fewer than seven different government departments or national agencies were directly involved in the three projects. These are the DHSSPS; Department of Finance and Personnel; Department of Work and Pensions; Northern Ireland Assembly Public Accounts Committee; Northern Ireland Audit Office; Information Commission; HM Treasury (UK). This list does not include agencies contracted to provide services to the Northern Ireland Department of Health, such as the Central Services Agency and the Service Delivery Unit, one or more of which were associated with each of the projects. The need for so many different government entities could not be explained by the projects being any larger or more complex than those in the Irish Republic. However, two of the three projects in Northern Ireland had their genesis in perceived national 'crises', and improved health information systems were assumed to be essential to their solution, and it may be that the political visibility of these projects exposed them to more attention from government departments. However, the project narratives do not suggest that this was the only reason for the involvement of government agencies. Of the seven high level government agencies involved, only the involvement of the Northern Ireland Assembly Public Accounts Committee (NIPAC) and the Northern Ireland Audit Office (NIAO) could be attributed to the perceived crises. In contrast, only one national level government agency was involved in the projects in the Republic of Ireland—the DoHC. This difference may partly be due to the effect of the contractual approach to governance in Northern Ireland. Table 3.3 highlights the involvement of different agents organized by their profession or associated interest group.

One of several similarities between the HCIS and the urban regeneration projects was the creation of project specific agents (PSAs), to facilitate interaction among stakeholders, to concentrate interest group input and to act as forums for decision-making. In the HCIS projects, these took the form of project 'boards' and were found only in Northern Ireland. These were not the same as the project 'teams', which consisted of the project manager, the user representative, hospital management, the ICT internal staff and/or consultants designing and implementing the system—which were present in both jurisdictions. Instead, the PSAs represented different stakeholders in the project who generally had significant decision-making authority, influencing direction. The boards of two projects in Northern Ireland included representatives of multiple government agencies as well as representatives from other stakeholders such as GPs, pharmacists and other health trusts. Also distinguishing the Northern Ireland projects from those in the Republic of Ireland was the need to get departmental approval for

Table 3.3   Agents in Healthcare Information Systems in Ireland

Agents	NI	ROI
Hospital/healthcare provider		
Clinical sponsor[§]	✓	✓
Hospital/organization management	✓	✓
'User' representative[†]	✓	✓
Clinical/administrative users	✓	✓
Information & Communications Technology		
Project manager	✓	✓
ICT manager in hospital	✓	✓
ICT consultants	✓	✓
ICT turn-key providers	-	✓*
Government		
Department of Health	✓	✓
Regional Health Trusts/boards	✓	✓
Project management 'board'	✓	-
Govt Departments other than DoH)	✓	-
Govt Agencies	✓	-
Other Stakeholders		
Patient (family) representative	✓*	
ICT industry standards bodies		✓

[§]This was generally a senior consultant in the organization, although GPs might also play this role.
[†]User representatives invariably come from a clinical background, with nurses playing this role to a large extent.
*One project only.

major projects. All three projects studied in the research required DHSSPS approval. In addition however, one project also needed the approval of the Department of Finance and another was funded through a programme sponsored by HM Treasury (UK). The only project in which departmental approval was mentioned in the Irish Republic was for the expansion of HealthLink from its original scope (centred around one hospital and local GPs) to a national project.

The first example of a PSA in the north was the case of the TMS, which had a project board that was, at first, made up of stakeholders in Belfast City Hospital only. When this project became part of the national strategy to provide theatre management in all major hospitals, the board expanded significantly, incorporating government representatives and a range of representatives from the various regional health trusts around Northern Ireland.

Health trusts (or 'boards' as they are referred to in the Republic of Ireland) played a fairly minor role in the projects in both jurisdictions, although again they were more noticeable in the North than in the south. Where they were most active was in the two examples of projects that involved the rolling out of an ICT system developed in one location, to other locations around the jurisdictions. Interestingly, it appeared that the health boards in the Republic of Ireland had more say in whether or not they would get involved in Health-Link, than did their counterparts in the North with regard to the TMS. It is also interesting to note that there did not appear to be a similar type of project board set up to oversee the roll-out of HealthLink—instead there was simply a project team that supported the incremental roll-out to hospitals and GPs as required (at the request of the end-users). These different approaches to national roll-out of ICT applications may be symptomatic of a more the top-down approach to HCIS projects in the North as compared to a bottom-up approach in the Republic of Ireland.

The second example of a PSA in Northern Ireland was in the EPES project– a national level project run by a project board established during project initiation. The project board was dominated by government agency representatives, but also included representatives of the direct users of the system, the family practitioners (GPs) and pharmacists. ICT consultants were the primary agents engaged by the project board to analyze feasibility and determine the basic functionality required, engaging in 'Competitive Dialogue'[4] with the project board to design the system and then entering into a contract with the DHSSPS to build and maintain the system over a five-year period. 'User' groups were involved in the project as it progressed, but largely as opponents (pharmacists), or, at best, as relatively uninterested participants (GPs). Patients did not participate in the project to any visible extent.

An unusual aspect of the approach to the EPES project was that the project board had authority over the ICT project itself, but had no authority over negotiations with the end-users on their eventual use of the proposed system. A different entity dealt with all contract negotiations with service providers in primary care– the 'Primary Care Directorate' of the DHSSPS. Not surprisingly, the negotiations with service providers on their future use of EPES became entangled with other contract negotiations, which slowed progress significantly.

As can be seen, the project boards in Northern Ireland were very influential, and included multiple participants from outside the 'host' organization. This is in contrast to the PSAs identified in the urban regeneration projects, which also had various degrees of influence in the projects, but, in the end, were never as powerful as the related government entity with overall responsibility. Nevertheless, it would appear that the more complex institutional environment in Northern Ireland contributed to the need for PSAs to play a similar role to that played by these agents in urban regeneration, i.e., to facilitate stakeholder interaction, build consensus and to drive solutions and implementation strategies.

PROCESSES IN HEALTHCARE INFORMATION SYSTEMS

Several of the processes engaged in by participating agents have been mentioned already: project initiation; requirements definition; agree/approve ICT solution; implementation/roll-out. Those familiar with ICT project management will recognize these as standard processes in any ICT project development process. They are also similar to those found in the urban regeneration cases as will be highlighted in the detailed discussion to follow. In addition, the process of 'creating project team/board' is similar to the process of 'activating agents' seen in urban regeneration, although the activation of existing agents in HCIS involves a change in role and a definition of the boundaries between the agent's activities within the project and those outside. In fact, the pattern in the HCIS domain appears to be quite similar to that in urban regeneration, suggesting that projects in public management—no matter what their level of organizational involvement—may involve essentially the same set of organizing process sequences. However, the intra-organizational ICT projects exhibited more demarcation between those activities inside and those outside the system, as well as between the different processes. In addition, the distinct separation between the processes of project initiation and project justification in the HCIS projects did not exist in urban regeneration. These similarities and differences will be explored in the discussion of processes below. The six processes identified in HCIS projects were: project initiation; project justification; requirements definition; project team/board creation; agreement/approval of ICT Solution; ICT systems implementation/'roll-out'.

Project Initiation

The HCIS projects had three possible initializing events: the 'political crisis' event, the 'new facility' event and the incremental set of 'ICT improvement' events. Political crises drove two of the projects in Northern Ireland– high waiting lists and low theatre utilization rates driving the initialization of TMS; the identification of fraud in prescription refunds driving the initialization of EPES. In the case of TMS, the resulting national project was bolted on to a hospital-based project that was well underway by the time the national ICT strategy was published. This may have contributed to an implementation strategy for TMS that was similar in some respects to the more incremental HealthLink project seen in the Republic of Ireland. From the data collected, it could be suggested that projects resulting from political crises are likely to have significant government involvement. Projects with similar scope, but different initialization events, in the Irish Republic had very little government involvement.

New facilities led to the initialization of the RABIU project in Belfast and the OCS project in Dublin. In both cases the ICT projects were part of a larger construction and organizational change project in which separate health services were brought together in a single facility in order to improve patient care as well as to create operational efficiencies. In the case of RABIU, the project brought together the in-patient brain injury services located in Foster Green Hospital and outpatient services located on Holywood Road. The OCS project was part of the Tallaght hospital project, which amalgamated three different hospitals in the Dublin area– the Adelaide, Meath and National Children's hospitals. One of the main challenges for the ICT projects was to integrate already existing, but separate, systems into one coherent 'systems architecture'. With this came the challenge of changing the organizational processes of the separate groups that now had to work together. In both cases, this led to a 'pilot' approach in which the initial scope of the overall system was pared down considerably in order to fit the prescribed budget (allocated as a small proportion of the overall budget), to minimize disruption of the medical and administrative processes and to lower the overall risk of the project.

The two remaining projects– HealthLink and the EHR– were not 'event' driven but emerged out of earlier ICT initiatives or government strategies. In both cases, a number of earlier projects, working group initiatives and/ or policy statements led, over time, to the development of these projects. It is worth noting that both of these were in the Republic of Ireland, in which this type of bottom-up approach to HCIS projects was more widespread than in Northern Ireland

Project Justification

HCIS projects all had to be explicitly 'justified' though some type of cost-benefit analysis undertaken by the sponsoring organization. Where the urban regeneration projects had legislative 'rules' upon which to draw for justification, the HCIS projects followed more business normative rules– a compelling financial, managerial or clinical reason to pursue the project had to be made. In the case of the new facility or crisis-driven projects, the events themselves provided the source of benefit to be gained, so the focus of the justification was on the cost of achieving those benefits. The politically sensitive projects did seem to access significant levels of funding (although this process took two years in the case of TMS), while the two projects linked to new facilities had limited budgets in the context of the overall project budget, and needed buy-in from clinical users at a very early stage. In the case of Health-Link, there were several justification processes that ultimately came together. These were undertaken by the Mater Hospital, in the first 'pilot' stage; by the GP IT Working Group in the decision to provide PCs to GP practices; by the Department of Health when it was decided to extend the project to hospitals and GP practices nationally; and finally by the GP practices and hospitals themselves in their decision to purchase the necessary hardware and software to connect to HealthLink. In the Northern Ireland projects, justification was highly structured as a 'business case' for approval by the DHSSPS.

Interestingly, the process of project justification in the Republic of Ireland did not appear as prominently in the narratives as a key decision point as it did in Northern Ireland. Nor did the budget constraints imposed by the justification project appear to have as significant an impact on subsequent decision-making. While the relatively better economic environment in the Republic of Ireland is likely to have been influential in this difference, it also appears that the more structured processes in Northern Ireland played a role too.

When comparing public service domains, this clear distinction between project initiation and justification processes observed in the HCIS projects did not exist in the minds (or comments) of interviewees in urban regeneration. In reviewing the case data, this was not due to differences in the organizational scope of the projects or the policy content, but rather to the existence of laws in urban regeneration relating to the circumstances under which action is justified. The existence of this legal justification, the inter-organizational nature of the projects and the difficulty in constructing and monitoring a project-wide budget under these circumstances appeared to de-emphasize the need for an overall cost-benefit analysis in UR projects. Instead, the project participants advanced directly to identifying the problem and agreeing to the solution. While this process of agreeing to the solution sometimes involved cost-benefit analyses of alternative solutions, no justification of the overall project itself was undertaken.

Requirements Definition

This process of requirements definition looked very much like the 'identifying the problem' process in the urban regeneration project cases. It was similar across all HCIS projects—although more structured and 'methodical' (using specific systems development methodologies) in Northern Ireland. In this process, the objectives for a given project were solidified (based upon the expected benefits arising out of the project justification process) and agreed to amongst the various participating agents. As in the urban regeneration projects, objectives took the form of agreed outcomes and 'functionality'. Specifically, a basic set of five decisions was made, concerning: what should the system accomplish; what functions/data were required to accomplish these things; who should 'own' the system; who should have access to the system; who should *not* have access to the system (the data security issue). The process was often engaged in simultaneously with the process, 'project team/board creation'– particularly when ICT consultants were hired to perform much of the process.

In urban regeneration, external consultants were almost always hired to perform all or a part of this process, while in HCIS, the host organization was likely to use its own staff—or to hire a project manager to join its staff—to perform most of the task. This difference may reflect the perceived value of outside experts in situations involving many different perspectives in urban regeneration, while HCIS projects are already more focused and generally contained within one organization.

Project Team/Board Creation

In the discussion of agents, the different types of agents involved were considered, and the nature of agents was highlighted as being largely an exercise in identifying roles. In essence, individuals within and from outside the organization took on particular roles on the project team and/or project board. While project boards were not always created, project teams were, and the first step in assembling a project team was the appointment of a project manager. The project manager may have been appointed before or after the project justification process, but was often linked to the identification of a specific individual to play the role of the user representative on the project team. This suggests that there is some kind of balancing dynamic in the formation of the project team roles. In some cases, the role of project manager was filled by the host organization's IT manager for the initiation, justification and even into the requirements definition, but it was highly unusual (and considered to be a problem for the project) not to have a dedicated project manager when requirements definition began. ICT consultants and/or internal ICT staff completed the project team, filling various functional roles depending upon the specific technical and managerial requirement of the project.

It should be noted that in all cases in Northern Ireland, ICT consultants were involved in the requirements definition and implementation/roll-out processes. The hiring of consultants was a quite structured process with rules governing how third parties were informed of the project (as a 'Request for Proposal'), how their proposals should be structured and conveyed and how proposals were evaluated. The basic rule framework for hiring consultants in the public sector was laid down by the EU under public procurement regulation, but these regulations appeared to have a different impact in each jurisdiction—playing a significant role in Northern Ireland, while being less commented upon as being significant in the Republic of Ireland. It is not clear whether this was due to the less prominent role of consultants in the Republic, or the more fluid process of hiring consultants in that jurisdiction. ICT consultants, once hired, reported to either the project manager, or in their absence, the IT manager.

As discussed in the section on agents, project boards were found only in Northern Ireland and their role was to facilitate interaction between a wide range of stakeholders, to be a central point for debating and agreeing on the goals of the project overall and to act as a final arbiter of project-related strategic decisions.

The 'Activate Agents' process in urban regeneration is similar in many ways to the project team/board creation process in HCIS. In both processes, participating agents are identified either through their own decision to participate or by their being directed via legislation or organizational fiat. In both processes, there is the potential for a PSA to be created—with a core function of facilitating agreement among other agents, but also with the potential to be tasked with managing other aspects of the project. However, the process of creating the project team/board was much more formalized in HCIS than in urban regeneration, and the role delineation between what the agent did inside and outside the system more likely to be quite distinct. Furthermore, agent activation in urban regeneration could result in agents pursuing the same activities outside the system as well as beyond the life of the project itself, while HCIS roles were bounded by the HCIS project and were not expected to continue beyond the life of the project.

Agreement/Approval of ICT Solution

In general, Northern Ireland project teams relied on outside vendors to propose solutions, while projects in the Republic of Ireland used consultants more sparingly. The Northern Ireland process was quite structured and formalized, and involved a considerable amount of political input from the numerous government agencies. In the Republic of Ireland, the process of agreeing/approving to a solution appeared to be more 'emergent'—as distinct from a 'planned' or negotiated process, along the lines of the strategic process distinction outlined in Whittington (2001). All of the projects in the Irish Republic had lengthy pilot stages and were modified significantly during and after these stages. Even when there was a pilot in Northern Ireland (e.g. the TMS implementation in Belfast City Hospital), this was in the context of a formal plan to roll-out the system across Northern Ireland hospitals as it was designed. In this sense, the 'pilot' was no more than the first, limited implementation.

As in the urban regeneration projects, the agreement and approval of the ICT solution involved two different sets of agents—with the 'agreement' sub-process generally involving the project team (including consultants, if present) and the end-users. If a project board was present, then approval could only be achieved through this agent and the sub-process involved a wider set of participants. In one case (EPES), the project board blocked project approval because of the presence on the board of representatives of end-users with little interest in seeing the project completed. One of the differences between this process and its counterpart in urban regeneration was that the solution process in that domain was often undertaken in parallel with the problem identification process (although not by design), while in the HCIS projects the project justification and requirements definition processes had to be completed before the solution process could begin. Of course, there were some modifications to the ultimate goals and deliverables of the ICT projects during the agreement and approval process, but this was not considered a revisiting of the project's overall problem domain. Rather, these modifications generally took the form of modifications to the functionality to be delivered rather than to the overall project goals.

ICT Systems Implementation/Roll-Out

Information systems traditionally follow a multi-step implementation plan, which can take one of two paths. In a linear 'planned' method, the major functions of the system are built and tested in a staged approach, although some functions can be implemented in parallel and then bolted together at an integration stage later on. Testing of the system is conducted first by the project team and then by the end-users—with this latter testing phase usually involving training in the use of the system. In systems terminology, this second phase of testing is called 'acceptance testing' and the system is not considered finished and ready for regular usage until such time as the end-users signal their acceptance, often via some formal sign-off document.

The other main approach to systems implementation is the development of pared down system modules that can be used right away by end-users as a 'pilot' for the envisioned system. During the pilot, problems can be fixed and performance tuned, and this approach may be used to refine the design or even requirements specifications. It is difficult for the majority of people to understand fully what design specifications will mean in the physical world—whether in relation to computer systems or houses and streets. While it is possible to build small 'pilots' that can create the 'look and feel' of the proposed design of a computer system, a pilot approach to requirements definition is not feasible for projects of the scale and complexity of urban regeneration, principally due to the cost implications of building pilots.

In all of the projects there was a staged roll-out plan, although this took a more linear/planned approach in Northern Ireland and a more emergent approach in the Republic of Ireland. None of the systems was implemented as a 'big bang' approach and two of the projects were significantly expanded after their initial implementation. In several cases, this was a question of implementing the same basic system across different locations, while in others it was a partial implementation, followed by adding on additional processes or user groups.

Until implementation/roll-out, the HCIS and urban regeneration projects had quite similar processes, but in the implementation process, major differences were revealed. Because of the differences between the policy domains, the 'content' of the problem(s) to be solved appears to be more influential than either the level of organizational activity or the overall governance environment. The main differences in implementation were: the amount of interaction among agents; the number of different contractors involved in delivering the solution; the length of time required to implement; the amount of end-user testing and influence. Each of these differences will be discussed in turn.

In the previous chapter, the observation was made that the amount of interaction among agents dropped off considerably as the urban regeneration agents got on with their tasks and focused on meeting deadlines, budgets and deliverables relatively independently. Apart from some planned and highly structured meetings among contractors run by a project manager, interaction between agents was limited. In the HCIS projects, on the other hand, interaction between participants in the project team stayed at the same level as before, with representatives from IT, clinical departments, management and government (if present) interacting regularly as the project progressed. Interestingly, HCIS functional objectives often shifted over the course of the implementation phase, although the overall objectives and project constraints did not. In the case of urban regeneration, on the other hand, the basic deliverables were less mutable, but the project constraints of time and cost did change.

In HCIS, there were never more than two ICT consultants involved in implementation, along with the internal IT staff and users. All other things being equal, this makes for a much less complicated set of interactions compared to the urban regeneration cases. In urban regeneration, there was a large number of specialist contractors involved, all contributing their particular skills with their particular norms and attitudes, making for a very challenging coordinating environment. It may be that the patterns of (less) interaction among agents in UR projects evolved over time as a coping mechanism to minimize the complexity of an already difficult exercise in organizing.

The third difference was in the length of time required to complete the HCIS projects. In urban regeneration the median timeframe was eight years, while in HCIS it was four years. It is difficult to compare the scale of projects from two such different domains, but from Figure 3.4 we can see that once a solution was agreed, the HCIS implementation time was significantly shorter than was the case in urban regeneration. This is cer-

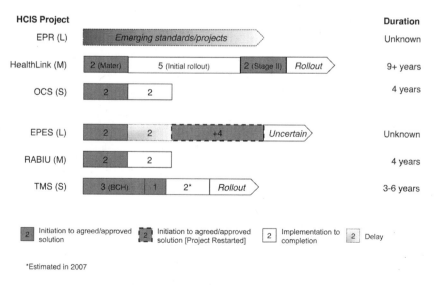

Figure 3.4   Healthcare Information Systems project timelines.

tainly related to the nature of the tasks being carried out in the different domains.

Perhaps as a consequence of the generally shorter timeframes in the HCIS projects, time elapsed did not appear to increase in importance in terms of driving decision-making– except in one of the two projects linked to the construction of a new facility (RABIU). In this case, the opening date of the facility and the perception of being 'ready' with ICT systems at least partially in place was an important driver for implementation and these factors drove decisions to cut back project scope and to go with partial implementation in the first phase.

The final difference observed was in the nature and influence of end-user testing of the solutions. In HCIS projects, end-users generally had the final say as to whether or not a system was complete, and they could propose changes in the system as it was being constructed. In urban regeneration it was quite unusual for potential residents or commercial interests to have much of a say once construction had begun—due to the cost of changes to design once the bricks and mortar were laid. However, it is well known that changes during the implementation phase of an ICT project are many times more costly than those same changes when decided during design, just as is the case in building and infrastructure. What is not clear is whether it is the relative cost of change that is responsible for the relative unwillingness in UR projects to adapt to residents' desires for change or simply different operating norms in the two different technical environments.

OUTCOMES OF HEALTHCARE INFORMATION SYSTEMS

In general, the intended outcomes for these projects were increased efficiency and new service support. Efficiency covered outcomes such as increased throughput (TMS), cost savings (HealthLink in the initial stages), eliminating fraud (EPES) and faster/easier information sharing between clinical departments and/or organizations (OCS, EHR and HealthLink in the later stages of the project). New service support was the driving force behind OCS and RABIU.

In several projects (mostly in the Republic of Ireland), the initial objective of increased efficiency was later expanded to include service extensions and/or improved service quality (OCS, HealthLink). There were also two cases in which implementation in one organization then spread to other organizations (TMS, HealthLink) even though this was not initially the plan. In both of these cases, however, the subsequent roll-out to other organizations was implemented by a different organization from the original sponsor.

The outcomes/outputs distinction existed in HCIS, but was different from that in urban regeneration in content, as well as in the scope of the targeted outcomes/outputs. It most cases in HCIS, the targeted outcomes were organization-specific—although they could be relevant to numerous organizations across the health system. For example, in the case of TMS, the targeted outcomes were the improved throughput in operating theatres (starting with Belfast City Hospital) and improved service quality. In EPES the targeted outcome was to achieve cost savings in prescription medicines and to reduce fraud among pharmacies, GPs and patients in Northern Ireland overall. In OCS, the targeted outcome was to improve the accuracy and speed of lab results in Tallaght Hospital, with a view to improving information-sharing across numerous departments in the Hospital. At first glance, these targeted outcomes look much more achievable and measurable than those established at the outset for the urban regeneration projects.

However, as had been observed in the urban regeneration projects, a mutation from outcomes to outputs occurred, over time, in HCIS projects. In the case of urban regeneration, project outcomes such as changing the mix of tenures morphed into specific numbers of dwellings to be built by social providers and private developers. In HCIS, theatre management throughput targets morphed into the implementation of particular ICT functions and the migration of hospitals to the new theatre management system. Post-implementation analyses neither occurred, nor were contemplated, in any of the projects studied, to determine whether the completed ICT system did in fact deliver the desired efficiency or service improvement gains. Claims were made, however, with regard to the OCS system's impact on lab test turnaround times.

Furthermore, the targeted outcomes did not play a role in feedback loops in project decision-making. Once the targeted outcomes were established and the justification of cost made in relation to these, the project and process goals became paramount and the only explicit feedback loop was the output of one phase of the project as the starting point for the next phase. The impact of project-related targets (cost/time) was much clearer in the HCIS projects than in urban regeneration, perhaps because intra-organizational projects are more easily tracked (and specific individuals held accountable) or because of the professional norms present in the ICT industry.

Similar to urban regeneration, *process goals* are made up of activities, checkpoints or documentation requirements agreed on among participants (or in some cases established in legislation), which may become rules depending upon the interaction and schema of the participating agents. Process goals address issues such as which agents are to be involved in which activities, the degree to which decisions should be by consensus, by majority or made by a particular agent, the format and periodicity of information-sharing among agents and the time periods in the unfolding process at which goals achievement should be reviewed by stakeholders. Process rules in HCIS were significantly more structured and detailed than those found in urban regeneration.

Throughout the projects, and from the very start, *project-related targets* were important results, which generally acted as constraining factors in agent decision-making. Cost, for example, was a major constraint that drove decision-making, particularly in the Northern Ireland projects. Unlike in the urban regeneration projects, cost was relatively straightforward to measure—at least in so far as it related to the direct costs of the project itself– and so it became a driver of decision-making. In urban regeneration, while attention was paid to time and budgets, it was unusual for the costs related to the activities of all of the relevant actors in a given project to be accounted for, and cost drivers did not feature largely in interviews and/or project documentation.

Table 3.4 provides a list of each of the different types of system 'results'—under the same categories used in urban regeneration. Even more than was the case in urban regeneration, the table shows how the main drivers of decision-making are the process and project results, rather than the outcomes and outputs that were the original reason for undertaking the project.

Table 3.4   Results for Healthcare Information Systems in Ireland

	Used as a Rule	Used as a Goal
Outcomes		
Improved throughput/utilization of resources	-	✓
Cost savings (value for money)	✓	✓
Decreased fraud	✓	✓
Faster/better information to management/clinicians	-	✓
Improved service quality	-	✓
Outputs		
Specified functionality/system	✓	✓
Number of departments/hospitals/GPs using system	-	✓
Process goals		
Conformance to EU/UK/NI/ROI public sector standards	✓	-
Required documents approved for each stage	✓	✓
Who should be included in decision-making	✓	-
Project-related targets		
Cost	✓	✓
Completion time	✓	✓

CONCLUSION: HEALTHCARE INFORMATION
SYSTEMS AS COMPLEX ADAPTIVE SYSTEMS

In this chapter, as in the preceding chapter, the basic elements required to describe HCIS projects as 'systems' using the complex adaptive systems (CAS) framework from Chapter 1 have been defined. In particular, the details of the agents, processes, environmental factors environmental rules and outcomes have been described, based on six cases in Ireland. The presence of each of these elements, and the goal-directed nature of the actions by agents within the HCIS projects studied, support the claim that these phenomena may be viewed as 'systems'. Furthermore, the successful mapping of the elements of HCIS projects to the proposed systems framework supports a more ambitious claim that the framework can be applied to heterogeneous public management domains as well as at different levels of organizational activity.

Figure 3.5 highlights the specific systems elements identified in HCIS projects in Ireland. As was seen in the study of urban regeneration, a box highlights the importance of agents in the system's environment—agents may or may not choose to enter the system over the course of its existence and bring with them their particular characteristics. The characteristics they bring, however, are different in nature as well as in impact from those in urban regeneration. This will be explored in more detail in the following chapter.

The system elements in italics represent those that are uniquely associated with the formation and operation of the system and represent the

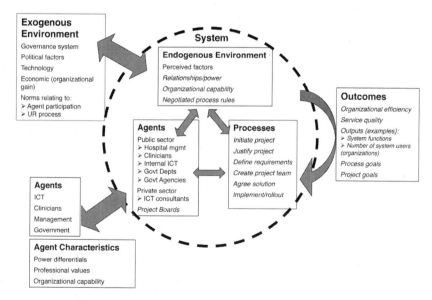

Figure 3.5   Systems elements of Healthcare Information Systems in Ireland.

changes that a system of this type brings about. These are largely confined to the processes and outcomes of the projects, although there may be some impact on the power relationships among individuals and their functional capability. However, unlike the urban regeneration cases, there appears to be less opportunity for adaptation overall, except in so far as processes affected by the ICT projects, engaged in by the organizations undertaking these projects, change as a result of the systems implementation. The creation of the internal environment, though certainly an exercise in mutual adaptation by agents, does not appear to carry over into the wider organizational environment to the same extent as in urban regeneration. The exception to this general observation is that in cases in which there is a multi-site (regional or national) roll-out, coupled with the project processes and outcomes impacting on the wider healthcare system, there may be some changes in power relationships and capabilities. An example of this can be found in the HealthLink project in which GPs became more informed (and therefore had more latent power) regarding their patients' lab test results; and in the EPES system in which the proposed system would have impacted significantly on the power relationships among pharmacists, GPs and the government departments involved in paying for prescriptions.

In addition to the general observations, noted above, regarding the features HCIS as a system, a number of observations arise from this analysis that are likely to have implications for public administration theory and practice in this domain:

- The boundaries of HCIS systems are clearly defined across multiple dimensions: an agent's role (inside versus outside the system); the organizational location—generally referred to as the 'sponsor'—of the system; and the budget parameters. A central activity in early stages of these projects is defining these boundaries which occurs in a highly structured way, consistent with the professional norms in management and ICT.
- As in urban regeneration, politics are an important factor in decision-making, largely having an impact on the project initiation and roll-out decisions. Social and economic factors are far less influential than in urban regeneration, although organizational gain may play a similar role in HCIS decision-making as economic (profit-opportunity) factors do in UR. Technology (capabilities and rate of change) and professional values and norms are much more important in HCIS than in UR.

1) Latent power relationships between professions and among individuals in an organization are a central characteristic of agents carried into the internal systems environment. Decisions about project objectives, process rules and participation are subject to influence

by these relationships, and the gain/loss of organizational power (both in the home organization and in the wider healthcare system) appears to be an implicit goal/effect of ongoing interactions.

2) Despite the existence of policy/strategy documents encouraging the inclusion of patients in decision-making in healthcare, there was little evidence of this in the HCIS projects. While this may partly be explained by the tendency for ICT systems implementation to be internally focused on organizational efficiency, several of the projects had direct impact on patient experience. The lack of involvement of community/patient representatives stands in direct contrast to the observations in urban regeneration.

- There appears to be an inflection point in the system lifecycle when the roll-out decision is taken (which may occur at various points in the system's history). If the decision is to expand the organizational scope—i.e., to roll-out the system to additional users in the organization/region– there is a significant expansion of potential stakeholders and agents, and the requirement for a PSA to resolve contentious perspectives increases.

4 Advancing the Case for Complex Adaptive Systems in Public Administration

INTRODUCTION

In this chapter, the analyses presented in Chapters 2 and 3 are summarized to support the use of the complex adaptive system (CAS) framework proposed in Chapter 1 for developing theory and practice in public administration. The empirical evidence supporting the use of the systems framework is supplemented by a theoretical discussion on how systems theory has developed to address a range of criticisms levelled at its use for public administration theory development over the last 50 years. This chapter functions as a bridge between Parts I and II of the book, concluding the argument for public administration projects as systems with the six core features outlined in Chapter 1, as a necessary precursor to the analysis of the unique CAS dynamics in the projects in Part II.

THE SYSTEMS 'NATURE' OF PUBLIC ADMINISTRATION PROJECTS

All human systems are characterized by purposeful activity (Ackoff and Emery 1972), and it is clear that the phenomena examined here fulfil this basic requirement of systems theory. In classic systems theory, however, the overall purpose of the system is assumed to be shared by the participants within the system and their interactions are aligned with this shared purpose. What we can observe in the case of the projects studied, however, is that there are many different purposes being pursued by the human participants engaging in the 'interlocking behaviours' that characterize human organizing (Weick 1969). This heterogeneity of purpose is difficult to incorporate into a classic systems theory approach, but CAS theory can accommodate this, in that agents with different schema are a fundamental aspect of CAS (Anderson 1999). Nevertheless, in order for a self-organizing system to emerge from the existence of heterogeneous agents, there needs to be something that causes the agents to interact. In the 12 cases studied, this impetus for interaction came in the form of policy objectives—whether legislative or managerial—and the initial stages of systems formation were largely focused on clarifying those objectives that may be jointly pursued, along with establishing the 'rules of the game' (Koppenjan and Klijn 2004). Over time, the interaction of agents was also observed to result in self-organization, adaptation, path-dependency, bifurcation and emergence– key dynamics of CAS– each of which is present to varying degrees in the projects studied. Before moving into the CAS-specific dynamics, however, it is necessary to review what has been observed so far with respect to the core elements of our basic systems framework: systems; environmental factors; environmental rules; agents; processes; outcomes.

The Boundary between Systems and Their Environment

We have already begun the discussion of the nature of the *systems* studied– that they are characterized by multiple purposes formed through agents engaging in largely self-organized interaction, which is stimulated by policy objectives. This was the case across all of the systems studied, with the intra-organizational Healthcare Information Systems (HCIS) cases being less connected to legislative policy than to organizational (departmental or hospital) policy and the reverse being the case in the urban regeneration (UR) cases. In addition, there was evidence of greater effort expended in the HCIS projects on defining and agreeing on the purpose for the system in the beginning stages and greater emphasis on defining the outcomes to be achieved and the overall cost of achieving these outcomes. In the UR cases, the initial stages of the projects tended to be more orientated to overall 'solutions', i.e. defining what would be done, where and by whom. Furthermore, agreeing to the physical boundaries for the systems activities in the UR projects was a crucial stage in the project, while the importance of organizational/professional boundaries in the HCIS projects was less obvious, but nevertheless still apparent.

Boundary definition is a fundamental and often contested process in system definition (Midgley 2000) and this was observed in both domains, but to a greater extent in the UR cases. Physical boundaries were highly contested in UR, while professional 'areas of competence' boundaries were influential in defining the roles of agents in HCIS projects, as well as contributing to definitions of the overall system scope. Defining system scope (including objectives) is a type of boundary exercise, and is often the first process of interaction in which agents engage. In both policy domains we could observe this in action, as agents came together to decide the physical and functional boundaries of the system in the early processes of project initiation, problem definition and agreeing requirements/solutions. No less a boundary exercise is the definition of time and budget constraints to be applied to the system processes and this, too, was observed in all cases but to a much greater extent in the HCIS projects than in UR. As the systems unfolded, time constraints played an increasingly important role in influencing decisions made—particularly in the UR cases—while budget constraints appeared more relevant in the HCIS cases. Finally, in the HCIS cases, there were clear boundaries in the perceptions of participating agents as to which of their activities and responsibilities were within the scope of the system and which were not, while this was less clear to agents in the UR cases. The topic of boundaries is taken up again in the initial chapter (Chapter 5) of Part II.

Features of the Environment: Factors, Rules and Agents

This brings us to the discussion of the systems *environment*—those elements that are perceived as being outside the system boundary, but nevertheless which may have an influence on the processes and outcomes of the system. The preceding discussion of the overall nature and boundaries of the system suggests that the distinction between system and its environment is found in the definition of the objectives that may be jointly pursued, and the boundaries (spatial, temporal, professional and financial) of the processes engaged in pursuit of those objectives. The environment, then, is anything that is not within this defined systems scope. The art of analyzing the environment of a system lies in the identification of those elements that have some relevance to the processes and outcomes of the system, but are not 'of the system'. In the first chapter, it was proposed that factors and rules made up the environment of a system, but in Chapters 2 and 3 the evidence showed that most agents participating in a given project pre-existed that project and, furthermore, that their (pre-existing) characteristics had significant impact on their behaviour within the system. Hence, the following discussion on the environment includes agents as features of the environment—although it is clear that agents are also a feature of the system itself.

Environmental factors in the UR and HCIS systems displayed the greatest variety of all of the elements analyzed. Environmental factors that were important to participants in one project were different to those in another project and, in fact, the importance of different factors varied across participants within the same project. It must be acknowledged up front that there was little in the way of observable patterns for factors (unless variation is a pattern!). Having said this, it is still the case that environmental factors, whatever form they took, did play a consistent role in providing the impetus for systems initialization. This was particularly noticeable in the UR cases studied in which social, economic and historical factors in the locations in which UR projects were undertaken were cited as the main justification for the projects overall. Socio-economic factors appeared to have no impact on the HCIS projects, nor did the legacy of the 'Troubles' in Northern Ireland have as much of an impact in these projects as they appeared to in urban regeneration. In fact, the 'environment' for the HCIS projects seems to be almost wholly made up of the rules established in legislation and in the organization(s) involved, along with the latent power and norms associated with the different agents participating. Furthermore, the exogenous environment was far less influential in the HCIS projects than in the UR projects, which suggests that there is a difference in the permeability of the system boundaries between the UR and HCIS domains. Whether this difference is due to the activity content or the organizational level of the cases is difficult to say, but it is worth noting that intra-organizational projects have two layers of 'insulation' from the outside world: the first being the project boundary itself and the second being the organizational boundary within which the project is managed. The absence of almost any community/patient participation in the HCIS projects further supports the hypothesis that the organizational boundary is a powerful deterrent to 'outsider' participation even if it is politically and legislatively encouraged.

Whatever the nature and influence of the exogenous environment, it is the case that the factors in play at the time of project initiation do act as 'initial conditions' which have a perceptible impact on the processes and outcomes of the systems. The impact of history and socio-economic conditions in the UR locations at the time of project initiation was clearly evident in the subsequent outcomes of housing density and tenure distribution, while the latent power differentials among agents in the HCIS projects had significant influence over the scope and processes of these systems. The state of information and communications technology at the time of project initiation also influenced the design of the HCIS projects and their targeted objectives. The reputation and capability of agents at the time of their entry into the systems in both policy domains was a factor in determining the roles undertaken by agents once in the system, as well as the degree to which other agents would engage with them in interdependent activities and/or co-production. In fact, in both policy domains and in both jurisdictions the characteristics and objectives of agents that chose (or were appointed by the government) to participate were influencing factors in decision-making and outcomes. This brings us to the next feature of the systems environment—the rules.

Environmental Rules and norms governing agent behaviour pre-existed, and often initiated, the beginning of the project. Definite patterns of rules could be identified which varied according to the policy domain as well as the jurisdiction. In Chapter 1, the types of rules that governed behaviour in a human CAS system were defined as relating to agents, processes, payoffs and time/place. What we found in the case studies was that these types of rule arose from various 'sources' that were embedded in the social, organizational and political fabric of society.

The primary sources of environmental rules affecting the projects studied were the legislation and policy relevant to the activities undertaken by agents. Policy could range from broad statements of intent or even aspiration– as in the case of the HCIS projects—to specific programmes of activity with associated funding streams and eligibility criteria for agents and beneficiaries—as in the case of the UR projects. Throughout the project, but most often in the early stages, rules stemming from public policy were considered to be important drivers of agent decision-making. Policy rules appeared to be considerably more germane, as well as clearer and more directive, in the UR projects than in HCIS projects.

Professional values, the second source of environmental rules/norms, were more pertinent in the HCIS projects than in UR. In these projects, the values of the medical profession relating to duties of care, individualization and data protection were often in conflict with those of the information systems profession, in which standardization, efficiency and data sharing were core values. Furthermore, reform efforts in the public management domain in both jurisdictions directly affected the decision-making in HCIS. This was seen to a lesser extent in the UR projects.

The third source, social norms, played a significant role in that they contributed to the schemata used by agents in their decision-making. Examples of rules arising from social norms were found in the UR process rules and time/place rules relating to the divided society in Northern Ireland and to the influence of the market versus social healthcare models in the HCIS systems in both jurisdictions.

The fourth and final source of environmental rules affecting the projects was the institutional governance structures in place in the two jurisdictions. The involvement of government agencies followed a similar pattern across both UR and HCIS policy domains, with projects in Northern Ireland largely driven from central government while projects in the Republic of Ireland were more locally managed. In addition, involvement by central government in the Republic of Ireland was generally located in a single lead department, while in Northern Ireland several government departments had jurisdiction over various aspects of the projects. Furthermore, in Northern Ireland a large number of other agencies and professional bodies were engaged in both the UR and HCIS projects while these appeared to play a much more muted role in the Republic of Ireland.

Agents, both organizations and individuals within organizations, were initially perceived as elements of the system rather than of the environment, but from the case data it became clear that most agents pre-existed the creation of any given system. Hence, we have included agents in the discussion of the systems environment. This does not suggest that agents are not part of the system as well—in fact, they are the actors that drive the processes and create the outcomes. We observed that agents often assume particular roles in a system based on their pre-existing characteristics, but that they may also change as a result of their participation in the system—whether by design or not. In the following discussion, we make observations about agents under four separate headings: the relevant characteristics of agents in the environment; the source of agents that can participate in a system; the nature of agent participation in the systems; and the patterns of agent leadership within the systems.

The main relevant characteristics of agents relating to their role in the projects studied were the sectors or professions to which the agents belonged outside of the system that influenced not only what the agents could or would do while in the system, but also how they related to each other. This was evident in both domains and in both jurisdictions and there were clear patterns of agent participation within and across jurisdictions. In the UR cases, there were specific roles for agent types defined both by their legal status (public, private, non-profit or community organizations) and their profession/function (i.e. architects, engineers, planners, developers etc.). The similarity of agent types and patterns of participation suggests that there is a larger organizational evolutionary system at work that generates a pool of specialized organizations, which may choose to, or be directed to, participate in any given project. If these case studies had been largely in the private sector, this evolutionary system would be referred to as a 'market'. However, as these systems were driven by public sector motives and resources, the ecology that resulted in the availability of the required organizations when they were needed is likely to be more complicated, since the dynamics of supply and demand and competition among firms are only a part of the story. Of course, the 'right' agents are not always available, or willing, to participate at the 'right' time and this may be one of the key challenges in large-scale public sector organizing, as well as a contributing factor to the emergence of project specific agents (PSAs).

As described in Chapter 2, the range of agents participating in the UR projects was similar in the non-governmental sectors in both jurisdictions. It was only in the public sector that the number and types of agents varied, and this was explained as having to do with the different political trajectories of the two jurisdictions and the influence of the 'Troubles' and the related changes in the governance structures in Northern Ireland. However, this pattern of agent similarity in the non-governmental sectors, and the diversity in the governmental agents, was also observed in the HCIS domain, where there was no obvious impact of the 'Troubles' or local authority housing issues. It appears, therefore, that the diversity of governmental agents between the two domains is not necessarily a result of history or social upheaval, but rather a pervasive difference in the approach to governance and government agency involvement in projects. As discussed above in the section on rules, in Northern Ireland, there was significant involvement in both UR and HCIS domains by a range of government departments, while in the Republic of Ireland the involvement of central government was more muted and tended to arise from one or, at most, two departments.

It has been noted above that agents bring pre-existing characteristics and relationships into the processes and interactions of the system in which they are participating and that these persist over time. This is not to say that participation in the system makes no difference to the characteristics of agents or that they behave the same way inside of the system boundaries as they do on the outside. In fact, it was clearly observed that agents did change as a result of their participation in the projects studied.

One example of the type of change observed was that individuals from the various professions in the HCIS projects perceived their roles in these projects as being distinct from their day-to-day activities and, in fact, their participation in projects resulted in them being referred to differently within the organization. For example, a clinical nurse would become a 'user liaison' and a hospital consultant would become a 'project sponsor'. These project roles often had quite separate responsibilities from the individual's professional role and, given that these roles had relatively short time spans, it was no surprise that an individual's professional training and norms tended to persist throughout the project. Nevertheless, there were indications that individuals in the HCIS projects learned something from their participation in projects, saw issues in a new light and/or built (or damaged) their own reputations in the context of HCIS development. Examples of this were the transformation of a hospital consultant's viewpoint on the need for information systems solutions to capacity and throughput problems, the knowledge of user requirements gained by a nurse assigned to act as a user liaison and the enhancement of GP computer literacy via the HealthLink project. This adaptation by agents was also observed in the UR projects, particularly in the case of community groups learning new skills, and in the capacity-building of private sector firms.

The final observation to make about agents is the tendency for a particular type of agent to take the lead in a given project domain. In the case of the UR projects, the lead agent was the government agency responsible for local housing development: the relevant local authority in the case of the Republic of Ireland and the Northern Ireland Housing Executive (NIHE) in the case of Northern Ireland. In the HCIS projects, the leadership role fell largely to the clinical staff in the main hospital involved. Having said this, the actual day-to-day management of the projects could be performed by a different agent. This was generally the case in HCIS projects in which the IS project manager had overall responsibility for allocating resources and ensuring that objectives were met. There were fewer examples of derogation of responsibility in UR, although when this did occur, the responsibility fell to a PSA, over which the government agency maintained significant influence. It would appear that authority (or power) and responsibility are less likely to be separated in the UR projects than they were in the HCIS projects.

Overall, the environment(s) of the 12 projects studied did consist of identifiable factors, rules and agents that exhibited patterns based on the policy domain and the governance structures in place. Environmental factors were the most variable across the projects, and the variation appeared to be connected to the perspectives and motivations of the agents involved in the projects. In fact, this dynamic of selection and mutation of elements of the environment within the system is a recurring theme for each of factors, rules and agents—a theme that is taken up below in the discussion of the processes and outcomes of the projects themselves.

Features of the System: The Processes and Outcomes

It should come as no surprise that it is in the *processes* element that the cases exhibited the most similarity. This is, of course, due to the types of phenomena selected for study, i.e. projects. Over the last 60 years or so, the practice and theory of project management has evolved towards a quite specific set of tools and approaches designed to maximize the efficient use of resources, develop effective solutions to organizational problems and opportunities and facilitate agreement among stakeholders (Young-Hoon 2005). The striking consistency across the Irish policy domains and jurisdictions bears witness to the broad acceptance of the project management approach at all levels of public management implementation. A definitive source for what is entailed in the project management approach may be found in *A Guide to the Project Management Body of Knowledge: (PMBOK Guide): Fourth edition* (Project Management Institute 2008) in which five processes are listed: initiation; planning; executing; controlling; and closing. In the 12 cases studied, the first three processes were clearly evident, while the last two less so. In addition, there was an explicit process of *activating agents* in the case of the urban regeneration projects and one of *creating the project team/board* in the case of HCIS projects which, broadly speaking, were similar processes aimed at clarifying who would participate in the projects. The fact that these processes of agent clarification appeared across both domains and in each jurisdiction suggests that in public sector projects, the process of agent clarification may carry more importance than it does in projects undertaken elsewhere.

The process of project initiation was evident in both the UR and HCIS cases in which several different drivers for project initiation were identified. Project initiation involves the identification of either an opportunity or a requirement for action in some sphere of organizational activity. In the case of HCIS, project initiation was 'event-driven' in five out of the six projects studied and events were classified as (a) political crises, (b) new facilities or (c) incremental information & communication technology (ICT) improvements. Arising out of these types of events was an awareness among one or more professional groups within the hospital (or in one case, in a government department) of the need for new information-processing capabilities. This awareness was resolved into a project initiation document in which the fundamental opportunities/issues were laid out and a high level case made for starting the HCIS project. In many ways, this project initiation document, and the interactions among agents to produce it, were similar to the legislation and legislative processes that gave rise to the initiation of urban regeneration projects. It is interesting to note that this project initiation process in HCIS was perceived as occurring within the boundaries of the project, while the legislative processes relating to UR were perceived as outside the boundaries of a given UR project. In fact, project initiation as a process within the UR projects was more aligned with the project *justification* process that occurred in HCIS projects. Project initiation in UR was more about justifying why urban regeneration should be undertaken in a particular place at a particular time and, in this, it was similar to the process of developing the business case (*project justification*) for an IS project in the healthcare setting. Furthermore, the initiation process in UR was tightly connected to the definition of the problem to be solved, while in HCIS, initiation and justification preceded the definition of the problem to be solved (called '*requirements definition*' in HCIS).

The above discussion may suggest that the process of project initiation is quite different in the two domains of public policy. However, the essential difference is not found in the content of the process(es), but rather in the location of the boundary between system and environment. In both the urban regeneration and HCIS domains the activities of identifying opportunity, justifying action and specifying the objectives for action are being performed, but in the case of urban regeneration much of this activity takes place outside of the system boundary—in the legislative and policy processes involved in specifying problems, policies and political expediency. In this we can observe the manifestation of the fuzzy boundary between policy and implementation, as well as how the activities of the policy process[1] (Kingdon 1995) are recreated within the boundaries of implementing organizations, i.e. the hospitals involved in the HCIS projects. The three streams model of the policy process proposed by Kingdon (the 'problem' stream, the 'policy' stream and the 'political' stream) are evident in both jurisdictions, but at different levels of institutional activity.

What is not an explicit part of Kingdon's model, however, is the process of identifying and/or activating participating agents. This process was observed in both domains and across jurisdictions and it is during this process that much of the action in terms of systems configuration occurs. As described earlier, most participating agents pre-existed the initiation of a given project, but it is the participation of, and relationships among, agents within the project that, in many ways, determines not only what can be achieved, but also the details of how the project will unfold and the nature of the complex dynamics that emerge. In both the UR and HCIS projects, agents were largely free to participate, or not, in any given project, and this fulfils one of the key criteria in complex adaptive systems models, that agents are independent actors operating with some degree of free will. Furthermore it supports the assertion that these systems are self-organizing. This was clearly evident in the cases studied, even with respect to the statutory bodies responsible for implementing urban regeneration policy as the decisions relating to where and when to undertake projects was left with these agencies. Moreover, as has been widely documented—and was observed again in these cases—the participation of various independent agents is as likely to redirect and even frustrate policy objectives as it is to result in their achievement.

The process of identifying and/or activating agents also incorporated other features of complex adaptive systems. The adaptation of agents over time (particularly evident in the community groups involved in the UR projects) and the emergence of new agents at higher levels of organizational activity (the project specific agents in UR and project 'boards' in HCIS) are both features of CAS. The specification of project roles for agents in the HCIS system exemplifies agent adaptation, as well as the process of aligning agent perceptions (schema) to facilitate interaction and define interdependencies. PSAs in urban regeneration projects explicitly undertook this latter process of aligning perceptions, with the result that problems and potential solutions expanded to incorporate the needs of heterogeneous agents. It would not be overly ambitious to suggest that self-organization is initiated here and that the CAS nature of these systems is grounded in this process of agent activation.

While it may be the case that agent activation sets the scene for CAS-type behaviour, it is in the processes of agreeing/approving solutions and implementation that CAS dynamics are most clearly observed. The most intensive interaction among agents occurred in the process of agreeing on and approving solutions during which time, outputs, resources, process rules, agent responsibilities and constraints are all defined—if not in all cases agreed– amongst agents. It was in this process that the vision driving the project became clear, with the attendant unpredictability arising from intense interaction among competing agent schemata. In addition, there was the boundary spanning activity of the *approval* process, which, in both domains and jurisdictions, occurred outside of the projects in government departments or 'quangos'[2] set up for this purpose. Furthermore, it was in the agreeing/approving process that the unexpected intervention from outside agents most often occurred, including intervention from politicians in the urban regeneration projects and the development of new technologies in the HCIS projects. Adaptation, emergence, bifurcation and path-dependency were all observable dynamics during both this process and the implementation process.

Having noted that CAS dynamics were observable in the implementation processes of the projects studied, this could not be said to arise from intense interaction among agents (as is generally assumed in CAS theory). In fact, implementation processes in urban regeneration tended either to be undertaken largely independently by the agents involved or, as in the case of construction, to be highly scripted interactions between different professions and/or trades following detailed plans and budgets. While there were agreed checkpoints in the process in which agents came together to review progress, these rarely had significant impact on the trajectory of the system or the fundamental nature of the outcomes achieved. Unpredictability in this process was created by divergences from agreed/expected activities or outcomes, which arose from unresolved differences in agent perceptions or motivations, along with the potential for physical (or fiscal) realities to frustrate or facilitate in surprising ways.

In the case of the Electronic Prescribing and Eligibility System (EPES) project in Northern Ireland, for example, the persistent resistance of the GPs and pharmacists to engage with the project led to its delay to the point of its no longer being cost effective under a new policy of free prescriptions. In the Fatima Mansions project in Dublin, the ability of the private sector agents to gain control over implementation led to a significant change in the number of private versus social dwellings. In the Order Communication System (OCS) project in Dublin, the agreed solution was abandoned by the Information Systems Department when it was found to be technically too difficult and costly. However, it was not always the case that projects changed significantly during implementation, as is evidenced by the unremarkable progression of Dublin's Hardwicke Street UR project. What is important about the implementation process in terms of its CAS nature is that the CAS dynamics observed in the 'implementation' process arise from a different source than those in the 'agree/approve solution' process. Future modelling or theory development using the proposed CAS framework must be careful not to ignore these different sources of unpredictability in the different stages of agent activity.

Patterns observed in the *outcomes* of the public management cases studied were, at the most general level, consistent with the literature on public sector performance management in the tendency for outcome targets to give way to output and/or process targets over time. The acknowledged difficulty in assigning individual or organizational responsibility for outcomes in complex systems involving many interdependent actors is a likely contributor to this diminution of project objectives, but this is only a part of the story. As highlighted in Chapter 3, the observed pattern of shifting from broad efficiency objectives to narrow IS system implementation objectives in the HCIS projects cannot be blamed on multi-actor complexity, as the projects were, by and large, resident in a single organization. Furthermore, in the HealthLink project in the Republic of Ireland, the interaction of many different actors in no way led to a narrowing of objectives, but instead broadened the original project goals from minor administrative efficiencies to a fundamental change in the way hospitals and GPs exchanged information to achieve major increases in efficiency across functions, as well as to improve patient care.

Having noted the general pattern of outcome objectives giving way to outputs and process targets, it cannot be said that outcome measures played no role in the projects studied. Where outcomes did play a significant role in organizational decision-making was in contributing to the justification for projects during their initial phases. For example, in urban regeneration projects, tenure mix, employment, safety, social inclusion and quality of life for residents were, to varying degrees, highlighted as targeted outcomes of the projects proposed. However, by the time the solutions were agreed on and implementation had begun, project goals had shifted to the number of dwellings demolished and replaced, the number/type of community facilities provided, the level of community participation and staying within agreed timeframes and/or budgets. In the HCIS projects, efficiency and new service provision were the driving forces behind the start-up of projects but these objectives were largely abandoned by the time the strategy for delivering the systems requirements was agreed and implementation had begun. There was little evidence of a project control strategy relating to the initial outcome objectives as these largely focused on project-related targets: budget and time constraints.

In the morphing of outcomes into outputs, processes and project targets, it was also observed that some of the latter began to assume the characteristics of 'rules' in the system. This was particularly noticeable in the case of process- and project-related targets in both domains. This means that these targets become embedded in agent decision-making as a fundamental part of the schemata that agents applied in determining behaviour. Interestingly, in traditional open systems theory, the link between outcomes and system behaviour via feedback processes is often modelled as a fixed rule; the classic example of the thermostat regulating a heating system based on changes in room temperature. However, it would be foolish to build this into a systems model of public management as the feedback processes operating here were not fixed but negotiated over time and subject to modification both at an individual agent level and at systems level.

Overall, while it was possible to identify specific policy outcomes that influenced the initiation and early problem definition in the cases studied, these rarely played an ongoing role in influencing agent behaviour. Instead, through the processes of problem definition, agreeing on solutions and implementing over time, these outcome objectives evolved into output, process and project targets, with the latter two types– process and project targets– having the potential to act as 'rules', as in a classic systems feedback model.

In summary, the cases studied exhibited each of the core six elements of a complex adaptive system as described in Chapter 1 (see Figure 4.1 for a summary of the key observations relating to each element). Furthermore, all of the projects exhibit the fundamental CAS dynamic of self-organization through the processes of agent activation and rule-setting engaged in by agents over the course of the projects. The remaining dynamics are less pervasive in their occurrence across the projects, but there is nevertheless enough evidence to suggest that all of the CAS dynamics are present. The remaining four unique CAS dynamics of adaptation, path-dependency, bifurcation and emergence will be discussed in Part II of this book.

Before moving to the observation of unique CAS dynamics, however, it is important to deal with any lingering doubts on the efficacy of systems theory in general to public administration and to problems of human organizing

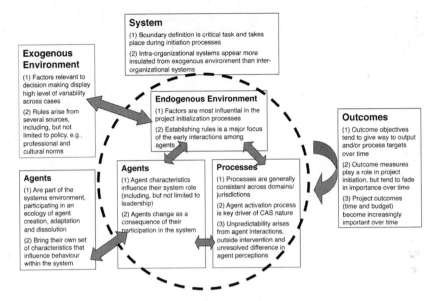

Figure 4.1 Key observations relating to CAS elements.

overall. This chapter concludes with a discussion on how developments in systems theory, and in the CAS framework in particular, address issues that have been raised about the application of systems theory to problems of human organization (including public administration) in the past.

THE ARGUMENT FOR A SYSTEMS THEORY APPROACH TO THE DEVELOPMENT OF PUBLIC ADMINISTRATION THEORY

In the Introduction to this book, the argument for adopting a complex adaptive systems theory perspective on public administration was put forward in the context of the need to 'reinvigorate' the discipline. The proposal was that CAS theory could provide an integrating framework for weaving together the various strands of theory that have developed over time into a more coherent basis for informing practice. In addition, it is suggested that CAS holds out the promise of a scientific basis for explaining, if not predicting, the unanticipated outcomes that characterize the real world of the public manager. In Chapters 2 and 3, the authors endeavoured to demonstrate how the proposed CAS framework could be used to describe empirical phenomena in public administration and thereby establish the basic foundations for developing CAS-based theory. In this chapter, this descriptive analysis has been summarized and the links between CAS theoretical elements and empirical observation made. The authors believe the links are compelling enough to take the next steps in the development of CAS-based public administration theory and practice.

However, before embarking upon the next stage of CAS analysis it is worth pausing briefly to review the more fundamental question of the value of systems theory overall as the basis for public administration theory and practice. Over the last 50 years there have been trenchant and devastating critiques of the use of classic systems theory in public policy and administration that resonate today in criticisms of more recent applications of complex systems theory to management (Rosenhead 1998). Eberhard Umbach (2000) provides a helpful summary of the range of criticisms of systems theory drawing largely from US and West German sources.

To begin with, there is the question of exactly what a system is. Marchal (1975) defines a system as any phenomenon that is made up of a set of elements that interact with one another in more or less stable ways over time. Granted, this is a very broad definition, and most likely it was definitions such as this that led to critiques of a systems perspective as having too broad a focus ever to result in meaningful or operational theory (Kornai 1999, Frederickson and Smith 2003). Caldart and Ricart's (2004: 97) more recent definition of a complex adaptive system, consisting of a 'mutually consistent ecology of parts, along with internal models and rules guiding them', provides slightly more specificity in relation to systems, but is still vulnerable to the critique of overly broad analytic scope. The careful definition of scope for the analysis presented here (i.e. projects in two specified domains of public administration in Ireland's two jurisdictions) was made partly in response to this critique. Furthermore, the discussion of boundary-setting processes recognizes the practical difficulties in defining the boundaries of systems that may underlie the theoretic fuzziness.

One of the earliest critiques levelled at attempts to apply systems theory to public policy domains is typified by Ida Hoos' (1972) critique of efforts in the US in the 1960s to implement a programme called the *Planning, Programming and Budgeting System* (PPBS) along with other examples of systems 'analysis' prevalent at the time. Hoos studied a range of programmes that had adopted a systems approach and found a litany of problems, including exaggerated promises, single-minded application of an 'engineering' mind-set, a lack of awareness of and/or reliance on participant knowledge in favour of external consultant input, over-reliance on quantification of variables and/or inadequate attention to accurate specification of variables, a focus on the model of reality rather than reality itself and, in the end, very few results to show for vast investments of money and time. Checkland (1981) characterized the systems approach described by Hoos as the 'hard systems' approach, in which systems are largely perceived as having the characteristics of machines that can be engineered for optimal performance. In contrast, Checkland proposed a 'soft systems' approach as a more realistic and flexible approach; firstly, to understand the nature of the system to be analyzed and, secondly, to try out various alternative strategies proposed by the stakeholders themselves for influencing the system in the desired direction. Referring explicitly to Checkland, as well as other later methodological developments, Umbach (2000: 20) noted that 'the critique of the 70s was the cause for corrections in the methodology of systems science'.

Over the course of this research, different systems models were reviewed in order to find one that could encompass the characteristics of the cases studied. The process of review was not a formal one but rather a more incremental process of trying out different models against the emerging conceptualization of public administration projects and eliminating those that were clearly inappropriate. The first systems models to be eliminated were those that relied solely on mathematic formulations such as the types described by John Casti in 1979.[3] While this was an 'easy' elimination in so far as the use of purely mathematical models to address complex problems of public administration had resulted in many of the harsh criticisms of systems approaches in the past, it was nevertheless the case that problems of urban regeneration and healthcare are often addressed using these types of model. Having acknowledged this, the interaction with practitioners as well as academics over the course of the research solidified the authors' convictions that a different modelling approach was required.

The second category of critique identified by Umbach covers the various levels of frustration expressed at the all-encompassing nature of systems concepts (Mueller 1996, Kornai 1999). As exemplified by the definition from Marchal quoted earlier, systems theory, in its efforts to provide the 'deep structure' of science (Bertalanffy 1968), can often fall into the trap of trying to be a theory of everything and ending up with statements that are empty of any practical meaning. Frederickson and Smith (2003) echo this critique in their warning about governance theory as tending towards an approach that includes everything, but runs the danger of explaining nothing. While acknowledging the tendency towards broad analytic scope in this research, the focus on particular manifestations of public management in this research (i.e. projects in Ireland) should go some way towards mitigating this problem.

The use of empirical case studies to explore the applicability of a systems approach also addresses the third category of critique as described by Umbach, which is the tenuous, and often non-existent, link between systems models and empirical data. Some infamous systems models of large-scale social systems in the 1960s and 1970s provided ammunition for these critiques, including the computer simulations of Pittsburgh and San Francisco in the early 1960s which were later seen to have been based on dubious estimates and assumptions about underlying variables and trends (for critique, see Brewer 1975).

Both Umbach (2000) and Stacey and Griffin (2006) describe a fourth type of criticism around the tendency for systems theorists to present their analyses in an ideological way that leaves little room for constructive debate and/or leads to pathological outcomes. While Umbach only briefly mentioned this as an issue related to the larger issue of overly broad scope and overly enthusiastic claims of relevance, Stacey and Griffin (2006) focused much of their criticism on this point. These authors suggested that a systems perspective, in particular one that is informed by cybernetic systems theory (Wiener 1948, Ashby 1956), results in a diminishment of the importance of the behaviour of individuals in preference to the behaviour of the system and a focus on how systems (and their human participants) may be controlled. In their view, this results in an ultimately dehumanizing view of people as mere systems components mindlessly responding to stimuli over which they have no control. The fundamental role of *independent* agents in CAS models goes some way towards mitigating this tendency of systems analyses as does the recognition that agents participate in setting the rules of their endogenous environments and that they can adapt over time. Overall, the CAS framework applied is consistent with a humanist approach to developing systems-based theory.

Another pathology blamed on the systems ideology of the 1950s and 60s was the belief that it led to an overly centrist approach to social planning—which was particularly problematic when combined with the engineering approach to systems analysis described by Hoos (1972) and Umbach (2000). Umbach suggests– and our analysis supports this claim– that recent developments in systems theory such as chaos theory, self-organization and complex systems theory are unlikely to result in the same sorts of pathologies observed as arising from earlier applications of systems theory.

This leaves the fifth and last type of critique of the systems perspective—that researchers and analysts display an over-reliance on metaphor or analogy to analyze and explain phenomena without being clear about the distinction between metaphor and reality. Stacey and Griffin (2006: 29) decry the gradual acceptance of the systems metaphor as a 'fact of life' over the course of the latter half of the twentieth century and the 'taking for granted that nature actually consists of systems'. They assert that when one begins to believe that a representation or model of reality actually is reality, one begins the slide toward a philosophical *cul-de-sac* in which nothing can be proven to exist outside the perception of the observer, and where any fact that is not consistent with the model of reality cannot be seen.

The research presented here engages directly with the idea that knowledge and even 'facts' are socially constructed, and recognizes that the systems model proposed in this book is only one of many possible frameworks for developing theory– valuable to the extent that it provides insights that were otherwise unattainable, or pathways to solving problems that were otherwise unsolvable, but not the only valid interpretation of the cases studied. Dennard *et al.* (2008) suggested the following in a recent compendium of articles on complexity and policy analysis:

Complexity implies that there is no one solution to any problem any more than there is one discreet cause. The good news is that an abundance of approaches to problem-solving is more productive that a reduction of methodology to one or two 'proven' methods or even interpretations. Complex adaptive systems are learning systems . . . [which] means that prior assumptions of methodology about what will or should work in any given context may fail or, more problematic, they may recreate the problem by re-developing the discourse that organizes those assumptions through regulation.

(Dennard *et al.* 2008: 12)

In addition to exploring (and rejecting) the application of mathematical systems models for use in public administration theory, Gareth Morgan's (1986) list of eight metaphors[4] were also considered and eventually rejected. There were two main reasons for rejecting the use of Morgan's metaphors as the framework on which to build public administration theory. The first was that they were principally aimed at understanding a single organization, and the systems under consideration here generally involved several organizations. Interactions among organizations receive minimal attention in Morgan's analyses, a clear weakness for the analysis of public administration systems. The other reason was that Morgan's metaphors were insufficiently developed to facilitate even a moderately precise specification of a model to support theory development. Morgan, himself, recognizes this fact and notes that the power of metaphor is to generate insights as opposed to developing theory.

Complexity and complex systems theory fell somewhere in between 'maths' and 'metaphors' in terms of the ability to incorporate all of the features of public administration while still being able to support the level of specificity required for theory building. In fact, complexity theory has been used to study systemic behaviour of phenomena ranging from sub-atomic particles to global economies. Complexity theory, of course, is an umbrella term that covers many different theoretical strands, but with a common focus on complex systems phenomena with many interacting parts and non-linear or unpredictable outcomes (Anderson 1999). Theories of complex systems are cropping up in numerous natural and social science disciplines, including meteorology, chemistry, biology, physics, education, management, economics and sociology. Complexity theory has also been identified, by public administration scholars, as having the potential to address the increasingly messy business of public service provision (Boston 2000, Blackman 2001, Weber 2005, Stacey and Griffin 2006, Koppenjan and Klijn 2008). And so, complex systems were selected as the category of systems models from which to draw to build a systems framework for public administration theory development.

As noted in the Introduction to this book, one particular type of complex systems model was eventually selected to construct the framework for analysis. This was the CAS approach, which Stacey *et al.* (2002) classify as one of three main types of complex systems models. The other two are *chaos* models and *dissipative structures* models. Of these three, CAS appeared a better fit for our empirical data than the other two, although the dynamic of bifurcation is more often found in dissipative structures models than in CAS. Like all of the other complexity theories, complex adaptive system theory is based on the idea that complex behaviour, at the systems level, can arise from the interaction of relatively few and even simple behavioural 'rules'—but in the case of CAS these are rules operating at the agent level rather than at the level of the system as a whole—which is a feature of the other two types of models. Furthermore, CAS models tend to be implemented in the form of computer simulations and 'fuzzy-logic' formulations, minimizing the need for quantification and precise mathematical formulations. CAS approaches are viewed as having significant potential in organizational modelling, so much so that an entire issue of *Organizational Science* was dedicated to exploring this potential (*Organizational Science* 1999, vol. 10(3)). More recently (and more relevant to public management) are the special issues of: (1) *Emergence: Complexity and Organization* (2005, vol. 7(1)) on the topic of 'Complexity and Policy Analysis', and (2) *Public Administration Review* (2008, vol. 10(3)) on the topic of 'Complexity Theory and Public Management', in which several of the articles drew on complex adaptive systems frameworks to explore a range of public policy and management domains.

However, the potential of a CAS framework for understanding complex social phenomena, such as exercises in public administration, may only be realized if it can be shown that the core elements of the framework may be observed in such phenomena. Frederickson and Smith (2003) refer to this as 'descriptive capacity', defined as 'a theory's ability to portray the real world accurately *as it is observed*' (Frederickson and Smith 2003: 230, emphasis authors' own). The discussion in this chapter has shown that, at least in so far as the core six elements and the fundamental dynamic of self-organization are concerned, the CAS framework has descriptive capacity across the range of Irish public administration projects studied. The rigorous methodology adopted and the range of cases selected suggests that this descriptive capacity may extend to other similar phenomena and achieve a reasonable level of generalizability, however this would need to be tested by replicating the study in different domains and under different political and cultural conditions. Replicating this study would be premature, though, without some further exploration of the four remaining unique dynamics of CAS as they may (or may not) appear in the case data.

In Part II of this book, we proceed with this next stage of applying the CAS framework and, in doing so begin to establish the nature of the 'explanatory capacity' (Frederickson and Smith 2003) of CAS-based theory based on the dynamics of adaptation, path-dependency, emergence and bifurcation.

In order to demonstrate this 'explanatory capacity' more directly, Part II is organized by public administration theme. Specifically, Chapter 5 explores the nature and dynamics of boundaries and their impact on decision-making and project progress; Chapter 6 looks at the dynamics of stakeholder involvement in public sector projects; Chapter 7 describes the role and effect of private sector agents; and Chapter 8 examines the tensions between the 'core' and 'locale' in setting and implementing public policy. Each of these themes has a rich history of academic research and analysis and in each the identification of CAS dynamics provides fresh insight into the cause and effect relationships that influence processes and outcomes within the theme. Chapter 9 draws together the strands of CAS analyses across the four themes and concludes that the CAS perspective does indeed provide additional insights to inform theory and practice in public administration.

5   The Impact of Boundaries
Identity, Community and Place

INTRODUCTION

The concept of 'boundaries' appears regularly in a wide range of literature concerning public management, administration, geopolitics, regeneration and organizational development. Discussions of boundaries focus on many things, from concrete physical manifestations and barriers, to virtual interfaces between one organizational unit and another, or even entirely theoretical demarcations between different schools of thought (Kaboolian 1998, Levi-Faur 2004, Agranoff 2004). However, managing 'beyond' such boundaries is a routinely recurring aspiration that transcends sectors and local concerns. Not surprisingly, there is an increasing understanding of the need to acknowledge and manage such boundaries (whether physical, social or organizational) within public management as a discipline (Currie *et al.* 2007, Fitzsimmons and White 1997, Boal 1992, Murtagh 1999). This chapter uses two of the unique attributes of a complex adaptive system (CAS)—path-dependency and bifurcation– to explore the impact of boundaries on public management strategic decision-making in the sectors of urban regeneration and healthcare. In particular, it focuses on demarcations to physical space, communal identity and within professional relationships in these sectors.

The first section of this chapter briefly defines what we mean by boundaries. It then goes on to explore issues that have emerged from our analysis of urban regeneration and healthcare, before looking at how the concept of boundaries is a recurrent concern across the sectors. This is followed by a brief review of the concept of boundaries within the public management literature generally. The main body of the chapter is taken up with an exploration of how a CAS lens can bring a new insight to the phenomenon of boundaries and decision-making in the two sets of case studies. This discussion will concentrate on path-dependency and bifurcation as CAS dynamics arising from, and helping to explain the impact of, boundaries. The chapter concludes with a brief discussion on the benefits of a CAS lens in an analysis of boundaries in public management decision-making.

BOUNDARIES AND PUBLIC MANAGEMENT

The core concern of this chapter is a discussion of boundaries, real or perceived, which demarcate communities, areas, activities and groups within and between neighbourhoods or organizations. While boundaries are a major issue of concern in the cases studied and in public management generally, the term 'boundary' is seldom defined. For the purpose of this chapter a 'boundary' will be identified as *'the interface between one thing and something else: the point at which two groups, contexts or entities meet'*. In turn, a 'border' will be defined as *'a part that forms the outer edge of something'* but also as a *'line or frontier area separating political divisions or geographic regions'*. Within the cases, a series of boundaries were identified. Within the urban regeneration (UR) projects these consisted of very visible manifestations such as walls, fences or railings as well as less tangible, or even invisible, highly sensitive neighbourhood demarcations such as bridges, areas of open space or street fixtures. Within the healthcare information systems (HCIS) case studies, boundaries were conceived of differently. They included differentiated areas of professional practice like those between doctors, dentists and pharmacists, interfaces between inter- and intra- organizational units such as hospital management, information & communication technology (ICT) department and clinical departments, and power delineations that separated one group of professionals from another (doctors and nurses, for example).

The topic of boundaries appears often in discussions of public management, and the issue of interest is often how such boundaries can be crossed effectively by people, knowledge or expertise, or how the adverse impact of their existence can be minimized (Kaboolian 1998, Levi-Faur 2004, Agranoff 2004). This should not be surprising; boundaries—physical, psychological or organizational– often represent a real impediment to effective and efficient working (Fitzsimmons and White 1997). It is clear from the case data that lines of demarcation, whether physical or organizational, often determined how strategic decisions were made, and how they could unexpectedly affect and shape the decision-making process.

In studies on urban regeneration it is well established that 'place' has physical as well as social, economic, cultural and political characteristics (Bryan 2005, Murtagh 2002). Boundaries within 'place' are often physical, or at least can be identified as having a physical location with or without a corresponding barrier. Most importantly, boundaries can be identified by people, particularly local people, with or without physical manifestations. Such boundaries relate closely to envisioned ideas of community, neighbourhood and in-group belonging (Anderson 1991). This essentially geo-political analysis of boundaries relates closely to communal identity, group identity and territoriality (Jarman 2004). Geo-political space is often 'contested', requiring that the needs and aspirations of opposing groups are negotiated and refocused. This is true of both urban and rural environments where commercial and regenerative initiatives have to be balanced with local environmental concerns and the additional requirements of community and social cohesion.

Within healthcare environments it is also well established that group and professional boundaries are significant in dictating organizational dynamics (Pettigrew *et al.* 1992, Currie *et al.* 2007). Within the organizational entities that make up a healthcare setting, boundaries can be discerned between organizational units, disciplines and professional orientations. Currie and Suhomlinova (2006) identify a clear set of boundaries for their study of knowledge-sharing in the UK National Health Service. For them, boundaries relate to specialized 'segments' within health fields (e.g. hospitals and organizations of higher education), different types of organization within a healthcare segment (such as primary care GPs and secondary care hospitals) and those between different professions within the general healthcare arena. They, and others, also cite power differentials between professional groups as both a contributory factor to the establishment of boundaries and an impediment to their removal (Fitzsimmons and White 1997). In an environment where interdisciplinary team collaboration is accelerating in significance, working across traditional boundaries without sufficient preparation and awareness can lead to group and role conflict. Professional training and different philosophical approaches to service delivery can also impede communication and partnership working. Finding a way through these difficulties requires organizational ingenuity by public management professionals and personal flexibility among healthcare providers. The next section will explore the difficulties of managing boundaries in urban regeneration and healthcare from a CAS perspective.

BOUNDARIES AND COMPLEX ADAPTIVE SYSTEMS

The impacts of physical, organizational and psychological boundaries on strategic decision-making are clearly apparent in the case studies analyzed. Such boundaries appeared in different contexts and affected decision-making in unpredictable ways. Two particular CAS dynamics—path-dependency and bifurcation– were regarded as significant. The most strikingly significant of these was path-dependency arising from the particular initial conditions that existed within the cases. The analysis of path-dependency here is focused on boundaries in an urban regeneration context and how the enormous impact of history, politics and communal identity affected decision-making. The very different characteristics of path-dependency that set the tone for boundaries in the healthcare cases are also briefly explored. The relationship between system bifurcations and boundaries is considered next. This allows an identification and analysis of clear and fundamental junctures that determined the path of events in both sectors.

Path-Dependency: People, Power and Politics

Political, cultural and economic history is reflected acutely in the development of the urban regeneration case studies. In both the Republic of Ireland and Northern Ireland, the historical legacy of division, decline and regeneration marked each of the areas under observation. This section will look at the role that path-dependency has played in the developmental trajectory of the urban regeneration case studies.

For the Northern Ireland cases, the collective trauma of 30 years of political violence, displacement and sectarianism had a profound effect on how communities developed within a broader context of social polarization and violence. In the urban regeneration cases, boundaries often existed as a direct result of initial conditions which include sectarianism, segregation and, until relatively recently, violent conflict. For communities in Belfast who bore the brunt of the 'Troubles' this was especially true. The three Northern Ireland urban regeneration case studies are indicative of the difficulties faced by many communities in Belfast and in other areas of Northern Ireland. For example, the historical legacy of sectarianism led to a degree of community segregation in which it was estimated that 90 per cent of public sector housing estates were segregated into predominately Catholic or predominately Protestant communities. The gradual entrenchment of such 'boundaried communities' led to significant instances of community isolation, segregation and interface conflict. Ongoing issues of personal safety saw the 'system' (the public and, at times, the private housing system) adapt by allowing individuals to self-select their community of belonging (and therefore the location of their home) which in turn, reinforced separation and allowed division to become both endemic and deep-rooted.

This reality was reflected in differences between Roden Street (and by extension the Greater Village Area) and Connswater as generally representing Protestant and Loyalist communities, and 'Clonard' typifying a Catholic/Nationalist/Republican (CNR) one.

Communities also displayed identifiable images that acted as clear territorial markers for those outside the community. Painted kerbstones, paramilitary murals and graffiti clearly identified community boundaries and communal identity. By the time the research was complete, many paramilitary- or 'Troubles'-related murals had been replaced with less conflict-based alternatives. For example, Loyalist murals close to Connswater were replaced with others commemorating the area's shipbuilding past and particularly the building and sinking of the Titanic.[1] Such identities were further reinforced by community groups, such as the Clonard ex-prisoners' group that acted as a support mechanism for former republican prisoners. Northern Ireland has around 40 'peace walls', many in Belfast, which separate Catholic and Protestant neighbourhoods, put up in an attempt to minimize sectarian conflict and violence. These interfaces (including those in Roden Street and Clonard) are often marked by high security walls and barriers and illustrate the architectural legacy of socio-political conflict.

Other less visible sectarian interfaces also existed. The motorway that bordered Roden Street effectively sealed it off from neighbouring West Belfast, a largely CNR quarter, and acted as a community boundary. Clonard, located within the confines of West Belfast, also contained a high security interface wall as it borders the Protestant/Unionist/Loyalist' (PUL) Shankill area. The proximity of Clonard to the Shankill contributed both to Clonard's own historical legacy and to the history of the Northern Ireland conflict. It contained the location of the infamous burning of Bombay Street (an important conflict trigger in the early days of the 'Troubles') and Clonard Monastery, the setting for talks that proved instrumental in brokering the Provisional IRA ceasefire and the beginning of the peace process. Clonard, like many areas of West Belfast, is a small and tightly-knit community. Northern Ireland Housing Executive (NIHE) housing waiting lists are illustrative of the fact that many people who are part of these communities continue to want to be housed within them. One of the issues immediately apparent to the NIHE during initial consultations for the Clonard/*Cluain Mór* regeneration project was the concern expressed by residents about moving away from the area. For many, this was a sensitive and difficult issue. Finding a site of such close proximity alleviated some of these concerns, and made the regeneration project viable. Naming the site in a way that linked it to the original location (Clonard– *Cluain Árd*– means high meadow in Irish: *Cluain Mór* means the big meadow), also helped cement cultural and familial linkages.

Roden Street and Connswater were also impacted by the same violent conflict as Clonard, and the Republican murals that dominated Clonard were matched by the Loyalist ones in these predominantly Protestant and Unionist communities. Paramilitary activity, and the intra-community conflict it generated, was another aspect of 'living history' within such segregated environments. Taking account of community boundaries, communal identity and community interfaces is an extremely difficult task for public managers. For example, paramilitary activity within the Greater Village Area in the early stages of the Roden Street development required the intervention of a respected local councillor who successfully negotiated a compromise so work could continue. While organized crime can often be a feature in urban regeneration projects, the particular circumstances that prevailed in the Village at that time made it extremely difficult and, indeed, unsafe to carry on clearing a site without political and community intervention. Localized 'political manoeuvring' of this type is a predicable outcome of such path-dependencies. The NIHE itself was regarded with general suspicion and concerns were expressed about its motives and the future of the community generally. This distrust can in part, be traced to the community's own historic decline and the parallel decline of other PUL communities throughout Belfast.

For Roden Street and Connswater, community conflict interacted with an economic downturn that dispersed and fragmented traditional communities. Intense violent conflict, the gradual erosion of traditional heavy industries, and a UK Government policy to encourage the development of new urban centres outside Belfast in traditionally Unionist areas left a legacy of inter-generational unemployment, social alienation and extremely poor educational attainment in some communities. By encouraging movement outside the city of Belfast, the UK Government exacerbated the decline of PUL working-class communities within the city. While this was unintended, it resulted in further ghettoizing PUL areas and in underlining a distrust of the NIHE, which had been established to ensure fair allocation of housing resources. It was clear to both the residents and local representatives that the Roden Street development was the first step in a general redevelopment of the larger Village Area.

This was a cause of great concern, principally because of the legacy of past regeneration initiatives in other Loyalist areas of Belfast which had resulted in depopulation and community dissipation, but also because of a complex parallel process within the community of house sales and lettings which left the community less cohesive and added to a general sense of vulnerability and a desire to retain old established boundaries.

These, then, formed the initial conditions from which NIHE needed to negotiate a careful path. In order to move forward, NIHE felt that it needed to build confidence in the community, and in order to achieve this, the housing executive worked in partnership with the South Belfast Trust and local community representatives to establish a new organization, which could act as a vehicle for local legitimacy and foster a partnership approach.

The impact of a specific regeneration history on the projects was marked, and at times also fed into communal memories. For example, Roden Street actively cited the 'hollowing out' of other traditional Loyalist communities in the Shankill and in Sandy Row (an area adjacent to their community) as a source of insecurity and their determination not to be the next 'victim' of change. Indeed, this background played out first as a resistance to change and then as a more focused attempt to mould that process to 're-establish' the community and re-negotiate the distribution of power. This in itself illustrated a lack of trust and confidence in NIHE, in contrast to the greater degree of confidence in the organization shown by the community in Clonard. In the Clonard example, it was the statutory removal of NIHE's power to build (a broadly based external intervention in housing policy by the 'centre') and the introduction of a new actor (Oaklee Housing Association) that was of more concern to residents. The re-negotiation of the balance of power that followed involved Oaklee as the new 'agent' establishing itself carefully within a potentially resistant environment.

For Dublin too, the economic harshness of the 1970s and 80s followed by the explosive economic growth in the Republic's economy in the 1990s led to unprecedented social, economic and demographic change. An improved economy, the development of new industries, investment and increased trade lead to unparalleled levels of wealth and prosperity generally in Ireland and in Dublin in particular (Kitchen 2002). While some commentators have referred to Dublin as an, 'ensemble of villages' (Kitchen 2002), Bannon (1999) sees it as 'a collection of communities and groups, which have their own identities while owing allegiance to the city'. Dublin in the early part of the twentieth century was characterized by a poor and densely populated core. The 1950s saw the rise of suburban neighbourhoods around this core, followed in the 1970s and 80s by a period of rapid urban expansion (Kitchen 2002). Inner city neighbourhoods in particular (of which Hardwicke Street and Fatima Mansions were two) went through periods of extreme social decline and deprivation accentuated by a dilapidated and aging infrastructure, with a rapidly falling population in the 1980s and unemployment rates that ranged from 35–80 per cent depending on location (MacLaran 1999). Housing projects (such as Dublin's Ballymun, Fatima Mansions and Hardwicke Street) were a response to an urgent and acute shortage of appropriate accommodation and were developed as such. The legacy of the Irish Government's 'surrender grant scheme'[2] and its ill-fated result in creating 'sink estates' out of relatively stable mixed neighbourhoods left a lasting legacy of distrust. Major shortcomings in the design and environment of the developments exacerbated community problems.

Fatima Mansions had a long history of social decline. As a working-class, inner city community, it was most vulnerable to the economic challenges. Because Fatima was notorious in terms of crime and addiction, boundaries between it and its surrounding communities were carefully protected– not by those within Fatima, but by those outside it. In particular, the fate of a wall that separated Fatima from some of its neighbours was a source of great concern and persistent debate. The 'sink' label affected Ballymun and Hardwicke Street in a similar way. In Hardwicke Street the situation was compounded by gangland violence and vigilante activity. For Ballymun, its history was one of physical, social, political and economic isolation and separation from the onset.

Within Ballymun too, one of the driving motivations of the regeneration project was the fear of repeating the mistakes of the past and unwittingly sowing the seeds of decline in the new environment (Ballymun Community Action Programme 2000). Its bleak history of initial hope followed by despair was topmost in the minds of residents and regeneration managers, resulting in an early awareness of their interdependence. While the cases discussed above involved relatively small communities, which were quite distinct within larger homogenous groupings, Ballymun represented the collective identity for a series of smaller neighbourhoods contained within its geographical area. Ballymun was subdivided into a number of neighbourhoods: Balcurris, Balbutcher, Coultry, Shargan, Sillogue, Sandyhill and Poppintree and the locus of power among them resulted in their emergence as actors in their own right within the regeneration 'system'.

In general, Ballymun had an almost worldwide reputation as a 'sink' estate with endemic social exclusion and deprivation. Media representations of the area (both directly and indirectly) publicized its problems. As a frequent film location, it became the backdrop of choice for urban decay and deprivation. Films such as *The Commitments* and *Into the West* used Ballymun as a location to symbolize the barrenness of urban life. Perhaps most prominently of all, its high-rise tower blocks featured in the U2 song *Running to Stand Still* (1987) to symbolize the chronic isolation of persistent social exclusion. Its name became shorthand for how not to conduct neighbourhood renewal in Ireland (Fahey 1999), and the initial conditions for the regeneration initiative were harsh. However, the sheer size of the regeneration challenge, and the inter-connectedness within and between the neighbourhoods listed above, were utilized effectively within the regeneration process. The very fact that the existence of these neighbourhoods was acknowledged showed a willingness and awareness of the need for the regeneration strategy to take account of initial conditions. By reflecting the neighbourhood structure within the consultation forums, the initiative was able to work with Ballymun as a whole, while preserving the community structures already in place.

Within the healthcare cases, the role of path-dependency is less obvious but still apparent. The implementation of information technology (IT) as a commonplace and important resource within the healthcare field has been a dramatic and relatively recent change to organizational practice. This has, no doubt, contributed to the general acceptance of IT solutions in all the cases. Long running bad news coverage arising from hospital waiting lists and the attendant bruising encounter of senior Northern Ireland civil servants with the House of Commons' Public Accounts Committee clearly contributed to an environment where a project such as the Theatre Management System (TMS), whose aim was to reduce hospital waiting lists in Northern Ireland, was initiated and readily supported. Such high political stakes may well have contributed to the engagement of the Department of Health's Service Delivery Unit later, as management of the project encountered staffing problems. By the same measure, the UK appointment of a 'Fraud Csar', a UK Treasury 'spend to save' initiative, and another difficult Public Accounts Committee hearing created fertile ground for the Electronic Prescribing and Eligibility System (EPES), at least initially. Backing at the highest organizational levels minimized the potentially stultifying impact of organizational, sectoral and professional boundaries. Legal barriers however, particularly with regard to freedom of information and data protection legislation were less easily transcended. Ironically, changes in the governance of Northern Ireland (a return to devolved authority) have resulted in recent plans for the abolition of prescription charges. Since EPES was originally conceived as an anti-fraud initiative, this may call into question the basis of the project as a whole.

Within the Republic of Ireland HCIS cases, an increasingly IT focused environment established favourable initial conditions and the path-dependency dynamics that were locally productive for the development of IT-related efficiency solutions. While no clear boundaries can be ascertained, the local development of the projects (in contrast to the centrally focused development in Northern Ireland) seems to indicate that project initiation was easier at that level.

The type of professional boundaries and power differentials identified within the case studies were a contributory factor in the significant staffing problems experienced by the Northern Ireland TMS project. The dual role of the first senior responsible officer (SRO) as a clinician and as a manager seems to have given the initial stages some credibility with clinical staff, and traction with departmental management. This credibility issue appears to have particular relevance within a healthcare environment that is operating around clear and firmly defined professional boundary roles. For example, a project manager within TMS (who held a doctorate in a non-medical discipline) was not regularly accorded the title Doctor—a situation that seems to have rankled and contributed to professional dissatisfaction. Attention to such seemingly minor, but at times vital, issues of professional standing illustrates the importance of boundary awareness and management within the cases. The 'boundary crossing' ability of the clinician/manager was also extremely significant in gaining momentum for the project, even while it competed with other similar projects for successful adoption. In the case of EPES, the clear professional boundaries and power dynamics between the Department of Health and the pharmacists created difficulties in terms of negotiation of project pilots and implementation. The boundaries between these professional groups were reinforced by a perception, on the part of pharmacists, that they had not been historically treated on a par with other medical professions, such as GPs and dentists.

In the Regional Acquired Brain Injury Unit (RABIU), the removal of former boundaries and the creation of new professional associations were key parts of the wider project. By integrating the inpatient and outpatient service in one new facility, RABIU had to integrate two sets of staff and also two existing IT systems. Having an IT project officer who was also a nurse broke down the possible communication and professional barriers that may have been present within the IT and medical groups during the project development, and allowed for accurate specification setting. The clear interdisciplinary nature of the wider project may also have contributed to a less 'boundaried' perception of the project's development.

Seeing a boundary as the interface between one thing and something else, or the point at which two groups, contexts or entities meet, allows us to look at the path-dependency dynamics arising out of the case's initial conditions and explore the boundaries and the professional delineations that operate within them. We have seen that boundaries can be physical or virtual, or both, and that boundaries within the mind are just as difficult and intractable as their physical manifestations. This focus on path-dependency is concerned with the 'back story' of cases and the dynamics between the people, power and politics within them. The focus on uncovering boundaries and their impact allows us to make sense of that back story, and to see how it determines the trajectory of future development. These cases illustrate that powerful defining forces are already at work and interacting when projects begin. Pinpointing identifiable boundaries offers a potential guide to, and through, the possible difficulties and opportunities that a project affords. We have seen in urban regeneration that boundaries were both physical and psychological: closely tied to communal identity. In healthcare, perceived professional borders played a bigger role in setting the scene for project implementation. In both domains, boundaries represented clear points of contention between groups and communities that were played out over the course of the projects.

Bifurcation: Setting New Boundaries

Bifurcations lead to sudden and unexpected changes in the system. In terms of a discussion on boundaries, relevant bifurcations include those in which boundaries are decided upon, or new boundaries are formed, creating new dynamics within the system as a whole. Securing the *Cluain Mór* site was a significant bifurcation point for the Clonard regeneration project, because the extensive waiting list for housing in West Belfast meant that only the availability of new land (in this case what had been an industrial site) would ease the strain on demand. However, it became apparent early on in the development that relocation was dependent not only on the availability of new land, but also on its proximity to the existing site. Residents were extremely reluctant to move away from what they regarded as 'their' community and since the 'put back' ratio for housing development was about a third of the existing cramped housing stock, the availability of land nearby was the major factor in the development going ahead. In order to ease the transition to a new site, both the NIHE and Oaklee Housing Association worked with residents at all times to reassure them that community integrity would be preserved, where possible. This extended to a sensitive relocation of residents in the new development so neighbours with existing good relationships were placed close together. Another bifurcation point occurred when older Clonard residents awaiting accommodation were unexpectedly able take up residence in a new sheltered housing development. The building, which had been a former convent, and had some considerable architectural merit, had not initially been considered for redevelopment until the indirect intervention of a UK Government minister who happened to come across it on a tour of the area. This intervention, and the sheltered housing development which resulted from it, had important consequences for reallocation of housing throughout the project.

Within Fatima in Dublin, the wall dividing it from the surrounding community was a subject of prolonged and intense discussion and debate for many years. Eventually, the decision was taken by a public manager in Dublin City Council to leave the wall, even though its demolition had been desired by Fatima residents and by the local authority itself. This decision acknowledged that the communities needed time to re-negotiate relationships and allowed breathing space before future re-engagement on the issue. The decision to keep the wall represented a change in the local authority's position and closed the debate at least temporarily, allowing the project to proceed with more stability, although with some lingering dissatisfaction on the part of some residents.

Within Northern Ireland's Roden Street case, plans to relocate residents led to intense dissatisfaction among tenants who were concerned about maintaining the cohesion of their community. While the eventual decision to build created a notable decision point in the general development discussion, distrust and dissatisfaction still surrounded plans for regeneration within the Greater Village Area. Boundaries, both psychological and physical, had already slowed redevelopment for many years and continued to do so. The lack of a significant change in resident attitudes resulting from this decision reflects the difficulties presented by the initial conditions, and the resulting path-dependency characteristics, creating high levels of distrust and robbing the project of momentum.

Within Ballymun in Dublin, a bifurcation arose from the placement of access and exit roads—issues relevant to the boundaries of intra-community neighbourhoods within the wider Ballymun community. Eventual agreement led to a more unified response among agents and allowed the project to move ahead again.

The experience of Fatima is significant in this regard, because it illustrates the coming together of diverse agents into one body, Fatima Groups United, which acted as a single voice and visioning mechanism for the development of the new community within eventually agreed boundaries. This creation of a new and powerful community agent reflecting a sense of direction and communal identity was a significant bifurcation in the Fatima case and had an impact on the forward trajectory of the project. By moving across organizational boundaries and creating a new set of relationships within the new structure, Fatima Groups United was able to exert new leverage.

In the healthcare cases, a boundary change in the span of the Health-Link project, from a small initiative that involved 12 GPs and one hospital to a national level project, significantly altered the working of the project and the agents engaged in it. The move required that software also be upgraded and integrated, both for the hospitals and for the GPs. The decision to expand was a bifurcation in itself and a change in both the project boundaries and the relationships between agents.

While boundaries were not the only causes of bifurcations in the cases studied, social, political and professional boundaries clearly impact on the likelihood of bifurcations occurring and contribute towards the conditions that create sudden and unexpected changes. In Clonard we have the clearest example of a bifurcation that is directly related to residents' concerns about boundaries and which impacted on the developmental trajectory of the project as a whole. The lack of significant bifurcation points in Roden Street is indicative of a wider project lacking momentum and being held back through difficult conditions within the case environment. Fatima shows us that changing boundaries and dynamics between agents can cause a bifurcation in the project and significantly impact on future outcomes.

WHAT DOES THE CAS FRAMEWORK BRING TO AN ANALYSIS OF BOUNDARIES IN PUBLIC MANAGEMENT?

This chapter has focused on boundaries and the concerns that surrounded them as one of the general themes that emerged from the cross-case analysis of CAS dynamics. It also looked briefly at the kinds of challenges faced by public managers in developing the projects and encountering boundaries that impact on decision-making. These challenges were significant because entire projects can run aground because of past events, perceived bias or community concerns. In providing this overview it sought to examine these processes through a CAS lens and to reflect on what particular insights this view brings to an analysis. In particular, it picked up on features such as interfaces, communal identity, professional roles and territoriality that were particularly relevant to path-dependencies within the cases. It set these projects firmly within a complex historical, political and organizational context and looked at how history and events of the past had impacted on the projects as a whole. In addition, the analysis highlighted how boundaries could be remade and reformulated in a way that allowed projects to progress and encouraged the active engagement of local agents.

Boundaries, viewed as initial conditions, proved to be extremely important in determining the future trajectory of projects, and it may be assumed that sensitivity to the presence and nature of boundaries would help to identify weak points or danger zones within public management decision-making. History and the legacy of the past were ever-present and powerful features of all the case studies. In urban regeneration they were particularly obvious, but in healthcare too, organizational design, power dynamics and contemporary concerns had significant impact on how projects developed and the way in which they moved forward. History creates a contested arena full of the concerns, wishes, prior damage and future desires that make up the decision-making context of the present.

For the urban regeneration cases, the initial conditions shaped their development and their approach to the process of re-energizing their communities. Through processes of community agent adaptation, seemingly immovable boundaries between groups were remade, resulting in new and different communal identities. The role of agents such as public managers in the facilitation of such adaptation was vital.

In the Republic of Ireland cases, the different political environment made the role of community agents different, but no less complex. Just as community organizations evolved in Northern Ireland with a focus on particular issues or in response to experiences, the three Dublin regeneration cases illustrate similar examples of community agents working to stabilize the boundaries of their communities in a way that fitted their sense of communal identity and belonging. The existence of a diverse, highly political and focused set of agents in Ballymun reflected the large, complex and visible regeneration process. The low level of community representation in Hardwicke Street (at least initially) reflected a community that was fractured, deeply troubled and finding it difficult to mount a focused response. However, initiatives like a self-conducted survey acted as a force to begin to mobilize members and create a more cohesive response. The experience of Fatima is also significant in this regard because it illustrates the coming together of diverse agents into one body, Fatima Groups United. This alone—the creation of a new and powerful agent that reflected communal identity– was a bifurcation point in the renewal process.

In Belfast's Roden Street the system also adapted, this time to a seemingly intractable obstacle of community collaboration, by the establishment of a new agent, Greater Village Regeneration Trust (GVRT), and therefore a new powerbase within the system. In terms of a community's ability to live comfortably, the case of Hardwicke Street saw significant emphasis placed on the security and needs of the residents with the development of 'friendly defensive space' for ground floor apartments. For Fatima too, security and the community's previous history were an incentive for the system to develop as many ways as possible to 'design out' problems. This was echoed in Connswater, where emphasis was placed on the 'secured by design' process with its anti-sectarian design of houses whose gable walls contained windows (making them unpopular with mural painters) and trellising, which make the erection of flags difficult. This adaptation of the regeneration design to the historical legacy of physical 'symbolism' within communities is significant in itself.

Within the healthcare cases, boundaries represented different and, at times, more amorphous concerns. The diversity of boundaries identified reflected the challenges that face those tasked with managing projects through a maze of sectoral, organizational and professional demarcations. The issue of power differentials between professional groups had the potential to create serious problems for some projects as they developed, and seemed to have done just that within the TMS case. In other circumstances the support of powerful allies (medical or non-medical) was beneficial for some projects, but less so for others. Managing these dynamics, however, was a vital issue for those developing projects in this environment. Boundaries also arose in terms of the scope of projects and a change in boundaries (as in HealthLink) can precede a fundamental change in the project as a whole.

CONCLUSION

While boundaries within public management can be identified in many different ways, it is clear empirically that they can present a real challenge to those implementing projects that involve a change or alteration in how or where a community defines itself, or that involve the inter-working of groups who already have established social and professional practices. We can see from our analysis that boundaries are not quickly established—rather they tend to be the result of long periods of development and involve deeply-felt concerns for group and individual wellbeing. By applying the CAS dynamic of path-dependency to the analysis of boundaries, the historical or organizational processes that established them, and their impact on project processes and outcomes, can be more clearly detected and understood. Furthermore, by looking at how changing boundaries can create bifurcations, future problems and fault lines in project development can be understood and at times, ameliorated. Looking at boundaries in this way also helps us to see how, in many cases, definitions of identity, communal space and professional space are not fixed, but can be changed with appropriate negotiation and sensitivity to the particular issues of concern that arise. Those implementing public policy on the ground are often aware of, and can take account of, boundaries within project development. But by putting an analysis of boundaries as initial conditions driving path-dependency and bifurcation dynamics to the forefront of project preparatory work, many of the seemingly insurmountable difficulties that can arise can be avoided or dealt with more effectively.

6 Vision and the Dynamics of Change

INTRODUCTION

This chapter uses complex adaptive system (CAS) analysis to assess how stakeholder involvement processes operated within the 12 case studies covering the urban regeneration (UR) and healthcare information systems (HCIS) policy domains. The cases studied in each of the two domains represented involvement processes between two different sets of agents, which nevertheless exhibited similar dynamics and could be profitably analyzed using the CAS framework proposed. The UR cases illustrate interaction between the public and state agencies, as part of the delivery of front line services, while the HCIS cases illustrate the interaction between functional groups within an organization, as part of the development of support services facilitated by information and communication technology.

In urban regeneration, the analysis concentrated on the relationship between the implementing agency and the 'community', as evidenced in ongoing partnership structures and *ad hoc* initiatives such as public meetings and surveys. The healthcare information systems case studies focused on the project implementation group and the relationships among members from different functional areas (which may or may not have been part of the core project team, or indeed of the sponsoring organization). The specific relationships and processes studied in this domain were between the users of the proposed system (or their designates) and the project implementation group, generally led by information & communication technology (ICT) professionals or representatives of hospital management. Involvement of users outside the project groups consisted mainly of surveys of user requirements or collaboration in implementation processes.

Stakeholder involvement is an important aspect of public administration, with literature reviews illustrating the point in relation to urban regeneration (Burton *et al.* 2004) and healthcare (Crawford *et al.* 2004). In spite of considerable efforts in both policy domains, this involvement often falls short of expectations, or has limited or even detrimental effects, due to inequalities of power (Daake and Anthony 2000, Taylor 2007).

It has been suggested that the reasons that governments encourage community involvement in urban regeneration include, to aid social cohesion, to foster social capital, to ensure effective planning and delivery of local services, to obtain agreement for the approach to planning and delivery of services and to uphold the right of the citizen to influence decisions which affect them (Burton *et al.* 2004). Crawford *et al.* (2004) have summarized the types of user involvement found internationally in healthcare as covering the following discrete areas: organization and delivery of local services; involvement of patients in their own treatment and care; development of clinical guidelines and treatment protocols, for example through membership of clinical governance committees; individual involvement in quality control measures, such as patient satisfaction surveys; healthcare planning; and attempts to improve public health. The emphasis is on a mixture of individual and collective representation, in comparison with a more collective emphasis in urban regeneration.

The chapter begins with definitions of community, users and stakeholders, followed by reflections from the literature on power imbalances and a review of the concepts of consultation and participation, all of which contribute to arriving at a definition of 'involvement'. Next, the CAS analysis is set out in detail. Five common themes were identified, which are discussed in relation to the CAS dynamics of path-dependency, adaptation and emergence, as set out in Table 6.1. No bifurcation points were identified, possibly because the involvement processes were iterative as well as dynamic, leading themselves to adaptation and emergence rather than to the sudden changes in direction which characterize bifurcation points. The most important finding was that a combination of adaptation features led

Table 6.1   Stakeholder Involvement Themes in the CAS Analysis

Theme	CAS dynamics
The impact of past experience on trust between participants	Path dependency
Building capacity for involvement	Adaptation
The role of key individuals as 'boundary spanners'*	Adaptation
The balance of power	Adaptation
The emergence of a shared project or programme 'vision' as a driver for change	Emergence

Note: * The term 'boundary spanners' has been used in organizational literature for over 30 years in relation to strategy, innovation and group processes (see Tushman & Scanlan 1981 for an early reference). Boundary spanners are individuals that link one organizational unit with another and/or link the organization with its environment generally. The main activity of a boundary spanner is the exchange of information between entities and the main challenge for boundary spanners is resolving conflicting schema and/or objectives among different entities.

to the emergence of a shared vision in the majority of cases, and that vision became the main driver for further change.

The chapter's conclusion reflects on the contribution of each of the five themes to the overall dynamics of involvement in the case studies, and the contribution of the research to the overall CAS analysis.

INVOLVEMENT AND PUBLIC MANAGEMENT

Who Is Involved: Definitions of Community, Users and Stakeholders

The urban regeneration case studies concentrated on the dynamics of community involvement in the planning and implementation of the programmes. It is acknowledged that other external stakeholders are involved in regeneration, including voluntary organizations, state agencies other than the implementing body and the private sector. However, these case studies were examples of programmes where governments expected communities, often meaning local residents (more so than the other groups mentioned above), to be able to state their views and to have these views taken into account by the implementing agencies.

A community has been defined as 'a group of people who interact directly, frequently and in multi-faceted ways' (Bowles and Gintis 2002: F420). Taylor (2003: 34) outlines three uses of the term: descriptive, denoting a group of people who share interests or interactions; normative, used to describe a place of 'solidarity, participation and coherence'; and instrumental, covering community as agency working for change.

Although community-based activity is generally seen as beneficial to society, it has also been recognized that inward-looking community ties, based on norms that are different from the rest of society, can have a negative impact (Putnam 2000, Portes 1998).

The HCIS case studies did not include direct representation of the interests of members of the public, but a wide range of other stakeholders was included in the programmes. The healthcare policy field refers more to service users than to community, perhaps indicating a different spatial approach to service delivery. While primary healthcare is delivered locally, specialist services including hospital care are not, meaning that the focus is more on the individual (or on groups defined by their health needs) than on the needs of geographically-based communities. Health service 'users' have been described as 'a variety of groups who use or may use the services . . . i.e. patients, carers, customers, consumers and members of the public' (Crawford *et al.* 2004: 21), although the term is sometimes also applied to workers in healthcare organizations (Coombs *et al.* 2002). Stakeholders are defined as individuals, groups and organizations 'who have an interest (stake) and the potential to influence the actions and aims of an organization, project or policy direction' (Brugha and Varvasovzsky 2000: 239).

Stakeholder interests can impact on healthcare planning through the involvement of specific groups, and through the consideration of the interests of those who are not present (Daake and Anthony 2000), such as future service users or those who are physically or otherwise unable to participate effectively. There are other examples of these dynamics occurring within information systems projects. Lorenzi and Riley (2003) highlighted the tendency of staff to resist the introduction of new information systems and the need, therefore, to communicate their benefits. 'User ownership' and 'positive user attitudes' towards information systems projects have been found to be crucial to their success (Coombs *et al.* 2002) and a model for 'user-centred' information systems development has even been proposed (Eason 2006).

Power Relationships

At its simplest, power involves getting someone to do something they would not otherwise do; other aspects of power that have been identified include mobilization of bias through control of agenda-setting; and the imposition of a dominant value system which excludes some options and generates the potential for latent conflict (Lukes 1974).

Power imbalances in urban regeneration are connected to the relationship between the state and civil society, and to power imbalances within civil society more broadly (Taylor 2003). The widespread experience of 'the persistence of oligarchy' (Somerville 2005: 123) and the exclusion of citizens from inner circles of decision-making (Skelcher *et al.* 1996) show how difficult it is to challenge the fundamental patterns of power inherent in governance structures. However, despite the power imbalance between state and civil society, other power differentials between and within state organizations can create opportunities for communities to network, negotiate and influence decision-making (Gilchrist 2000), for example in partnership structures (Taylor 2007).

In healthcare, power relationships are evident between service users and healthcare providers (McEvoy *et al.* 2008) and among functional groups within the healthcare system. It is the second area that concerns us in the research reported here, as service users were largely absent in the case narratives based on the interviews conducted. However, in the case of ICT projects, the 'users' of the system are often in a similar position vis-à-vis the ICT project team, as is the community in UR projects vis-à-vis the implementing agencies. Interactions between clinical staff and managers can be fraught: managers need clinicians for legitimization of new systems (Myers and Young 1997), but clinicians adopt strategies of resistance if they do not agree with change (Doolin 2004). Particular issues can arise if clinicians think information systems will be used to limit their professional judgement in the interests of financial control (Doolin 2004).

Towards a Definition of 'Involvement'

The term 'involvement' is used here to cover all aspects of consultation and participation. Many factors can affect the quality of involvement, including power relationships within and between the organizations involved, networks and regimes from which communities may be excluded, and wider economic, social, political and cultural forces (Muir 2004).

Although the terms 'consultation' and 'participation' are often used interchangeably, their meanings are different. Arnstein (1969), writing in a spatial planning context, defined consultation as a process where citizens are asked their views by decision-makers but there is no guarantee that these views will be taken into account. Participation depends upon a more equal relationship between the parties involved: 'the redistribution of power that enables the have-not citizens, presently excluded from the political and economic processes, to be deliberately included in the future' (Arnstein 1969: 216). Arnstein's 'ladder of participation' between different levels of involvement is often the starting point for a discussion of participation,[1] but has been criticized as somewhat simplistic (Murphy and Cunningham 2003, Taylor 2003). However, it is still useful to acknowledge that participation involves a deeper and more prolonged association between parties (including an element of power for participants to endorse or veto initiatives) than consultation.

A definition of 'involvement' that can be applied to both sets of case studies, despite their many differences, is proposed as: *the interactions between agents in the project arena and policy environment through which a temporary or permanent accommodation between different interests and different levels of power is achieved.*

A CAS ANALYSIS OF INVOLVEMENT

In the analysis of the case study data around user/community involvement, the CAS dynamics of path-dependency, adaptation and emergence were relevant and found to lead to important insights. A summary of the case study features relevant to involvement and organized by these dynamics is set out in Table 6.2. As pointed out earlier, no bifurcation points were identified. The most striking observation was how up to three adaptive processes helped to shape the emergence of a shared project or programme 'vision'.

Path-Dependency: The Impact of Past Experience on Trust

The past experience of participants with each other, or the passing on of past experience through organizational memory, was an initial condition in the cases that created different 'paths' of trust, or distrust, that evolved over the course of the projects, and created either advantages or disadvantages for each project. In five of the six urban regeneration case studies, past experiences of involvement with the implementing agency, or of involvement in

Table 6.2 Stakeholder Involvement Themes by Case Study.

	Urban Regeneration				
	Path Dependancy	CAS feature			
		Adaptation	Adaptation	Adaptation	Emergence
	Impact of past experience on trust	Building capacity for involvement	Role of key individuals as 'boundary spanners'	The balance of power	Shared 'vision' as a driver for change
Ballymun	✓	✓	✓	✓	-
Fatima Mansions	✓	✓	✓	✓	✓
Hardwicke Street	✓	-	✓	-	✓
Clonard/*Cluain Mór*	✓	✓	✓	✓	✓
Connswater	-	✓	-	✓	✓
Roden Street	✓	✓	✓	-	-

Continued

Table 6.2 Continued

	Healthcare Information Systems				
	CAS feature				
	Path Dependancy	Adaptation	Adaptation	Adaptation	Emergence
	Impact of past experience on trust	Building capacity for involvement	Role of key individuals as 'boundary spanners'	The balance of power	Shared 'vision' as a driver for change
Electronic Health Record (EHR)	-	-	-	-	-
HealthLink	✓	✓	✓	-	✓
Order Communication System (OCS)	-	✓	-	✓	✓
Electronic Prescribing and Eligibility System (EPES)	✓	-	✓	✓	-
Regional Acquired Brain Injury Unit (RABIU)	-	✓	✓	✓	✓
Theatre Management System (TMS)	-	-	✓	✓	✓

other regeneration or renewal programmes in the area, influenced the level of trust between communities and implementing agencies. In cases where organizations representing residents and (sometimes) other local interests already had the knowledge, networks and skills to communicate their views effectively to the implementing agency, a trusting environment put residents in a better position to ensure the programme met their interests, and to negotiate for change if necessary. A good working relationship resulted. In cases with good relationships initially but little experience in the community groups, residents needed to develop consultation structures and were able to work with agencies to do this because the basic trust existed, due to the previous experiences of the agency by individuals.

In cases where negative experiences in the past led to distrust, a poor working relationship was evident at the start of the programme and, in some cases, did not improve. An example of this occurred in Ballymun, where residents had campaigned for the regeneration of the estate over many years through various community-based organizations, including the Ballymun Housing Task Force. Over the years they had had negative experiences with Dublin City Council, which set the scene for the working relationship with Ballymun Regeneration Limited (BRL), an organization closely connected with the Council. There was a lack of trust between community organizations and BRL; conversely, BRL staff felt that community activists did not represent the views of the majority of residents. This dynamic affected consultation on the draft regeneration master plan, as well as the ongoing negotiations between the community and BRL.

In two of the HCIS case studies, the type of past experience of another information system (either manual or electronic) was significant, especially if its operation had affected working relationships between different staff groups. As in urban regeneration, past experience could lead to paths of trust or distrust. The lack of trust identified within some of the health organizations was connected not only to actual past experience but also to the wider phenomenon of resistance to change in organizations. There was no resistance to change identified in urban regeneration; on the contrary, residents led pressure for change.

An example of organizational memory creating difficult initial conditions and affecting trust occurred in the Electronic Prescribing and Eligibility System (EPES) project. The interests of pharmacists were presented on the project team by the Pharmaceutical Contractors' Committee, whose relationship with the Department of Health, Social Services and Public Safety (DHSSPS) in Northern Ireland had been strained in the past due to perceived inequities in their treatment compared to GPs.

Adaptation

Up to three adaptation processes were evident: building capacity for involvement; the role of key individuals as 'boundary spanners'; and the balance of power. All the case studies included one or more of these processes and four case studies included all three (Table 6.2).

Building Capacity for Involvement

Building capacity for effective stakeholder involvement required the provision of extra resources in the form of either money or time. There were distinct differences in how this was achieved in the two policy domains, with additional funding and the time of residents being more important in urban regeneration, and staff time taking priority for HCIS. The process of building capacity was more common in urban regeneration, being found in five out of the six cases, whereas it was identified in only three of the healthcare projects.

All the urban regeneration case studies had dedicated funding for promoting community involvement, either from state organizations or from voluntary or charitable sources, or a combination of both. The funding usually provided for extra paid staff with a community advocacy remit, located in community-based organizations, but training for local residents, and activities such as surveys and consultation events, were also included. In general, funding helped to 'level the playing field' between communities and state agencies, and addressed some aspects of power imbalances. Positive aspects of this approach included strengthening the capacity of residents' associations and advocacy bodies, and the development of expertise, for example in the planning process. Funding also allowed community-based organizations to commission consultants to carry out surveys and other research, independent of the implementing agency. In some cases, however, funding appeared to be perpetuating dysfunctional involvement structures.

In Connswater, additional resources made a positive difference. The residents' association was set up at the start of the regeneration process and members received funding, advice and training from the International Fund for Ireland and the East Belfast Community Development Association. After a couple of years they produced a ten-point priority plan for the area and began to campaign against the closure of a local school. The funding would not have brought about this success without the additional time contributed by local residents; on the other hand, it is improbable that the group could have progressed so fast on a voluntary basis alone.

Stakeholder involvement was built into the budgets of HCIS projects through processes such as requirements surveys and pilot stages. Staff time from stakeholders outside information technology (IT(departments was an important resource, however, and capacity was built through greater knowledge of how clinical requirements could be operationalized in the information systems under development, leading to better quality user feedback. The use of outside expertise was an additional capacity-building resource, for example the use of IT consultants to carry out requirements surveys and to write strategies. The HealthLink project provided an example of how staff time was used for stakeholder involvement, through the participation of GPs at both local and national level. The pilot project involved GPs in the initial consultation and then they had to learn how to use the new technology, on which they provided feedback. The project team was also part of the Department of Health's National General Practice Information Technology Group, which provided funding for expansion after the pilot phase as well as facilitating information exchange and training.

The Role of Key Individuals as 'Boundary Spanners'

Chapter 5 discussed the more general importance of boundaries in both the policy domains. The role of key individuals who could reach out across institutional boundaries was crucial in both sets of case studies. The important boundaries were those between community interests and the implementation agency in urban regeneration, and professional boundaries in HCIS.

All but one of the urban regeneration case studies involved people who played a 'brokering' role in the projects through making connections between agents across organizational boundaries, for example to exchange information or to address conflict. This process was beneficial to working relationships, even if it was not possible to overcome the problem under discussion. It is worth noting that it was not only community activists who were involved in putting forward community interests. Others included 'street level' bureaucrats, who were frequently located in offices on or near the regeneration area, senior bureaucrats in the implementing agency or in another public body and local politicians. The project leader from Fatima Groups United (FGU) was an example of a boundary spanning community activist. He had been involved in local community groups on a voluntary basis for many years, including as chair of FGU, before taking up his salaried post. He had experienced the entire regeneration process in Fatima Mansions, including the breakdown of negotiations with Dublin Corporation in the late 1990s, which had led to FGU commissioning its own report on options for the future (O'Gorman 2000). Later, he helped to negotiate community benefits from the public-private partnership (PPP) agreement.

Boundary spanning activity occurred in four of the HCIS projects. One of the three staff on the project team of Belfast's Regional Acquired Brain Injury Unit (RABIU) was an ex-nurse. She carried out the year-long 'requirements gathering' process, which gave the project team a comprehensive knowledge of the concerns, expectations and aspirations of the clinical staff. There was concern from the project team that unrealistic expectations had been raised by the degree of consultation, but good working relationships were also established and, when budget problems arose, it was possible for project staff to work constructively with clinicians to resolve matters. Once the contract had been awarded and the software development stage was under way, the ex-nurse was able to explain technical terms to clinicians and vice versa, thus continuing to minimize misunderstandings between the two groups.

The Balance of Power

The earlier definition of 'involvement' was based on recognition of the importance of the dynamics of power and interests. Therefore, it was not surprising to find that, in the majority of case studies, different levels and types of power occurred, and a permanent or temporary accommodation of power relationships needed to be achieved in order to move the project forward.

In all but one of the urban regeneration case studies, interactions were shaped by the balance of power between community-based agents and others. If one agent was more powerful than others, conflict or overriding of the community's views resulted. If there was a balance of power, then consensus-building through negotiation and mutual learning could take place. Although state agencies controlled resources and decision-making structures, this did not mean that they always had an advantage. One of the most important adaptive features within the dynamics of community involvement was the introduction of mechanisms to distribute power, and the shifting of power from one agent to another. In particular, it appeared that funding independent residents' advocacy groups to build capacity was an effective way of decreasing the 'power gap' bet ween communities and the state, and of enhancing the ability of residents to build positive working relationships and social capital. However, the degree to which communities could shape programmes to their own requirements was still limited by the wider context of funding and policy guidelines that had to be followed by the implementing agencies.

An example of negotiating within a finely balanced power relationship was the response of the Clonard Residents' Association to the introduction of a new agent into the Clonard/*Cluain Mór* programme. In a contested area during the 'Troubles', the power of government agencies and housing associations to implement the redevelopment was limited without an accompanying endorsement from residents, who had been concerned that housing need in the area could not be met through the planned demolition and replacement of existing homes. A nearby industrial site became available for new housing, but the government required the new housing to be built by a housing association rather than by the housing executive, which was highly thought of in the area. The support of the Residents' Association for the chosen housing association was crucial for the success of the new development, which became known as *Cluain Mór*.

The balance of power was also important in four of the HCIS cases. Here, the interests of larger number of agents needed to be taken into account, including IT staff and consultants, hospital managers, clinicians and allied staff such as pharmacists and phlebotomists. In national level projects, civil servants and politicians were also involved. The multiplicity of agents might suggest that many power struggles would take place during the project implementation process and that great difficulties would be encountered in reconciling interests. However, the fundamental power divide in these projects was quite simple: clinicians and allied staff versus the rest. At times when these two groups of interests could be reconciled, working relationships were productive and projects moved forward. Clinical and allied staff possessed latent power to obstruct project design and implementation, whereas project teams (made up of ICT professionals, management and in some cases government agencies) were, in theory, able to threaten to impose new systems. The two sets of interests were finely balanced overall.

A demonstration of these dynamics occurred in Northern Ireland's EPES project which, as mentioned earlier, was opposed by community pharmacists, whose representatives were key partners on the EPES management committee. At the time, a new contract was being negotiated between pharmacists and the DHSSPS, and cooperation with EPES was used as a bargaining counter. This led to a process of 'brinkmanship', which ended with the DHSSPS declaring unilaterally that they would cease accepting claims for payment made through the old prescribing system after a certain date. In this case, unlike the urban regeneration example, negotiations were over-ridden in an expression of the superior power of administrators at that point in the process.

Emergence: 'Vision' as a Driver for Change

The most important finding about stakeholder involvement was the emergent factor of a shared programme or project 'vision' as a driver for change, which was developed and expressed through written documents and through dialogue between agents. A vision of some kind emerged in all the case studies and in eight of them the vision was shared, rather than contested (Table 6.3). It was the vision, rather than the detail of outcomes, outputs and implementation structures, that appeared to motivate participants.

The adaptation and emergence features of the CAS analysis were closely linked, with different combinations of the three adaptive features described above– capacity-building, the role of key individuals and the balance of power– helping to shape the vision or contributing to problems in doing so.

Four types of vision were evident, as summarized in Table 6.3:

- A strong vision, shared between participants, with consistency between past, present and future, in two of the case studies;
- A defensive vision, based on protecting territory or professional boundaries, in three cases;
- A vision driven by a single agent, in four cases; and

- An adapting vision, in which all participants negotiated change together and agreed to a way forward, in three cases.

However, there was no connection between the number of adaptation features and the type of vision in a case study, or between the number of adaptation features and the coherence of the vision. In Ballymun, for example, all three adaptive features were present, and yet the vision was ultimately driven by the strongest partner, the regeneration agency, and was not shared. Alternatively, in the RABIU project, all three adaptive features were also present, contributing to an adapting vision that was shared amongst all participants.

In the urban regeneration cases, the vision centred on what the community would look like at the end of the regeneration—in other words, the quality of life in the area. The community vision at the start of the regeneration programmes was, unsurprisingly, for better conditions for existing residents. In contrast, implementing agencies had a wider strategic vision, for example to introduce mixed tenure or to integrate the area more closely with surrounding districts in order to reduce stigma. In four of the case studies, the vision of the future community, held by different agents, converged towards that held by the implementing agencies. If convergence towards an agreed vision did not take place, then either the project was delayed (Roden Street) or the state took the lead and left the community behind (Ballymun).

The most interesting urban regeneration example of a shared and converging vision was that of the adapting vision in Fatima Mansions. Here, the regeneration vision altered substantially between 1995 and 2004, including changes to the planned new housing profile to increase total units from 364 to 601 units (an increase of 65 per cent), but to reduce social housing from 364 units to 150 (a reduction of 59 per cent). We see a number of reasons why such a huge change was accomplished without serious conflict. Firstly, Fatima Mansions had a strong history of community involvement and residents had a strong and capable voice through FGU. Secondly, social housing was only part of what residents wanted, and new social and leisure facilities were included in the final PPP contract. There may have been an element of pragmatism from FGU in accepting the some of the changes at various times, including agreeing to a private finance option rather than the more limited choices options that would have been available under direct state funding. Certainly, it is an unusual story of major change being negotiated successfully over a relatively short period.

In the HCIS projects, the vision was about how effectively the system would contribute to improved service delivery through its efficient operation. Four projects, Order Communication System (OCS), HealthLink, RABIU and Theatre Management System (TMS), were directly connected to service delivery at local level. Electronic Health Record (her) and EPES were national level projects, which sought to create a framework for better local services, through better record-keeping and a more efficient anti-

Table 6.3   Types of Vision and Their Coherence in the Cases

	Urban Regeneration				
	Type of Vision				
	Strong shared	Defensive	Single driver	Adaptating together	Was vision shared?
Ballymun	-	-	✓	-	NO
Fatima Mansions	-	-	-	✓	YES
Hardwicke Street	-	✓	-	-	YES
Clonard/*Cluain Mór*	✓	-	-	-	YES
Connswater	-	-	✓	-	YES
Roden Street	-	✓	-	-	NO

Continued

Table 6.3 Continued

Healthcare Information Systems					
		Type of Vision			
	Strong shared	Defensive	Single driver	Adaptating together	Was vision shared?
Electronic Health Record (EHR)	-	-	✓	-	NO
HealthLink	✓	-	-	-	YES
Order Communications System (OCS)	-	-	-	✓	YES
Electronic Prescribing and Eligibility System (EPES)	-	✓	-	-	NO
Regional Acquired Brain Injury Unit (RABIU)	-	-	-	✓	YES
Theatre Management System (TMS)	-	-	✓	-	YES

fraud system respectively. In all cases, the vision was developed through information-gathering exercises of various kinds, which allowed stakeholders to indicate their support the vision, which in general they did. Where the stakeholders did not support the vision, problems and delays followed.

RABIU's project developed an adapting vision, which sat within a wider vision for the new regional unit– an integrated care service for people with acquired brain injury in Northern Ireland, in line with a 'centre of excellence' approach. However, this did not lead to a welcome for the project initially, due to staff concerns that increased responsibilities for data inputting would remove them from contact with patients. The long 'requirements' exercise dispelled these worries and led to endorsement of the project vision by clinicians, so that the software development stage was supported despite various problems. It is worth noting that both Fatima Mansions and RABIU included key individuals who assisted adaptation processes connected with the emergence and support of the vision.

HOW CAS CONTRIBUTES TO AN UNDERSTANDING OF THE DYNAMICS OF STAKEHOLDER INVOLVEMENT

In examining the issue of stakeholder involvement in public administration projects from a CAS perspective, this chapter has reviewed definitions of community, users and stakeholders, has considered the place of power imbalances in the dynamics of involvement and briefly examined the concepts of consultation and participation. Based on this, a definition of involvement was proposed as: *the interactions between agents in the project arena and policy environment through which a temporary or permanent accommodation between different interests and different levels of power is achieved.*

We then used this definition to explore how the CAS dynamics of path-dependency, adaptation and emergence contributed to an understanding of the evolution of involvement and identified five themes within this: the impact of past experience on trust between participants; building capacity for involvement; the role of key individuals as 'boundary spanners'; the balance of power; and the emergence of a shared project or programme 'vision' as a driver for change.

The emergent dynamic of a shared vision as a driver for change was the 'big picture' that inspired and motivated involvement in eight of the case studies, while in four projects the vision was contested and implementation suffered as a result. The vision was, of course, not the end of the story; rather, it provided a framework for future stakeholder involvement and the continuing mediation of different interests throughout the implementation process.

The dynamics of adaptation drove the emergence of the vision, but not in straightforward or predictable ways. In some cases, the provision of resources to build capacity for involvement gave participants who began with less power to represent their interests a greater ability to negotiate with others and to make best use of their opportunities within the system. In other cases, the provision of resources made no difference or perpetuated negative patterns of interaction. The role of key individuals as 'boundary spanners' reminds us that it is human behaviour within systems that delivers the goods. Interactions between agents are complex, and these individuals often provided alternative channels of communication at times of stress, through which power imbalances could be bridged and different interests could be discussed. Analysis of the balance of power revealed that different agents held power at different times and in different ways, such that they had the ability to veto decisions or even to block activities by direct action.

Finally, the influence of past experience affected the path-dependency of trust, or distrust, between stakeholders at the start of the programme or project. It could provide a positive environment for the beginnings of the initiative or it could influence working relationships adversely.

The complex dynamics between agents involved in all the case studies meant that there was no direct relationship between the number of themes identified in each case study and the quality or extent of involvement. However, it could be said, in general, that the extent of involvement was greater if a larger number of themes had been identified. The question of the nature of working relationships between participants was also interesting. In general, the projects with more themes identified had the better working relationships, but in one case, Ballymun, involvement was high but the dynamics were not positive. It was also possible to find projects with less involvement where what had taken place had created good working relationships, for example Hardwicke Street and OCS. If there was a theme that related more closely to positive working relationships, it was the existence of a shared vision (Table 6.3).

The CAS analytical framework deepened our understanding of the interaction between process, context and individual behaviour, as well as the influence of power. Given the differences between the two policy domains from which the case studies are drawn, our ability to identify five examples of CAS dynamics (three of which were adaptive processes) that contribute to effective stakeholder involvement across these domains shows the strength of the theoretical framework. The analysis also shows that CAS dynamics contributing to stakeholder involvement are unpredictable in terms of their content, the times at which they occur and their effect on involvement. Nevertheless, the various dynamics appear to be interrelated and may have a sort of cumulative effect on the quality of involvement by community or user groups. The connections between the five themes are not surprising given the dynamic nature of stakeholder involvement, in which power relationships are key.

7 The Role and Effect of the Private Sector

INTRODUCTION

One of the features of public management reform at the end of the twenti-eth century was a strong push to introduce market mechanisms[1] and pri-vate sector firms into the provision of public services (Hood 1991, Pollitt and Bouckaert 2004). There have been numerous critiques of the effec-tiveness of this aspect of 'New Public Management' (Dunsire et al. 1994, Peters and Savoie 1998, Kay 2002, Propper et al. 2004), as well as various attempts at explaining why theory didn't work in practice. These expla-nations included the effect of institutional context (Pollitt and Bouckaert 2004), the ideological as opposed to practical nature of reform efforts (Brunsson and Olsen 1993), the conflict between different value systems (Moe 1994, Lynn et al. 2001), a failure to implement fully the proposed reform (Moynihan 2006) and the unanticipated costs of engaging with the private sector (Prager 1994).

In spite of the questions surrounding the use of market mechanisms in public management, there remains an identifiable shift towards mixed-market service provision that has directly impacted on urban regeneration and on healthcare in Ireland. Examples include urban regeneration tax incentives and the introduction of public-private partnerships (PPS) in the Republic of Ireland, and the shift in housing provision role from the North-ern Ireland Housing Executive (NIHE) to housing associations in Northern Ireland. In the healthcare policy domain, we see the introduction of private health insurance and hospital 'co-location' policies in Republic of Ireland, and 'purchaser/provider' re-organizations in Northern Ireland healthcare. Furthermore, private firms and non-profit organizations are, and have been for decades, key participants in these policy domains. In addition, there is evidence from the case studies that the involvement of the private sector contributes in specific ways to the unique complex adaptive system (CAS) dynamics identified in Chapter 1—namely, path-dependency, adaptation, bifurcation and emergence. Hence, the role and effect of the private sector in public services is an important theme for the analysis of complexity in public management.

In this chapter we will summarize how private sector agents are present in the systems overall. To do this we will briefly review the key findings from our case studies presented in Chapters 2 and 3 as they pertain to private sector involvement, under the headings of the six core elements of CAS systems framework. Following this discussion, we will then explore in more detail the effects of private sector involvement in terms of the unique dynamics of CAS and conclude with the implications for theory and practice of these observations.

A CAS ANALYSIS OF THE ROLE(S) OF THE PRIVATE SECTOR IN PUBLIC MANAGEMENT

This section revisits the six basic elements of CAS identified in the 12 case studies, focusing in on the role of the private sector in each of the policy domains. The overall sense one gets from this review is that the private sector plays, and always has played, a significant role in the delivery of these public services. How that role, or roles, affect the complexity of public service management is the focus of the later sections, but first we will deal with the six core elements of system, environmental factors, environmental rules (discussed with environmental factors), agents, processes and outcomes as they relate to the *private sector* in urban regeneration and healthcare information systems (HCIS).

System refers to the particular projects themselves, which have objectives, a particular time span and geographic location, and in which private sector agents may choose to participate. Participation by the private sector is discussed under 'agents', but it should be noted here that there did not appear to be any discernible pattern between the scope of the projects (i.e. size, organizational level, heterogeneity) and the degree to which private sector agents participated. Having said this, the evolving objectives of projects were affected by the participation of private sector agents, a feature that is discussed in more detail later in this chapter.

Environmental rules and factors—the exogenous environment of the projects studied was strongly influenced by the private sector, largely with respect to the economic and technological factors that drove the establishment of the projects, and the rules that governed the behaviour of professionals during the projects. Specifically, economic circumstances in each of the jurisdictions drove the initiation, scale and outcomes of urban regeneration (UR) projects, while technological advances in information & communication technology (ICT), largely arising from private sector activity, drove the objectives, design and outcomes of the HCIS projects. Professional norms in architecture, planning, engineering, development, ICT and healthcare were highly influential in the problem specification, solution and implementation activities in which these professionals participated. The vast majority of these professional norms evolved over time through the actions and interactions of individuals working in the private sector, and through the explicit decisions of private sector professional standards bodies. Even without private sector involvement, these norms were influential to the extent that individuals working in a particular role (e.g., ICT professional, architect, planner) in the public sector would consciously apply the norms of their profession to their own behaviour. As discussed in the earlier chapters, professional norms were particularly influential in the HCIS projects.

In addition to being a key influencer of the exogenous environment, private sector agents in the projects also introduced different rules and factors into the endogenous decision-making environment. An example of this is the focus on social issues and network building by non-profit housing associations and on economic gain (profit) by developers or builders. In the HCIS cases, the private sector consultants were highly influenced by budgetary issues, while the public sector focused on functionality and user acceptance. Norms governing who should defer to whom in different professions were also in evidence in the decision-making processes, with different professions occasionally coming into conflict.

Different rules and factors among agents regarding decisions created the need for agents to expand their decision-making perspectives and, in many cases, also generated the need for project specific agents (PSAs) to create agendas of common objectives and decision-making processes that met or modified power/influence expectations of different participants. Hence, it was observed that PSAs paid a lot of attention to process objectives, i.e. who must be included in decision-making, how the decisions will be made, and who has final 'say'. While in some of the urban regeneration cases PSAs did not appear, this was only in those projects in which a public sector agent had almost complete control over the objectives and processes in the project. Where there was a more balanced distribution of power between agents, there was a need for 'honest brokers' to engage with the various agents to find space for joint decision-making or 'covenanting' (Klijn and Teisman 1997, Koppenjan and Klijn 2004). We return to this point later under the discussion of emergence.

Finally, organizational capacity was a key factor in private sector decision-making, influencing not only what the organization would commit to, but whether or not it would participate at all. The survey conducted in the urban regeneration domain suggested that organizational capacity was less relevant to decision-making for public sector agents. In addition, perceived risk was something that private sector organizations— principally the 'for-profit' firms—also evaluated in deciding if, and how, it would participate. While the main risk considered was financial, there were also concerns about reputation (although this could go both ways, in that some projects were seen as having the potential to enhance a firm's reputation and some were not). Firms managed perceived risks by creating new entities specifically for the purpose of participating in the project (kept financially separate from the rest of the firm), and/or establishing clear boundaries in the contractual relationship(s) with the commissioning public sector agent. This latter action tended to take the form of agreeing to specific outputs to be delivered and the contingencies that would need to be managed by the public sector.

Agents—the private sector agents engaged in each of the policy domains have been described in some detail in Chapters 2 and 3. In this chapter, these agents are grouped in categories to facilitate easier comparison across the two policy domains. It is clear that the private sector involvement in terms of these categories is similar across the two domains, with the exception of the categories of project specific agents and 'market facilitators'.

Project specific agents (PSAs) have been thoroughly discussed and—although they appeared in both policy domains– these types of agents (referred to as project boards) were created within the 'host' agent in the HCIS projects and were therefore more aligned with the public sector than the private sector. PSAs in urban regeneration will be discussed in more detail later in this chapter as an example of emergence.

Policy/strategy consultants were present in both domains and include a broad range of organizations and/or individuals that specialize in identifying the problem(s) to be solved and/or the potential solution(s) to identified problems. Policy experts, economists, planners, ICT consultants and community/patient advocates are examples of these types of private agents.

Technical experts/contractors were also present in both domains, providing specific products/services to contracting agents largely in the public sector. This group of agents included architects, engineers, developers, builders, housing associations, ICT solutions providers, programmers and computer equipment providers.

'Market facilitators' include bankers, estate agents, lawyers and marketing consultants whose fundamental task was to facilitate the exchange of goods, services and money among buyers and sellers. As noted in Chapter 2, these only appeared in the urban regeneration projects and were only mentioned as key participants in one of these projects. The feature will come up again in the section on bifurcation.

It is also important to note that community sector groups (while they are technically private organizations in so far as they do not have public sector remits) are not included in the list of private sector agents as they are generally considered to be representative agents for the wider citizenry, without the sort of organizational imperatives of profit and/or financial sustainability that drive for-profit firms and not-for-profit organizations such as housing associations. As discussed in Chapter 6, the user community groups in urban regeneration may be compared to the user representatives in the HCIS projects as both have as their central purpose to ensure that the interests of users/residents are considered and incorporated into the plans and activities of the private and public sector agents.

Processes—each of the agents described above tended to be involved in particular processes within the projects. For example, policy and strategy consultants were involved in the problem/requirements definition processes while technical experts/contractors were involved in proposing alternative solutions and implementation. It is worth commenting upon the observed 'specialization' of the private sector agents, with different processes tending to involve different agents. There is no *a priori* reason that the private sector should arrange itself in such a way as to produce different types of agents for different processes in the delivery of public services, but this was evident in these projects. The public sector, on the other hand, tends to be organized such that we see one or, at most, two agents with umbrella responsibility across the entire set of project processes. While there are clearly a large number of other public sector agents involved, they tended to be structured in a kind of 'star' formation, with the main planning/implementing agency in the centre of the star and the other agents providing input to that agent (either as policy/direction providers or specialist advisors). The nature and impact of this interaction among public sector agents is further explored in Chapter 8.

Outcomes—the majority of the *outputs* (which superseded outcomes over time—see Chapter 4) in the projects studied were produced by private and/or non-profit agents contracted by the commissioning public sector agency or supported by government subsidies in the form of tax incentives or discounted land sales (in the case of urban regeneration). In Northern Ireland, all new social housing is built by non-profit housing associations and private housing is built by private developers. All of the HCIS systems in that jurisdiction were delivered by IS consultants. In the Republic of Ireland, social housing may be built by public or non-profit agents, while private housing is built by private developers. The HCIS outputs were generally delivered by contracted ICT consultants and/or solutions providers. All in all, a fairly unexceptional set of observations with respect to the most tangible of system outputs—i.e. new buildings, roads, computer systems—the production of which was achieved by those who specialize in these outputs.

What was more interesting was the circumscribed role of these agents in relation to other project outcomes. In fact, interviewees from the private/non-profit sectors in urban regeneration explicitly described difficulties encountered by their firms/organizations when trying to expand their remit into other areas, e.g., community, social and economic objectives. For example, hiring of local people (to achieve socio-economic outcomes) proved difficult because of the lack of basic skills or because building sites were vandalized or robbed. Efforts to sell properties to investors (to achieve tenure mix objectives) became side-tracked when legislation was brought in to limit rent potential. Non-profit firms were barred from providing affordable[2] housing and received limited funds to build/staff community services. In essence, there were clear boundaries around what these sectors were expected to do and very limited opportunity to go beyond the defined areas of operation. This was also the case in the HCIS projects, however there was little evidence of private sector efforts or desire to expand their remit in the projects studied.

The limiting of the non-profit/private sector role in urban regeneration appeared to have the full support of residents and community activists in both jurisdictions under the assumption that the government could and should be expected to provide the community, economic and social services required to achieve the aims of regeneration. In fact, in the majority of UR cases, involvement of the private, and even non-profit, sectors was looked upon with mistrust by the community who sought to keep their involvement to a minimum.

While the main objectives for involving the private sector, as described by public sector interviewees, centred around increased efficiencies (in terms of time and cost) and, in some cases, higher quality/capacity to deliver the desired output, there was little evidence that this was achieved. Budget data was, unfortunately, rarely provided by interviewees, however had there been significant cost savings arising from private sector involvement we would have expected to hear about it. More often than not, interviewees avoided the question of budgets and, even if they did provide some financial information, it rarely related to actual expenditure. However, publicly available reports from audit bodies in both jurisdictions support the anecdotal evidence from the projects that cost savings are not typically the results of private sector involvement in public sector projects.

In terms of time required, urban regeneration projects of similar size but with a higher proportion of private sector involvement did not appear to be completed any faster than those with less private sector involvement. Nor was it the case that HCIS projects in Northern Ireland (delivered by IS consultants) took a shorter time than those studied in the Republic of Ireland, which were generally delivered by the public sector. This finding cannot be regarded as conclusive, however, as the selection of projects for the study was performed in consultation with the relevant public authorities in each jurisdiction. It is unlikely that the public authorities would have chosen projects that reflected badly on their performance relative to the private sector. Nevertheless, the observation that involvement by the private sector did not generally result in shorter completion cycles is consistent with other observations from the cases, such as the pervasive influence of the public sector across all projects and the need for extra time to align different perspectives on the decision environment in order to make progress.

What did seem to be achieved with respect to economic outcomes was that public funding was (partially) replaced by private funding when private and non-profit organizations became involved, at least with respect to urban regeneration. In the case of the Fatima Mansions public-private partnership (PPP), the investment in social housing and amenities was 'funded' by the profits made by the PPP on the development and sale of private housing. In other words, the social housing units were provided by the PPP for 'free'. Of course, this is not actually the case, as the land on which the private housing was built had been owned by the council and this was turned over to the PPP for development of the scheme. A similar arrangement operates in Northern Ireland where housing associations are encouraged to access private financing to part-fund social housing construction. Again, the NIHE may donate the land, or sell it at less than market price to the housing association, thereby decreasing the assets owned by the state agency. In both cases, the private sector is funding (or part-funding) the construction costs for social housing in return for low-cost land on which to build.

However, in addition to the decrease in state-owned land banks, there are other costs to the public sector of these types of arrangements. In the case of the Fatima PPP, there was a significant decrease in the number of social housing units that were provided on the site—from 363 social dwellings before the project began to 150 social and 70 affordable dwellings planned under the PPP. In order to fund these, 380 private dwellings were built. In the North, rents for housing association-provided dwellings are generally higher than the NIHE and they are expected to rise as more private money is put into this sector. Therefore, while the taxpayer may benefit from the shift of funding responsibility, it appears that there are offsetting losses experienced by the recipients of social housing in the form of fewer dwellings and/or higher rents.

On the benefits side, it does appear that in Fatima Mansions and Ballymun high quality amenities were provided by the private sector that would not have otherwise been available. This could be due to the negotiating skills of the public and community sectors, but may also be due to the positive effect that quality amenities have on the value of private dwellings. The economic logic of providing parks, community facilities, security features, etc. to encourage private buyers and renters to pay more also increases the utility and satisfaction of the social housing tenants and affordable housing buyers, thereby providing more social 'value', along with increasing the profits achieved by developers. Furthermore, the quality of the amenities, along with a more mixed socio-economic profile of residents is expected to reduce the stigma associated with living in the estates going forward. On balance, then, it is difficult to say whether there is clear advantage or disadvantage from the shifting of funding from the public to private sector, except in a narrow public accounts view, in which the advantage is clear.

In conclusion, we may observe from our cases that in spite of the rhetoric of market-based reform in both jurisdictions, and the involvement of a range of private sector agents, urban regeneration and HCIS projects are dominated by public sector agents, in terms of the 'boundaries' of the system, the rules which govern project participation and the setting of agendas and desired outcomes. The role of the private sector (including housing associations in so far as they participated in the urban regeneration projects) appears to be relatively narrowly focused on proposing solutions and delivering on a set of relatively circumscribed outputs. Furthermore, the private sector appears to engage in greater specialization than does the public sector, with different agents being involved in different processes. The private sector also has more of a regard for the financial and reputational risks (as well as rewards) of project involvement, further narrowing the range of activities in which these types of agents will participate.

Consistent with much of the literature critiquing the privatization agenda of public management reform, the expected savings in time and/or cost did not appear to arise from the inclusion of private sector agents. However, this general observation has three caveats: in cases in which private/non-profit agents were responsible for funding significant proportions of the physical development activity, this did decrease the cost to the taxpayer—although there was no evidence to suggest that the overall cost decreased; the shift of funding responsibility appears to be associated with a decrease in the benefits received by social housing tenants either in the form of fewer dwellings being provided or in higher rents being charged; private sector involvement also appears to be linked to higher quality amenities, the enjoyment of which benefits both the social and private residents of the area. It must be recognized that each of these results could be 'predicted' without resorting to CAS theory—which brings us to the crux of the analysis—what, if any, observations suggest the presence of CAS in the empirical data?

Path-Dependency and the Private Sector

Earlier we referred to the 'strong' influence of the private sector on the systems' environment(s), impacting on specific environmental factors as well as on the norms that govern the behaviour of professionals. In essence, the industry and economic systems that operated in the wider economy had a direct impact on the perceived need for the public sector projects, as well as on the capacity of private sector agents to participate. Housing market cycles influenced urban regeneration, and ICT innovation cycles influenced HCIS. So far, there is little to surprise us. However, looking a little deeper into how the influence manifested itself suggests that the features of the industry cycles—one relating to demand and supply and one to innovation—have the hallmarks of initial conditions, the state of which create different path-dependent processes and outcomes in the projects.

Taking the urban regeneration cases first, in each of the two jurisdictions, different housing market conditions were observed; Belfast was experiencing a long period of decline in housing demand and, in Dublin, housing demand was rapidly increasing. These were economic facts that, while recognized by the participants, were not considered as the main drivers of the projects. Instead, the projects focused on improving conditions for the residents of the targeted areas. Nevertheless, in Dublin, the outcomes of two out of the three projects featured an increase in density of housing in the area, a decrease in the number of social dwellings available and an increase in private housing—largely justified by the public sector agents involved as contributing to social mix in the area and increasing the quality of amenities and services. In Northern Ireland, all of the projects resulted in decreased housing density, with more or less the same number of social dwellings and fewer private dwellings. Here the outcomes were justified by the public sector agents as being necessary to improve housing conditions, to eliminate derelict buildings and to improve neighbourhood safety. Whatever the justification, the fact remains that the 'state' of housing demand cycles at the time of urban regeneration project initiation was linked to path-dependencies—in terms of housing density and tenure. Of course, the likely housing outcomes are interlinked with the community outcomes and so these, too, will be affected by the housing market conditions, as well as by those characteristics related to boundaries discussed in Chapter 5.

In the HCIS cases, the link between the industry initial conditions and project trajectories was less apparent, but still worth noting as a potential CAS path-dependency. However, it was not the economic states of either the IS or healthcare industries that appeared as relevant initial conditions, but rather the state of the innovation cycle in ICT that was a driver of HCIS outcomes. In particular, the introduction of powerful and relatively inexpensive communications technologies along with standards for using these, primarily those that facilitated the creation and promulgation of the Internet, appear to have affected the outcomes of the HCIS projects in unanticipated ways in the Republic of Ireland in particular and, to a lesser extent, in Northern Ireland. The most obvious case of this sensitivity to innovation cycles is in the Republic of Ireland's HealthLink project. In this project a fairly 'low tech' and circumscribed scope project designed to enable communication between one hospital and a handful of GPs expanded to a country-wide communications standard with 50 per cent of GPs and 19 (out of 70) hospitals participating as of May 2008. The enabling technology in this case was the Internet, which, by the time it was incorporated into the infrastructure of HealthLink, was already in its fourth decade of development.

The combination of widespread use and rapidly falling cost in communications technology created opportunities for applications across a wide spectrum of users, and the healthcare industry was no exception. Health-Link was a particularly clear case in which the original objectives were overtaken by events in technology, but this was also evident in the Order Communications System (OCS) project—in which the second stage of the project, which was expected to be an extension of the communications links to other departments within Tallaght Hospital, was instead considered for extension to users outside of the hospital via a Healthlink-type protocol. One of the interesting aspects of the Electronic Health Record (EHR) project is the constant referral by various stakeholders to technology and standards developments in ICT as key drivers of change and opportunity in the delivery of healthcare.

In contrast to observations in the HCIS cases in the Republic of Ireland was the relatively contained impact of ICT developments on the projects studied in Northern Ireland. Certainly communications technology innovation and improvement underpinned two of the projects, Electronic Prescribing and Eligibility System (EPES) and, eventually, the Theatre Management System (TMS), but interviewees were much less forthcoming in their acknowledgement of this and the project narratives barely mention ICT developments as a key factor. In the north, it seemed as if developments in technology were much less relevant than were political factors and power considerations in driving the evolution of the projects. Of course, this perception may have been somewhat influenced by the backgrounds of the researchers conducting the interviews. In the Republic of Ireland, the researcher had an ICT and management background, while in Northern Ireland the researcher came from a policy and management background. However, as can be seen in other observations of the difference between these two jurisdictions, the cases in Northern Ireland do appear to be more heavily politicized than do those in the Republic, and it is possible that some form of 'crowding out' of the technological considerations occurred here.

Adaptation In and Around the Private Sector

Adaptation, at both agent and systems levels, is actually one of the objectives of public management reform for the participation by private sector agents in public service systems. The theory is that private firms, community organizations and/or non-profit organizations inject new thinking—not to mention competition– into public sector bureaucracies to improve performance (Osborne and Gaebler 1992, Peters and Savoie 1998). As highlighted in the introduction to this chapter, it has yet to be conclusively shown that performance, either at the systems or agent levels, does improve with the introduction of private sector agents, and our data is no exception. However, that there is certainly evidence of adaptation—in both the public and the private sectors—arising from the participation of these agents in the cases. Interestingly, adaptation was more obvious in the urban regeneration cases, which operated on an inter-organizational level, and in these cases it was the adaptation of the private sector that was most apparent.

The adaptation of private sector agents in the urban regeneration cases took three basic forms. As discussed in Chapter 2, new private sector agents were created, some of which were facilitated by the public sector and some which were driven solely by imperatives in the private sector. New agents included the PPP in Fatima Mansions, a new subsidiary of a building firm to pursue public sector business in Ballymun and a range of new community organizations in UR projects in both jurisdictions. While these agents were created specifically to pursue opportunities for profit (or other forms of gain in the community) arising from the projects themselves, they were also expected, by the founders/participants, to have an existence beyond the lifespan of the project. It is worth noting that the creation of new agents was largely a private sector activity and was driven by the need to conform to requirements established by the public sector and/or to minimize risk to an existing firm arising from participation in an urban regeneration project.

The second form of adaptation was to existing private sector agents, in which various aspects of their operating goals and processes were modified as a direct consequence of their participation in the project. The most extreme example was the reorientation of existing community organizations to focus on the opportunities presented by the project, but there were also adaptations of private sector for-profit and not-for-profit agents. Private building firms hired local staff (not always successfully) and created local offices to manage and monitor progress. Non-profit housing organizations also created local offices, with an expanded role beyond that of private firms of interacting with local community representatives and even, in one case, providing office space and supplies to local groups. Both private firms and non-profit organizations became engaged with 'affordable' housing projects within the overall regeneration project—sometimes with the encouragement of the local authorities and sometimes not.

The third type of adaptation in private sector agents was a kind of 'second order' adaptation linked to the adaptations discussed above. When the manager of a firm or a community organization makes a conscious decision to become involved in a public sector project, they are doing so to achieve objectives that are specific to their organization. These objectives may, or may not, be fully aligned with the explicit objectives of the project and/ or with the public sector agent(s) managing/facilitating the project. However, by engaging with the public sector project at all, the *reputation* of the private agent changes—particularly if the private agent has not previously been involved in public sector initiatives, and/or has been openly hostile or dismissive of public sector organizations or endeavours in the past. When private sector interviewees or advisory group members spoke of the risks of becoming involved in the public sector projects, the financial and operational risks were often secondary to what they referred to as 'reputational' risks. These risks appeared to have two main aspects: the first being the risk of a higher level of public and media scrutiny should the firm/organization fail to deliver (or even be perceived to fail) on its commitments, and the second being the risk of 'guilt by association'. The second risk has its roots in existing negative perceptions of the public sector by the media, industry and citizens relating to broken promises, inefficiencies and corruption. By getting involved in public sector projects, some private sector agents felt that they ran the risk of being 'tarred by the same brush'.

It was difficult to tell from the case data if this reputational risk actually bore out over time, although public ridicule of a major developer in Dublin who pulled out of a number of urban regeneration/social housing PPPs in 2008 suggests that at least the first type of reputational risk is real. Having said that, it is also the case that several of the private sector interviewees commented that their decision to participate in these projects was to get into the public sector 'niche' and build their firm's reputation and brand in this manner. This was observed in both the urban regeneration and HCIS cases and is consistent with private sector strategy for building up a firm's profile and product portfolio in the market. The public sector market segment in construction and ICT is significant in each industry and, while fraught with difficulty, can be a lucrative and steady income generator.

Moving on to the adaptation of other agents and/or the system overall, specifically in response to the participation of private sector agents, we also observed three forms of adaptation. The first of these was discussed in the Chapters 2 and 3 and consisted of the need for public sector agents to consider different decision factors than they otherwise might have done in pursuing their own as well as joint objectives. This expansion of perspectives on the nature of the problem and the features of the environment that constrain or enable action was clearly visible in the case studies as public sector agents recognized the need to attend to the economic 'realities' of the project context and the social and community needs and capabilities that could and should be incorporated into project objectives and processes. However, this adaptation—or perhaps, more accurately, learning process—generally did not happen without the input of a facilitating agent, i.e. the PSA.

We also observed a second type of adaptation that appeared as a more systemic shift than one centred around specific agents. This was the gradually increasing focus on the imperative of time as a factor that drove decision-making the longer a project ran. This was most apparent in the urban regeneration cases in which interviewees specifically referred to the increased pressure to complete a task or deliver a set of outputs related to a 'phase' as driving detailed decisions about outputs and processes. In the HCIS cases, deadlines were a feature of project planning and management and were particularly salient in the projects that were linked to the construction of new facilities. This focus on deadlines and elapsed time was noticeably greater in the urban regeneration cases, however, which suggests that time becomes more of an issue when there is a significant participation of private sector agents. Furthermore, there are many more comments from private sector agents about the inordinate amount of time required to 'get anything done' when dealing with public sector-based projects and counterparts.

Finally, there is the third form of adaptation consistent with the long-standing participation of private sector specialists in these projects. It relates to the role of these specialists– researchers, strategic consultants, IS consultants, architects, private planners, etc.—in creating proposals/analyses for the public sector 'principals' to consider in identifying problems and solutions. In UR these agents make a key contribution to the emergent 'vision', while in HCIS they are more likely to be focused on the 'solution'—with occasional input into the requirements definition. While some might consider this stretching the definition of 'adaptation', given that it is a designed element of the overall process, the phenomenon must still be acknowledged as part of the process. The problem definition and the solution objective(s) driving the activities of all participants to a greater or lesser extent are the result of the interaction of private sector 'specialists' with their 'generalist' public sector counterparts. During this process each has an opportunity to learn and adapt, incorporating these changes into their body of knowledge and experience which may then be applied (or not) in future endeavours.

To conclude this section on adaptation, we have observed that the participation of private sector agents in public sector projects involves several different forms of adaptation; some intended and some not. The 'intended' form may be characterized in complex systems terms as an institutional approach to 'boundary spanning' (Hazy *et al.* 2003) in which agents from different sectors, environments or industries are encouraged to engage in public sector projects to contribute their expertise, as well as to facilitate the exchange of knowledge and experience that leads to accelerated learning. In the course of this intended adaptation, unintended adaptation was also observed to occur, including the adaptation of private sector agents seeking to engage in the projects, changes to the reputations of private and community sector agents and shifts in the processes and time sensitivities of the project participants overall.

Bifurcation Arising from Private Sector Agent Entry

Bifurcation, defined as the sudden change in the trajectory or state of a system, was observed as arising from private sector participation in only two of the 12 cases studied, one each in the urban regeneration and HCIS policy domains. Nevertheless, we would argue that this is a crucial feature of public sector systems and the impact of private sector involvement. In each of the cases in which bifurcation was observed it led to dramatically different outcomes of the system as well as a 'tipping point' for private sector involvement driven by positive feedback processes.[3] The appearance of a bifurcation point, the nature of the feedback dynamics and the impact on outcomes in each case is discussed below.

In the urban regeneration policy domain, the bifurcation point was observed in the Fatima Mansions project and appeared during the period in which the PPP was created to take over the delivery of the project from the local authority. Immediately prior to this period, the local authority had finally begun the long-awaited regeneration of the area following a master plan that had been agreed by all of the stakeholders, including the community representative group, Fatima Groups United, the Dublin City Council, the Planning Board and the Department of the Environment. This master plan was itself the product of intensive negotiations among participants and included a number of new elements (at least in regard to previous urban regeneration projects in Dublin) relating to social and community objectives. The demolition of vacated social housing blocks began in mid-2003 and this first phase (moving existing residents and demolishing vacant dwellings) was completed by the end of the year, and funded by Dublin City Council. However, while the negotiations in Fatima were underway, the Department of Finance had established a major investment fund in the National Development Plan 2000–2006 to support new initiatives using a PPP model. €2 billion was set aside to support such initiatives with the objective of providing seed and/or matching funding to projects that engaged in PPPs for major infrastructure development. Government departments responded by setting up PPP task forces to look for opportunities in their respective policy domains. In the case of the Department of the Environment, there was already a PPP unit in place prior to the establishment of the National Development Plan fund, however the creation and size of this fund gave new impetus to its activities.

Much to the surprise of the community, Dublin City Council and the Department of the Environment decided, in late 2003, to proceed with the regeneration of Fatima Mansions via a PPP. This decision was taken, according to local authority interviewees, because it was 'clear that all of the required funding for the Master Plan would not be forthcoming from the Department.'[4] How and when this became clear was not explained, however what was clear was that it was a departure from what had been assumed by the community stakeholders, and was resisted by them at the outset (Punch, Redmond and Kelly 2004). Nevertheless, the PPP went forward and a private sector joint venture between a developer and a construction company, Moritz/Elliot, was awarded the PPP contract in early 2004. The role of Moritz/Elliot was to deliver the overall project in consultation with the Fatima Regeneration Board (established in 2001 to oversee the physical and social development of Fatima Mansions) and the Dublin City Council (DCC).

It was following this insertion of a private sector agent into the project that significant changes occurred. Firstly, the project got 'unstuck' in so far as it could now move forward with some certainty of financial resources being available. Secondly, as discussed in the Outcomes section of this chapter, the mix of social and private housing planned for the area shifted significantly, from the 250 social dwellings and an unspecified number of private sector dwellings originally envisioned, to 150 social, 380 private and 70 'affordable' dwellings. It should be noted here that, prior to regeneration, the stock of housing in the designated area was 363 social housing dwellings. Thirdly, the locus of power in the implementation phase moved from the Fatima Regeneration Board (FRB) and the DCC to the PPP.

This shift to the PPP and the related shift of influence towards the private sector appeared to be a 'tipping point' for involvement by the private sector in a particular project. In this project, a number of additional private sector agents were involved in the project after the PPP was created. A range of 'market facilitators' were involved in the Fatima Mansions project, including banks, law firms, marketing consultants and estate agents. These agents were involved directly with the PPP agent, Moritz/Elliot, as was another property development company, Urban Capital, which facilitated the deal between Moritz/Elliot and DCC. While agents of this type may well have been involved in activities in the locale of the urban regeneration projects studied, they were not mentioned by any of the interviewees, nor did they appear in documentation as having been direct participants in the project itself except in Fatima Mansions. It would appear that the introduction of a PPP structure creates opportunities for participation by a larger segment of the housing/construction industry in urban regeneration as well as for the development of new market niches for firms such as Urban Capital.

In the case of HCIS, the bifurcation arose from the development and adoption of new technologies and new standards in the information technology (IT) industry along with a private sector 'tipping point' similar to that described above. Bifurcation was observed in the HealthLink project in which the maturing of the Internet in Ireland, the adoption of the health-care-related communications standard (HL7) and the participation of GPs and software vendors of GP office management applications all combined to facilitate the roll-out of the system to a vastly expanded user community than was originally envisioned. The specific period of bifurcation was in 2002 after the HealthLink project had been up and running for approximately five years. At that time HealthLink was running as a stand-alone communications system linking the Mater Hospital in Dublin to approximately 50 GP practices in the area. Running in parallel with the HealthLink project, but not connected to it, was a national initiative around the introduction of general practitioner information technology (GPIT). This initiative was undertaken by the Department of Health and Children (DoHC) in conjunction with the Irish College of General Practitioners to introduce the use of technology into GP practices. However, the initiative made little progress other than funding the purchase of desktop computers and printers for GP offices, many of which remained unused. Nevertheless, in some cases—particularly in GP practices that were more enthusiastic about the adoption of IT—this initiative did have the effect of highlighting the lack of integration between the HealthLink stand-alone modems, printers and software, and the desktop computers and Internet links that were steadily making inroads into the administrative functions of these offices.

In 2002, the then newly-formed Health Board Executive (HeBE) set up another project to adopt a national messaging standard for healthcare information, and included a representation from the HealthLink team. This group selected the international messaging standard HL7 as the preferred standard to be adopted by all Irish healthcare providers (DoHC 2004). In parallel, the HealthLink project team decided to take the opportunity to migrate its system to run over the Internet; this would address the GPs' issue with the specialized and expensive communications kit required to set up HealthLink, provide a development window to migrate to the new communications standard HL7 and also justify getting additional funds from the

DoHC as a national project. To further improve and integrate the system with existing GP administrative processes, the project team worked with the leading GP office software providers in Ireland to integrate HealthLink with their software. These firms were then able to charge an extra licensing or, in some cases, a messaging fee for the connection to HealthLink—making it extremely attractive to the firms to promote the connection to HealthLink as a new service facilitated by their software upgrades.

In late 2003, the new 'HealthLink Online' system was launched and was a tremendous success with GPs. Usage quadrupled in one year with over 200 GPs using the system by late 2004. HealthLink Online became a national project funded and managed by the Health Services Executive (HSE), which had replaced the HeBE in 2004. It is worth noting that a 'second order' positive feedback dynamic—that of the 'network effect'[5] also operated in the case of HealthLink in that each time a new hospital became linked into the system, the value of the system to all GPs (and to other hospitals) increased significantly. This was due to the increase in the amount of information and linkages that each new hospital brought into the network when it came online. This network effect, in addition to the positive feedback processes of software (and other technology) vendors, contributed significantly to the exponential increase of HealthLink usage by healthcare providers in Ireland.

This begs the question: why did we not observe similar developments in Northern Ireland where the same information technology factors were present? While the projects studied in Northern Ireland did not include an application such as HealthLink, all of the projects involved some potential information links between healthcare providers. Nevertheless, there was no evidence of a 'take-off' of usage as was observed in HealthLink and, in one case—that of EPES– potential users fought against adoption of the system, in spite of its purported aim to improve their productivity in much the same way as HealthLink. Of course, the main purpose of EPES was to eliminate fraud at the point of prescription; an objective that would not endear the system to the pharmacists or GPs who may have felt themselves targets, instead of beneficiaries, of the proposed system. Nevertheless, it is also possible that the rather more centralized and structured approach to ICT in the North limited the opportunities for innovation and private sector initiative to impact on projects.

Overall, private sector-influenced bifurcation in projects appears to be a relatively unusual event that is triggered by a significant change in the technical, market or political environment(s) of the project and which leads to a much expanded role of the private sector and a sudden change in the outcomes of the project. In the case of Fatima Mansions, private sector involvement increased greatly after the introduction of the PPP, with private sector agents that were invisible in the other projects suddenly coming to the fore. In addition, the number of private dwellings planned for the area increased enormously while social housing decreased. In the case of HealthLink, the changeover from the proprietary stand-alone communications system developed in the Mater Hospital to an Internet-enabled standard communications link into GP office software presaged a dramatic increase in usage and penetration of the system throughout the Republic of Ireland.

Emergence of New Private Sector Agents

As discussed in Chapter2, while the agents involved in urban regeneration were broadly similar (albeit present in different proportions and with different levels of influence and responsibility), in three out of the six projects studied, new agents came into being after the project commenced, each having varying degrees of influence, but all with a similar task of fostering collaboration among agents and facilitating participation by community groups and political representatives. These agents were called project specific agents (PSAs) in the urban regeneration context and were compared to the 'project team' agents that played a similar role in all six of the HCIS projects discussed in Chapter 3. However, the HCIS project team agents were set up by the project sponsors as an explicit and required element of the pursuing the objectives of the project, while the PSAs *emerged* out of the interactions of various agents over the course of the project with quite different characteristics and links to these other agents.

In Ballymun in Dublin, the local authority involved in the project created and owned the project specific agent, Ballymun Regeneration Ltd (BRL), which had overall strategic and implementation authority across all aspects of the project. Although BRL's board consisted of community representatives, local politicians, private sector representatives and local authority executives, the ultimate control of the agent and of the project remained in the hands of the local authority. BRL was in a position of power with respect to the private, non-profit and community sectors and had responsibility and authority for the coordination and purchasing of all services required to achieve the goals of the project. As such, BRL operated as a super-agent in the system, managing a network of implementing agents, all of which reported into BRL, but which also had to coordinate with each other to achieve complex outcomes.

A very different position (and genesis) was observed for the Greater Village Regeneration Trust (GVRT) in the Roden Street/Greater Village Area project in Belfast. This organization was founded by political and community representatives and did not have any members from the relevant government agency—the NIHE– on its board, although the NIHE did provide half-funding for one employee of the organization. While the NIHE was supportive of the GVRT's establishment as a 'legitimate' representative of the community, it is questionable whether or not the NIHE considered the role of the GVRT to be central to the NIHE's own urban regeneration objectives. In effect, the GVRT was able to represent the views of residents to the NIHE, but had very little direct influence over problem definition, solution or implementation. Nevertheless, the GVRT's link to politicians in the area strengthened its position in negotiations with the NIHE and allowed it to foster strong relationships with board members of the NIHE and other influential government agencies in the South Belfast city area. This enabled the GVRT to operate as an influential network node and to pursue joint outcomes consistent with its own objectives.

Finally, the FRB in Fatima Mansions, Dublin, was created at the behest of Fatima Groups United, a coalition of community groups in the area, following the rejection by the community of local authority plans for the regeneration of the area. The FRB included representation from public, private and community organizations and had an independent chair agreed by all stakeholders. The FRB played a key role in helping to define the problems in Fatima Mansions and in developing and agreeing solutions, but had much less influence over the implementation stages of the project than did BRL in Ballymun. In addition, mid-way through the project the local authority turned implementation authority over to a PPP run by a privately held joint venture company. During implementation, the FRB functioned more like a network hub than a hierarchy or a network node, having relationships with all major stakeholders and being at the centre of decisions to act, if not at the centre of acting on those decisions.

In each of the three cases above, the PSA had a central role in liaising with local residents to gather their views on regeneration and to facilitate consultation and cooperation among community groups. Where no PSA existed, residents' groups played this role– but to a much more limited degree. We noted that in each of the projects that developed PSAs there were significant difficulties in the relationship between residents and the responsible government agency prior to project initiation. Long histories of failed attempts at regeneration and communication breakdowns between government and residents preceded the initiatives, which may have been a factor in the establishment of the PSA. This may also account for the anecdotal reports that the existence of a PSA and the associated increased level of community participation did not result in significant increases in satisfaction levels amongst residents compared to non-PSA projects where there were less acrimonious histories.

Another characteristic of PSA behaviour was their facilitating of other community organizational activity under the umbrella of the urban regeneration project that might not have otherwise occurred. In the projects studied, this took the form of assisting organizations to apply for funding (which may be project-related or from outside funders with tangential goals to urban regeneration), providing space for organizations to carry out regeneration-related activities or spawning new organizations to address problems identified by stakeholders but not addressed by the agreed solution. In this way, the PSA acted as an 'incubator' for social action that increased the size and complexity of projects and whose manifestations (in the form of new or redirected community organizations) may continue well beyond the existence of the PSA itself.

IMPLICATIONS OF THE CAS ANALYSIS ON THE ROLE OF THE PUBLIC SECTOR

Overall, the cases studied indicate that public sector projects in Ireland are dominated by public sector agents, in terms of the boundaries of the system, the rules that govern project participation and the setting of agendas and desired outcomes. The role of the private and non-profit sectors appears to be relatively narrowly focused on proposing solutions and delivering specific outputs in fulfilment of project objectives. Given this, it was unsurprising that the outcomes of the projects studied, in terms of time, cost or quality, did not appear to be significantly impacted by the inclusion of private/non-profit agents. However, this general observation must be tempered with the observations of a number of subtle changes in the outcomes and processes of the system and the agents themselves, arising from private sector involvement. The introduction of private funding into the urban regeneration projects can decrease the cost to the taxpayer, but appears to shift the cost to current and/or future residents in the form of higher rents and loss of publicly-owned land. Private sector agents appear to be more sensitive to budget constraints and to the passage of time, creating pressure to cut back either (or both) specified functionality or attention to process elements. In contrast, however, the use of private sector agents with particular expertise can increase the quality of the resulting outputs.

The use of the CAS framework for analysis also highlighted features of, and the impact on, the policy domain, which may otherwise have been overlooked. For example, the analysis of decision factors by agent-type suggested that the introduction of private and non-profit agents increased the complexity of decision-making due to the different perceptions of the environment/objectives. This, in turn, contributed to the emergence, in some cases, of PSAs whose role it was to facilitate joint decision-making and 'covenanting' among agents—i.e. the process of identifying opportunities that exist for alignment of perceptions across agents in order to move the project ahead. Where no PSA emerged, this role was left to the public sector, whose focus on process, politics and 'soft' objectives was cause for frustration among the private and non-profit sector participants. Initial conditions arising from industry and market dynamics proved to have important implications for path-dependencies in system outcomes, with the housing market affecting the density and social mix of regenerated neighbourhoods, and technology innovation cycles affecting the potential rate of take-up and direction of HCIS development. A range of different types of adaptation—some intended, some not—was observed, which affected both the immediate project as well as having a potentially wider impact on future activity in the private sector. In addition, it resulted in the creation of new knowledge in both the private and public sectors.

The most interesting CAS-related observation was the identification of a possible 'tipping point' in projects arising from the introduction of a critical level of private sector responsibility for solution definition and implementation. This appeared in the case of Fatima Mansions and HealthLink projects, in which the role of the PPP (in the case of Fatima Mansions) and the involvement of software vendors (in the case of HealthLink) presaged a significant shift in private sector involvement as well as an acceleration and expansion of the projects concerned. In both of these cases, the sudden change in the project appeared to have a largely beneficial effect, but this may not be representative of all private sector-induced tipping points. Nevertheless, the role and dynamics of private sector involvement in public sector projects appear to display many of the unique features of CAS, suggesting that policy and public management theory could benefit from the incorporation of CAS dynamics into their models and assumptions, as well as preparing for the unexpected in their plans, particularly in activities involving significant participation from the private sector.

8 Core and Locale
The Tension Between the Governing Intent and the Implementing Outcome

INTRODUCTION

This chapter represents the last thematic analysis of the cases. It differs slightly from the earlier themes in that it explores connections between governmental policy-making at a central, 'core' level and implementation activity at a local level, the 'locale'. It examines how policy decisions formed *centrally* are enacted *locally*, and describes the interplay between the implementation processes at work locally in the cases, and decisions taken at central level that were not necessarily directly related to the focal policy implementation on the ground. The chapter sets out to define 'core' and 'locale', and embeds these definitions within the context of studies dealing with public policy implementation and complex adaptive system (CAS). It then looks at the tension between core and locale within the case studies and then turns to an analysis of how these concepts interact with CAS model features. The chapter concludes with an exploration of implications of the CAS analysis for policy makers and public managers.

THE GOVERNING 'CORE' AND THE 'LOCALE' IN PUBLIC MANAGEMENT

The terms 'core' and 'locale' are widely used in many disciplines to denote the relationship between an administrative core, or centre, with its more distant operational locale (McAuley 1999). While the concepts of core and locale have generally been approached in a multi-disciplinary way, one of the principal points of origin for the concept is Weber's contention that there is a tendency for power to be centralized at the apex of an organization, within its bureaucratic 'core' (Weber 1948). This analysis is specific to western political thought and concentrates on the existence of a single 'centre', which itself produces a role for peripheral or marginalized places (Chondroleou, Elcock *et al.* 2005). In the case studies, locale is not marginalized or peripheral, rather it is the location in which policy-making from the centre is 'operationalized' and realized on the ground. Here, locale is the site of implementation and includes the agents and institutional structures that are engaged in the implementation process.

Implementation is a contested topic in the literature on public management. The classical framework of public administration assumed that top-down structures, working by authority and rules, rendered implementation a minor matter: what was decided was done. However, with the collapse of the classical model, new conceptualizations were required to contend with the nature of implementation processes and growing concern with an implementation deficit. The so-called 'implementation approach' (Lane 1993, Lane 2000), with its exploration of implementation strategy and policy outcomes, and of implementation as both process and result, arrived at a consensus that decentralized implementation was more effective than top-down implementation. In this view, policies are only finally 'made' when they are implemented: policies may be intended centrally but they are emergent locally, echoing Pressman and Wildavsky's (1979) earlier work. Moreover, their emergent reality may vary from location to location or from one implementing unit to another (Pettigrew 1992).

Following Lane's (2000) survey of models of public sector management in the twentieth century, it is clear that while the 'policy approach' and related 'implementation perspective' began to make implementation a significant conceptual issue, other models and approaches also incorporated implementation elements in important ways. Work on policy networks proposed that policies become practice through the interaction of networks of stakeholders and that these might even be more efficient than the bureaucratic hierarchy. By contrast, new public management, with a central focus on efficiency, is seen as placing contracting at the heart of public sector governance, conceptualizing the implementation puzzle as a principal-agent and transaction cost challenge.

Most attempts at replacing the classical model stress the intertwined and inseparable nature of policy-making and policy implementation. They variously call attention to the reality of policy as negotiated, brokered and emergent, involving power, dependency, cooperation, learning, feedback and evolution. This set of perspectives causes disquiet because of the indeterminacy it attributes to policy intent. Yet there can be no return to the classical model of 'perfect' implementation of the centre's intent. Against this background, the attractions of the new public management formulation, centred on contracting as a foundation stone of governance, offered a route back to more secure, predictable and controllable ground. It is in this context of conceptual divergence and competing models that the case data will be examined from a CAS perspective.

CORE AND LOCALE IN URBAN REGENERATION AND HEALTHCARE INFORMATION SYSTEMS IN IRELAND

While the descriptions of core and locale focus attention on the theoretical content of the concepts to be explored, it is important to define how they appear within the data of the case studies. The 'core' is defined as representing national government (in this case, the Irish Government, the UK Government and the short-lived Northern Ireland Executive[1]). Correspondingly, the 'locale' contains local government agents or entities and other agents with whom they interact during the course of a project, at a local level to implement governmental (or central) policy. Central government is therefore defined as a powerful element of the environment.

These definitions are complicated by two factors within the Northern Ireland cases. The first is the existence of two possible 'centres' for decision-making. The first of these is the Northern Ireland Office (NIO) and the second is the Northern Ireland Executive. The NIO was established in 1972 when the Northern Ireland Government was dissolved in the face of a worsening security situation and the onset of the 'Troubles'. During the period of this study, the NIO had responsibility for Northern Ireland's constitutional and security issues, in particular, law and order, political affairs, policing and criminal justice. For a short period of time (December 1999–October 2002) economic and social matters were the responsibility of locally-elected Northern Ireland ministers when power was devolved to the Northern Ireland Executive. However, the Government of the United Kingdom suspended the Executive in October 2002 and from then to the end of the research, the Northern Ireland Office, and the British ministerial team located within it, re-assumed responsibility for these functions. The Executive was re-established and power again devolved in May 2007. The delineation between the structure of the NIO, its relationship to British Ministerial responsibility and the Northern Ireland Government's departments is an important dimension within the core-locale definitions/distinctions in Northern Ireland.

While the period of the study covered the suspension of the Northern Ireland Executive there is little doubt that the dynamic and power relations that existed during devolution were different to those that operated through the system of 'direct rule' from Westminster. It is also likely that the possibility of the re-devolution of power had some impact on those within the decision-making structures through the period.

The second complicating factor in relation to Northern Ireland deals with agents operating within both contexts of core and locale. Within the Northern Ireland urban regeneration cases, the principal 'agent', the Northern Ireland Housing Executive (NIHE), operating at the locale was also acting at the core. The NIHE has a dual role as a governmental agency and but also a local actor, with a local presence within the regeneration initiatives.

Within the healthcare cases too, the role of the Northern Ireland Department of Health, Social Services and Public Safety's Service Delivery Unit (SDU) also straddles the core-locale continuum. While clearly being a feature of the core, its direct local intervention in the Theatre Management System (TMS) project brought it into direct contact with the project at its implementing level. This intervention seemed to reflect the significance of the project both to the reputation of the health service publicly and to the internal audit requirements of the SDU, or may have been a feature of the more 'interventionist' nature of the Northern Ireland Government in local projects as discussed in previous chapters.

In terms of core-locale, the Republic of Ireland context was much more straightforward. The core was defined as the traditional governmental structure with its corresponding ministerial departments and policy-making functions. At the local level, the city or county development boards were tied in to the local government structures (city and county councils) and specific programmes focused on urban regeneration.[2] In the case of the healthcare information systems, locale was represented by GPs and hospitals.

Core and Locale: Dominant Characteristics

As the last of the CAS dynamics themes, core-locale appears because of the extent to which, throughout the cases, there was an active interaction between policy-making at the core and its implementation at the locale. Particularly in the case of the urban regeneration cases, the outcome 'on the ground' was a distinctly emergent phenomenon. This was the case also in the healthcare cases—although less dramatically so. While it might be argued that policy, as the intent of the core, was realized, this could only be supported in the most general sense. A regeneration project or an information & communication technology (ICT) initiative might be characterized as being completed, but its general character—not just its detail—was locally constructed to a significant extent. This general feature of the cases therefore seemed to invite inspection from a CAS perspective. Next, before interrogating the data from a CAS perspective, some general features of the case data are examined.

Policy Intent

It was clear, from a core-locale perspective, that intent for urban regeneration policy was largely a national level phenomenon located in, and emanating from, central government and its key departments and agencies. Additionally, there appeared to be a difference in emphasis between regeneration in Northern Ireland, which took housing as its central focus, and regeneration in the Republic of Ireland where the focus was broader and encompassed other aspects of economic regeneration.

For the healthcare cases, North and south, policy intent was a more diffuse national and supranational phenomenon. Located at a central government and health agency level, it was also reinforced at EU and supranational level by public sector health care ICT forums and the expectation of common ICT platforms, as well as by the institutional apparatus of global ICT professional practice and ICT consultancy.

Resource Availability

The availability of resources was also significant in determining the course of events. If resources are defined as representing the financial and other organizational attributes (reputation, knowledge, skills, etc.) that enable an agent to move towards its intended goals, then funding is the most visible– but by no means the only important– resource within the cases. A number of sources of funding were utilized in each case study to move the projects forward. Most of these were from the state core and were distributed either directly, or through a facilitating organization. However, the cases show that the projects were also impacted by the effects of funding aimed at other issues, such as social exclusion or community sustainability. This interaction with other projects working outside the project system with different aims and objectives will be discussed below.

Core-Locale Interaction

Core-locale relations and the interaction (intended and otherwise) of policies of the core with events and activities at the locale proved important. Such interaction was deeply bound up with tensions and issues involving power, intention and outcome. Just as it was shown to be difficult to anticipate the mix of resources that would impact on community development, it was equally difficult to be clear in advance about the impact of other policies and initiatives of the core that had significant, unintended and unpredictable outcomes for the project. The impact of the policy backdrop and the initial conditions that precipitated project development are explored below.

The impact of a number of power relationships was observed. One was the conventional political dynamic of 'clientelism' or socio-economic mutualism in both jurisdictions, which is still a powerful political force (Kirby 1997). However, other dimensions of power relationships were also in evidence. For example, personal 'expertise' power was exerted by individuals and groups associated with influential reports in many of the cases such as Fatima, Ballymun, and in the Theatre Management System. However, the 'expertise' power exerted in many of the projects at the locale was trumped by the structural or institutional power of the core at some point in the project. For example, in Fatima the introduction of a public-private partnership (PPP) late in the project process is a demonstration of classical top-down bureaucratic fiat. This effective use of 'structural' power (Finkelstein 1992) is an important example of how the core can 'stamp its authority' on a project, when it feels necessary.

Dispersion of Authority from the Core

A key theme of many revisions of the classical public administration model is the delegation and 'dispersion' of the traditional power and authority of the administrative core to actors in the locale. While this is a clearly recognized attribute of public management reform in general (Birrell 1994), it is also within the cases the result of intervention in the form of external funding and capacity-building mechanisms (EU 'Peace' funding in Northern Ireland, for example) and with it, a proliferation of non-state organizations, semi-state organizations and quangos. How such dispersion should be undertaken and governed remains a matter of debate—whether through government agencies with considerable autonomy, networks of stakeholders, non-governmental organizations (NGOs), the not-for-profit sector, the private sector or other third parties. All the cases revealed examples of dispersion of central authority from the core—sometimes by design and sometimes *de facto*, as a feature of the processes involved in shaping and implementing policy. It has been argued that such dispersion lays the ground for complexity when compared to the assumed top-down, unitary model of decision-making and implementation at the heart of the classical model.

CORE AND LOCALE FROM A CAS PERSPECTIVE

The previous thematic chapters have engaged with different subsets of the CAS dynamics. As a theme, core and locale is of particular interest because it presents a perspective on all four unique CAS dynamics that became evident in the interactive nature of the policy-implementation relationship. The core-locale relationship was heavily dependent on, and propelled by, path-dependencies arising from the environmental context of the public management process. Second, the 'push-pull' nature and top-down versus bottom-up tension of the core-locale relationship was especially important in encouraging the adaptation of agents in the systems. Emergence was a feature of working out the core-locale relationship—not least the creation of project specific agents that managed part of tension between core and locale as well as between the agents within the locale. Bifurcations most commonly arose at the nexus of intent and implementation, at the intersection of core and locale.

Path-Dependency

All of the cases demonstrate the importance of path-dependency in the translation of the core's intent into action realized locally. In the urban regeneration cases, there was a record in many of the cases of government policy having unpredictable and unwelcome effects on earlier community development. Both north and south of the Irish border, the governing core has implemented policies that had led to a lack of trust within the communities. In the Irish Republic, the lack of adequate maintenance of housing and infrastructure, inadequate security and poor planning for necessary services all contributed to a legacy of mistrust. As a specific example, the historic legacy of the 'surrender grants scheme' left policy implementers with an uphill struggle to persuade residents of the value of the new urban regeneration initiatives. The scheme, launched in 1984, provided an incentive to local authority tenants to leave their rented accommodation and to move into the housing market through the purchase of a private house. The scheme was intended to alleviate overcrowding and free up housing stock. Instead, it emptied areas of people in regular employment (those who could secure mortgages), leaving within those areas those who were most in need of community assistance and support. While the overarching aim was to free up social housing for those most in need by making it attractive for others to enter the housing market, a major effect was to create zones of social exclusion, alienation and hopelessness. By tinkering with a delicate social mix while having little understanding of the consequences, the government plunged the already struggling working-class areas into a spiral of deprivation from which it was very difficult to break free. For all three Dublin urban regeneration cases (Ballymun, Fatima, and Hardwicke Street) the surrender grants scheme created initial conditions from which the regeneration projects developed, but also left people concerned about the possible unforeseen impacts of future projects and instigated the construction of powerful alliances to avoid 'the mistakes of the past'. The implementation process was confronted by residents suspicious of central intent and determined to negotiate its outcome with the government and its local agents.

The impact of the inattention to maintenance and security, the paucity of community services and the surrender grants scheme resulting in significant marginalization and deprivation, was heightened by the visibility of extraordinary growth in the Irish economy and a consequential sense of even greater deprivation. This increasingly obvious disparity between the booming Irish economy and those who regarded themselves as socially excluded from it, also reinforced the political impetus to 'assist' those left behind by the Celtic Tiger. The 2000 Planning and Development Act was an initiative that made a number of legislative changes aimed at enabling the advancement of a sustainable development ethos in the planning system. The structural shift towards mixed tenure included in the Act focused on building social housing within a community context, rather than entertain the danger of ghettoization. The Act is interesting for its policy consequences: it impacted on pockets of extreme urban social exclusion and represented a legislative recognition of the mistakes of the past—imposing specific conditions on which future projects had to be based.

The type of path-dependency that characterized regeneration in the Northern Ireland housing cases was very different from the cases in the Irish Republic, but also reflected the role of the governmental core in failing to develop trust within marginalized communities. Sustained violent conflict had left a legacy of sectarianism in all areas of society (Murtagh 2002), with segregated housing as a default setting in the public (and much of the private) sector. The harsh regeneration environment faced by those promoting development in Roden Street/Greater Village Area has already been documented in earlier chapters. Most of those difficulties centred on a lack of community confidence in the governmental core's intentions and, by proxy, the intentions of the NIHE as the governmental agent in the locale. The lack of a cohesive 'voice' to consult and negotiate on behalf of the community further exacerbated fears. The creation of the Greater Village Regeneration Trust (GVRT) filled this gap to some extent, but as a community organization, it reflected in a focused way the original difficulties. This lack of confidence in the core, found in both the case studies in Northern Ireland that affected Protestant/Unionist/Loyalist communities, had its origins in what respondents described as the 'hollowing out' of traditional neighbourhoods in other Loyalist areas of Belfast. This demographic change arose from a series of initiatives from the 1970s onwards to create new urban centres outside Belfast, and more recent redevelopment pressure on these traditional inner city communities. As a result, the subsequent histories of these projects were set to unfold within a cycle of mistrust between core and locale—a tension that was key to the development of an organized community voice in GVRT and its attempts to change the intended course of regeneration implementation. Hence, path-dependencies triggered both adaptation and emergence.

The dynamics of path-dependency in the healthcare cases are very different, but also illustrate how the foundations upon which policy is built impact on its 'outworking' within healthcare contexts. While there appeared to be general agreement that ICT innovation was an appropriate way to create greater efficiencies within healthcare and to create tangible patient benefits, the implementation trajectory of projects North and south differ significantly in their genesis. For example, in Northern Ireland, ICT policy in healthcare was firmly situated under the umbrella of an integrated Department of Health, Social Services and Public Safety ICT Strategy developed in 2002, which itself with a subset of the UK Government's ICT healthcare strategies. The Republic of Ireland's healthcare cases revealed a very different developmental background. Arising from initiatives at the periphery, rather than through the central mechanism of governmental policy, the cases illustrate the significance of activities on the ground and of bottom-up processes that shape central policy. While central policy existed with regard to healthcare information services (HCIS) in the Republic, it was aspirational and visionary in content rather than specific. Together with global and EU 'visions' of ICT in healthcare, this broad policy umbrella helped to legitimize ICT innovation at the local level (GP, hospital, hospital department). Furthermore, when some of these local innovations proved successful they expanded, yielding a realized policy at a regional or national level where no centrally planned implementation had existed.

The two jurisdictions provided contrasting illustrations on top-down and bottom-up processes of policy in action, which were influenced by the nature of the differing governing approaches. This difference in origin is also reflected in the expanding scope of the projects in the Republic of Ireland; a feature that was not apparent in the North where the cases developed generally as anticipated. Where the Northern Irish cases did expand, this widening of scope occurred very early in the project's development as a part of central government strategy. For example, while TMS was initially conceived of as a stand-alone project to solve one high profile problem (that of long hospital waiting lists for elective surgery in Belfast City Hospital), it was transformed into a much larger and more ambitious project by the time the project specification was agreed.

Bifurcation

Bifurcations represent a distinct 'tipping' point at which a system changes quickly and radically in response to an event. Because of the significance of bifurcations to how projects develop it is no surprise that they often occur in the complex interactions between the core and the locale. For example, the establishment of Fatima Groups United represented a significant bifurcation in the development of the Fatima project and, more significantly, it represented the wresting of power within the project back to the communities who had an enormous stake in its success. However, later in the project's development, the core took control back with the imposition of a new PPP structure.

Within Clonard, the project could not have commenced in any real way without the allocation of land nearby by the Northern Ireland Department of the Environment. The availability of this land ensured that the community could be relocated in an area close to the original site, which was an important requirement for individuals personally and for community sustainability. This allocation of land created a bifurcation in the project and was triggered, to a significant extent, by the core's acknowledgment of the community's concerns.

The selection of TMS over its rivals, late in its project development, as the main template for theatre management systems in Northern Ireland illustrates the importance of structural power and agent association to the success and selection of one project over another. Both the public nature of the problem (hospital waiting lists) and the close involvement of the core from the project's initiation gave TMS a strategic competitive advantage against its rivals from an early point in its development. A re-organization of the administrative framework through which health and social care are delivered in Northern Ireland (the Review of Public Administration) contributed to a weakening of the position of other systems and a strengthening in of the TMS position. This 'push-pull' dynamic illustrated by project bifurcations conveys the ability of both the locale and the core to alter project dynamics fundamentally.

Adaptation

Within both urban regeneration and healthcare, instances of agent adaptation were observed. For example, feedback from the locale to the core, resulting in system adaptation or policy change was one important consequence of the role played by research carried out by the Economic and Social Research Institute (ESRI) and part-funded by the Katherine Howard Foundation.[3] This research, entitled *Building Communities: Housing as an instrument of social inclusion*, and the series of conferences arising from it, used Fatima Mansions as a case study of living conditions and social housing trends. The process was regarded as having placed integrated social housing back on the public and policy agenda, resulting (among other outcomes) in the Planning and Development Act, 2000. There is no doubt that policy 'feedback' from case locations within urban regeneration (like Fatima, Hardwicke Street and Ballymun) influenced this fundamental policy shift and it represents adaptation to a coalition of agents' concerns.

The unexpected interaction of agents within and outside the urban regeneration system in relation to the Connswater case illustrates a situation where the NIHE was initially keen to move ahead with the centre's intent for the regeneration process, and was unconcerned about the weak community infrastructure in the area. This weak infrastructure had a negative impact on the ability of the community to engage in, or demand, consultation on the initiative. While this did not seem to be a concern for the NIHE, the East Belfast Partnership (a body funded by the EU and Department of Social Development) considered it problematic, and it assisted members of the Mersey Street Residents' Association in receiving training and administrative support. This was an important intervention for the project. The focused and articulate residents' group that emerged was much less compliant and was more confident of its position and role. Implementation became a process with a locally-negotiated dimension and this forced a re-think of aspects of the planned process. The policy intent of the core (and the NIHE) began to evolve through stakeholder consultation and bargaining in a manner that had not been planned. Interestingly, the focus of the East Belfast Partnership was not one of 'regeneration', but of 'renewal', a subtle distinction, but one that reflected the Partnership's concern for the sustainability of local communities within the broader regeneration framework.

The creation of GVRT in 1999 also represented adaptation in an attempt to resolve the difficulties in the development of Roden Street. However, GVRT in the strategically important Village Area also represented the emergence of an important lobbying mechanism for the local community. By attracting funding and additional staff, the organization grew quickly to employ around 30 people and represented one of the most important lobbying organizations for the regeneration of Protestant/Unionist/Loyalist communities in Belfast. The role of GVRT and other community-based organizations pushed the regeneration of their communities up the political agenda, at a time of concern about keeping working-class Protestant communities engaged with the peace process. [4] At a more micro or street level, adaptation to specific situations can also be identified. During the demolition and rebuilding process in Roden Street, there is evidence to suggest that compromises had to be reached with local paramilitary elements. For managers in the locale, dealing with such a naked exercise of power is firmly outside the normal dimensions prescribed in regeneration. Nevertheless, within this context, adapting to the existence and presence of such actors was vital for both the success of the project and the safety of those delivering change on the ground (Birrell 1994).

The introduction of a new agent in Clonard in the form of Oaklee Housing Association (as the result of NIHE's loss of the power to build) saw the local community adapt to work with the new agent. However, this example also illustrates the adaptive behaviour of NIHE and Oaklee, who both explicitly and implicitly recognized the need to give Clonard residents the space and time needed to become comfortable with the new environment. Fatima residents and their NGO network, Fatima Groups United, were also able to adapt successfully to extreme structural change with the introduction of a PPP arrangement during the regeneration process. This adaptation was facilitated by local skilled leadership and the existence of a relationship of trust between the main actors and the residents. In both of these cases there was a recognition by those with 'structural' power (NIHE, Oaklee, Dublin City Council) that those with 'ownership power'– residents– also had to have their position and authority respected.

With the healthcare cases, adaptations between core and locale were more 'micro' in scope. For example, the loss of the project manager during an important phase of TMS left the venture in a potentially difficult situation. The problems of 'going live' without the main member of staff were compounded by the difficulties encountered in finding a suitable project manager in the first place. While the project officer who was still in post was extremely competent, the volume of work required that additional resources be found. By intervening directly in the project, the Department of Health, Social Services and Public Safety (DHSSPS), through its internal SDU, went from being an overseeing and monitoring body to becoming an integral part of the project's day-to-day running. In taking on this role, the Department illustrated the core's ability to adapt its role when it regarded the stakes (and the public price of failure) to be sufficiently high. The intervention of SDU was a clear adaptation by the core (DHSSPS) to an implementation imperative of the project and the locale. Such an adaptation did not occur within the Economic and Social Research Institute (EPES), principally because the project remained relatively stable, even though it encountered significant delays with regard to data protection and in negotiations with the pharmacists.

One of the most interesting aspects of adaptation was the 'boundary spanning' activity that occurred in TMS and Regional Acquired Brain Injury Unit (RABIU). Within these projects, boundary spanning linked healthcare professionals with their information technology (IT) colleagues in a way that ameliorated the effects of some of the boundaries and barriers that existed. Boundary spanning also existed in Order Communications System (OCS), but the difference between these cases is that in OCS, the use of 'IT Sisters' on wards was an integral implementation mechanism of the project—not an adaptation. This term identified nurses with a particular interest and responsibility for the implementation of the IT project. However, within TMS and RABIU the IT-trained project officers engaged in the cases also, by chance, had a nursing background. They adapted smoothly to fill the roles of in spanning boundaries. Both readily acknowledged that their nursing history had significantly improved their ability to gather appropriate information in the system design phases, to engage in successful knowledge transfer during the development of the project and to assist with appropriate implementation of the hardware and software schemes at the end. This ability of the individual agents to adapt is significant.

Emergence

The creation, in a number of the project cases, of new organizational mechanisms to facilitate core-locale interaction, illustrates emergent properties of the system and the project-altering interaction of the core and locale. The PPP used in Fatima is one obvious example of this, as was the use of Ballymun Regeneration Ltd. The use of a PPP, by its nature, introduces an additional set of actors into the system, but also creates another point of contact and another power relationship with the core that facilitates the transfer of information between actors. However, it also creates an additional layer of bureaucracy– a gap between the core and the locale– leaving open the possibility that responsibility for the initiative could be lost within this bureaucratic layer.

Another example of emergence was where funding, which had been aimed at addressing problems of social exclusion, gave rise to an impact on regeneration projects. Government funding had been allocated centrally to

'Making Belfast Work' under a social exclusion programme. In the process of implementing this programme, it was decided to support the employment of a worker within the Clonard regeneration process. This worker was tasked with maintaining an office, and a presence, on site to keep up lines of communication with the community, NIHE and Oaklee (the Housing Association involved). This 'cross-over' funding had a major, unplanned and unpredictable impact on the course of the Clonard project, because it allowed the residents to engage at all levels in the process.

A similar situation occurred during the development of the Roden Street regeneration project where funding was solicited and received from the South Belfast Partnership (SBP) and the NIHE to fund a 'community sustainability' post in the Greater Village Area. The SBP was set up to represent the local community and provide an opportunity for locally elected politicians to work together and was part funded from EU 'Peace funds'. By recognizing the need to develop coherent community representation, and working in tandem with NIHE, the SBP was able to use funding to create new linkages and move the regeneration process forward.

IMPLICATIONS FOR POLICY FORMULATION AND IMPLEMENTATION

Core-locale relations are complex and multi-faceted. They represent the point at which the administrative and policy orientated core comes into contact with the implementing locale at which decision-making becomes realized. Four particular characteristics of this core-locale relationship were identified in the cases. The first was the recognition that, for urban regeneration, policy was largely a national level occurrence, in contrast to healthcare where it was a more diffuse national and supranational phenomenon. The availability of resources and their distribution through facilitating organizations was the second significant characteristic identified. The intended and unintended interaction of policy at the core with activities in the locale was the third. The final one was the dispersion of power from the core through the establishment of semi-state organizations and quangos. Unlike other thematic areas addressed here, the core and locale theme exhibited all of the CAS dynamics of path-dependency, bifurcation, adaptation and emergence.

For those making and implementing policy, there is a series of significant findings. The first of these is the importance of initial conditions, and the path-dependencies that result from them, to the developmental trajectory of a project. By having a firm understanding of initial conditions, and of the positive and negative consequences of core-locale interaction in the past, policy makers and implementers can be aware of potential problems and can craft policy and its implementation accordingly. We can see from the cases that large-scale interventions by either the core or the locale can result in project bifurcations that have a significant effect on the way the project develops. Adaptation is also apparent, both on the part of the core and of the locale, and is often the key to moving beyond seemingly intractable problems of implementation. We see emergent phenomena within the project too, in the role of new organizational mechanisms to facilitate project development. Most importantly, the strength of the linkages between core and locale, and the level of communication was a marker of project success. Where relationships of trust existed—or were built– and compromises could be made, projects worked well. More difficult relationships resulted in much more challenging policy implementation. The cases show how the detail of interactions between the core and locale take place and can impact both positively and negatively upon projects. By appreciating this interaction, and ensuring that agents are working as much as possible towards similar objectives, project outcomes can be facilitated.

It is clear that history is a significant factor. An appreciation of the relevant path-dependencies is essential to effective decision-making. The clock does not start on policy and its implementation at the moment of formal decision process initiation—some specific time zero, t_0. Instead, it starts at t_{-n}, some significant period before the need for decision has perhaps ever been considered. Moreover, because several elements of social history and action may have to be brought together by a policy initiative, it is important to realize that their different path-dependencies may be the raw material of complex interactions and non-linear outcomes.

The nexus of core and locale, of policy and implementation, is the fulcrum of effective action and is exactly where the best, most aware and most adaptive managerial agents are needed if emergent phenomena are to be positively directed, bifurcations grasped quickly and adaptations to be made positively. Without this guidance capacity the fulcrum can collapse and the nexus take the form of a vortex.

Contrary to many of the inherited assumptions about implementation that consider 'good' implementation as blueprinted and exactly carried through, it is clear that emergence and adaptation are 'normal' and most often essential to effectiveness. Implementation from a CAS perspective is a process that should feature significant open-endedness *ex ante*. The appropriate capability for implementing agents—either in the core or the locale– is therefore high on adaptation, and governance mechanisms need to incorporate measures and rewards that support the deepening of such capacity and its deployment. Given the likelihood of bifurcations, the actors and governance mechanisms need also to assume that surprise events of considerable importance will occur and that 'surprise management' is a valuable skill to cultivate.

9 In Conclusion

This book, and the research on which it is based, was driven by a number of ambitions. The authors shared an intellectual concern arising from the collapse of the 'old' public administration and the unresolved contest between various 'new' frameworks that claim better approaches and insights. It was, therefore, intended to make some contribution to advancing public administration theory and to improving the capacity for governance in public service systems. The route chosen for this purpose was to explore the relevance and application of complex adaptive systems (CAS) theory. This approach was selected for a variety of reasons but not least because it seemed to have the potential to integrate various strands of theory rather than to erect yet another contesting and exclusive conceptual framework.

The book was also driven by a desire to support practitioners by adding to their understanding of the phenomena for which they carry a burden of stewardship. The question here was if a CAS framework could provide new and better insights and enable better decision-making and action-taking. The nature of complex adaptive systems thinking clearly contrasts with traditional approaches to decision and action, and with many of the new public management principles. This is particularly the case in terms of its orientation towards identifying patterns in system behaviour, in assuming uncertain outcomes and in informing real-time adaptation. Most of the traditional and the more recent public management approaches have sought to eliminate unpredictability and surprise. Their analytical and philosophical orientation is to engage rational-analytical thinking and modelling in such a manner that policy decisions should be translated unambiguously into strategies for action and that action itself should follow through in an undisturbed line of command and control. Complex adaptive systems theory, by stark contrast, assumes that interactions in human and organizational networks will intrinsically generate unexpected consequences and that this unpredictability is natural and not open to elimination.

The practising manager is therefore faced with a difficult challenge: how to navigate in a shifting environment. The context and nature of managerial action is much closer to Lindblom's incrementalism. Lindblom's (1959) model of disjointed incrementalism has been commonly held out as an illustration of the pathology of public management systems but it may in truth be very close to the reality of life in a complex adaptive system. Quinn (1980) proposed a variant of Lindblom's model with his characterization of successful strategy as based on logical incrementalism. For him, the logic guiding piecemeal and emergent decision-making lay in an overall pattern of intended outcomes that decision-makers kept clearly in mind and used to guide their incremental moves. In the same way, it might be argued that those managing in complex adaptive systems contribute best by retaining clarity about ends (although acknowledging that these may have significant ambiguity and may change with feedback from action and intervention by external forces) and then concentrating on navigating the emergent reality which arises from taking action and the interactions of people, organizations and institutions. The familiar sailing analogy may be appropriate. It is possible to navigate winds, currents and tides and to arrive at an intended destination but it is impossible to manage those same winds, currents and tides. A concept of 'complex incrementalism' may therefore offer a framework for managerial behaviour in complex adaptive systems.

A third ambition underlying the book was that of dealing directly with the challenge of making complex adaptive systems theory operational in the context of empirical research. A familiar critique of the systems theory base, especially in its use in the social sciences, is that it is over reliant on 'armchair' theorizing and 'argument by analogy'. There are relatively few empirical studies grounded in extensive field research that help us to tease out how theoretical concepts may be operationalized, measured and analyzed. The research on urban regeneration and healthcare information systems sought to confront this gap in the literature head-on. By focusing on quite specific projects, bounded in time and place, the researchers were forced to render theoretical generalizations into practical field research measures and method. This necessitated the design and specification of a model framework with enough specificity to guide data collection and analysis, and to bridge the gap between the more general theory and underlying constructs of complex adaptive systems, while accommodating the need to put these into practice at the point of action taking by participants in the systems studied. The hope is that this may contribute to progressing a second generation of research in the field that is empirically-based and generates testable hypotheses—advancing along the theory building cycle proposed by Carlile and Christensen (2006).

THEORY

The theoretical journey involved in pursuing the book's first ambition was relatively straightforward. As noted in Chapter 4, it started by making the case that public service provision may be characterized as a 'system' and, particularly, one that may have multiple concepts of purpose, involving many agents interacting with one another, triggered into action by policy objectives that may be jointly pursued. Systems theory has had its time in the doldrums, having been the subject of a wide and sharp range of criticisms. The broad critique of systems theory has ranged from the deficiencies of an 'engineering' approach involving models too far removed from reality, to the frustration experienced by many with the early literature that too often had ambitions for a general systems theory that, in trying to explain everything, explained nothing. Systems theory and models have been criticized for their remoteness from empirical data, for an over emphasis on control theory to the exclusion of human agency, for encouraging a centralized grand-planning approach to the challenges of public service provision and for too much reliance on argument by analogy. Despite this established critique, it was felt that time and theory had moved on apace since the first flush of enthusiasm for systems theory and that a more 'mature' approach was both available and offered significant potential for new insight.

The next challenge was to recognize that systems models, as they might apply to social phenomena, have been differentiated and elaborated considerably in the past decade or more. This necessitated a choice of model appropriate to the empirical research on hand. The process of inquiry focused on complex systems theory. Among theories of complex systems, that of CAS, rather than chaos theory or the theory of dissipative structures (Stacey *et al.* 2002), was selected for its apparent immediate usefulness. The particular attraction of CAS was that its models represent a system by characterizing the behaviour of agents as they interact and produce emergent patterns of behaviour at system level. As CAS are self-organizing, there is no need to assume a unitary controlling entity or agent, a feature that was seen as particularly important in the study of public service provision in a so-called networked world, and in the wake of public management reforms with their introduction of private and not-for-profit actors into policy-making and implementation. CAS systems are also, by definition, adaptive so they enable a capacity to learn from experience. Adopting this specific approach to description and explanation then generated the second research focus on investigating uniquely CAS dynamics.

The theoretical journey therefore led to a two-part sequence in research and analysis: the characterization of the public sector projects studied as system phenomena followed by the posing of the question of whether they could also be characterized as CAS phenomena. The combination of these two research processes created a researchable '6+4' *analytical framework*, consisting of the six core elements of the CAS framework, namely *system, environmental factors, environmental rules, agents, processes,* and *outcomes* plus the four unique CAS dynamics of *path-dependency, adaptation, bifurcation* and *emergence*.

The answer to whether the first step could result in a system characterization was never in much doubt *ex ante*, but we were much less sanguine about the likely presence of CAS dynamics in the case studies. As may be

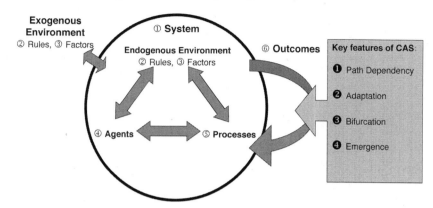

Figure 9.1   CAS model: the '6+4' analytical framework.

seen in Chapters 5 to 8, significant evidence of CAS characteristics was observed across all cases, suggesting that at least these instances of public sector activity are open to interpretation as CAS and that such interpretation has some interesting and worthwhile insights to offer the theorist and the practitioner. Overall, it proved possible to develop a sufficiently detailed operationalization of the CAS framework to allow extensive descriptive exploration of the cases and to support analysis of the adaptive forces at work. The theory therefore bears the burden of confrontation with the reality of policy-making and implementation—in other words, it works. It works because the general features of CAS theory as developed in recent years in the literature are shown to be amenable to development in sufficient detail for them to be used at very specific levels of public sector project formulation and implementation.

The CAS analysis was based on cross-case investigation for common themes or patterns. The principal themes affecting all 12 cases in urban regeneration and healthcare information systems and across two jurisdictions were the impact of boundaries, the dynamic nature of project vision and the agent involvement on which it was based, the role and effect of private sector involvement and the nature of the core-locale relationship. All these common themes exhibited aspects of the four CAS dynamics: path-dependency, adaptation, bifurcation and emergence, although not all four were features of all cases. Considerable variation in the importance and working of each dynamic was also observed. If not all CAS dynamics could be observed in all cases, does this suggest that not all were in fact behaving as CAS? It is our view that this is not a necessary conclusion because the chosen start and end points for the research may have excluded other CAS features and/or because of limitations on the insights that could be gleaned through the research methods used. The variation in the how each CAS dynamic was observed to work its way out in the cases is a lesser concern, as such variation would seem to be intrinsic to the assumed unpredictability of process and outcome.

In examining the common themes, initial conditions and the resulting path-dependency are seen to be of great importance to process and outcome. Initial conditions set boundaries since they were constructed through time and were fundamental to the capacity to find a shared vision and to shaping agreement on objectives and outcomes. These were, in turn, central to project success and to the time required for implementation. The nature of boundaries is seen to be quite variable between the urban regeneration and healthcare settings: in the former, physical boundaries were vital; in the latter, professional boundaries were essential. But despite this, the manner in which boundaries exerted influence was common: assumptions based on past interactions across the boundaries and the existence of trust, based on experience, were pivotal to the launch and life of the projects. Initial conditions, often with long, emotional or institutionalized path-dependencies were powerful forces. The capacity of the system to span boundaries through the actions of various agents and processes was consequently important to success. Changes in the accepted definition of boundaries was seen to lead to bifurcations, or to their avoidance, in project histories and sometimes proved essential to unlocking major blockages in implementation.

Adaptation was a general feature across all the themes. It was seen that boundaries could be redefined through active agent engagement, through the work of boundary spanning individuals, through the creation of project specific agents (PSAs), or through the intervention of agents initially 'outside' the system and, on occasion, by fiat where the most powerful public sector agent took a unilateral decision. The emergence of a shared vision for the urban regeneration projects was achieved through various adaptations among the agents in the systems and was substantially affected by the power they wielded and the ways in which power relationships were modified through interaction among traditional and new agents. While the involvement of private and not-for-profit agents was seen as having limited impact on projects, it was nonetheless clear that they added complexity to decision-making, prompting adaptation to conceptions of possible outcomes and project vision within the system, and on occasion bifurcation in a project's history. The relationship between the core policy agent and those implementing policy at local level (in the 'locale') was also an adaptive one, with influence running in both directions and sometimes marking breakthroughs in previously intractible standoffs between policy intention and local action.

Bifurcations were not universally observed but were nonetheless apparent. Changes in assumptions about boundaries led to significant bifurcations, overturning some of the constraints of initial conditions and their roots in path-dependency. The introduction of a critical level of involvement by private sector agents was also seen to precipitate changes in project vision and outcomes, especially in the cases of urban regeneration. Such bifurcations could be beneficial, opening up new possibilities and flexibilities, new approaches to cost and its allocation and new learning for all agents. Decisions by powerful agents on either side of the core-locale relationship also precipitated bifurcations, drawing attention once again to the importance of agent power and its use.

Emergence was observed principally in the shaping and re-shaping of project vision and in the creation of PSAs. The shaping of project vision was critical to progress in what were often very difficult situations that had to carry the burden of path-dependencies and initial conditions riven through with conflicting assumptions, mistrust or professional territorialism and power battles. The emergence of PSAs was important to a project's processes and outcomes in a practical sense. Their emergence also demonstrated the self-organizing capacity of CAS in quite a dramatic manner in so far as the systems were seen to generate new order-producing mechanisms from the interactions among agents.

In general, the '6+4' CAS framework may be seen to have 'worked' theoretically. It unambiguously supported a descriptive approach to research and analysis. The analysis of the four unique CAS dynamics goes beyond the descriptive to provide insights into important causal factors at work in the origins and trajectories of the project cases. This insight provides the real payoff from the analysis, and provides a basis on which to argue a case for advancing to further empirically-based research on public sector systems as CAS.

PRACTICE

The second objective of the research arose from the desire to contribute to the practice of public management by testing whether CAS concepts 'in action' could provide new or enriched insight for the practitioner. This potential was tested in a limited manner in the course of the research through formal interaction and project briefings with representatives of the practitioner commumity. To date, a barrier to insight from CAS in the professional and applied field has been its use of a specialized and often obscure language that has relied unduly on analogy with phenomena in the natural sciences. Furthermore, specifically social science-based empirical research has been limited, so that purely conceptual reasoning and argument by analogy has been overly dominant: features not likely to generate great confidence among the community of practice. In addition, our experience of this research programme suggests that power relationships are inadequately addressed in CAS theory, despite the fact that they are intrinsic to the world of the public sector manager.

It is believed that the '6+4' framework offers a more readily-grasped and accessible entry to CAS reasoning and understanding for the public manager.

Implementing the framework through research at the level of public sector projects also grounded the method and theory in a very immediate context with which managers are familiar. For many public sector managers, the data reflects the kind of managerial experience and responsibility in which they are immersed daily, and the theoretical constructs have been rendered 'practical' in order to operationalize them for research purposes.

In terms of how a manager's practice might be affected, we believe that the implications of the four CAS dynamics are the most important. They challenge the professional to engage in prior and real-time analysis that is not always central to the traditional process methods and assumptions of either the classical bureaucratic model or the rational-analytic, rational choice models that underpin much of the new public management tradition. The deep importance of path-dependency and its creation of initial conditions indicates that the 'start' date of a project should be viewed as a continuum stretching back into time, rather than as time-present. As with all system and human phenomena, setting time boundaries is a challenge— when does history begin and end for any management project or undertaking? A clear message from the research is that ignoring history is likely to be a recipe for ineffective action, or even disaster. As public service systems become more diversified in the numbers and kinds of agents involved, this is a matter of concern. In a more networked world, many of the agents are highly specialized and have little interest in, or capacity to understand, the path-dependencies that set the initial conditions. That some of the agents should undertake to understand the path-dependencies is vital, and this seems to fall to core agents in policy-making and implementation roles. If agents cannot, or choose not to, make the appropriate analysis of history, they seem doomed to mis-specifying purpose, vision and the path of implementation and to bedevilling the initial stages of projects with potentially avoidable conflict, time delays and budget over-runs. Understanding how the initial conditions have been set and anticipating their likely consequences should, on the evidence of this research, ameliorate these undesirable effects. To do so adequately involves interaction among these core agents at the pre-launch stage, and the recognition of a need for new mechanisms such as the PSAs as seen in several of the cases.

While the analysis of initial conditions may be integrated into the more traditional project methodologies based on rational-analytical principles, the implications of assuming that there may be important bifurcations, emergent activity and considerable continuing adapatation in the system are more challenging in terms of normative approaches to managerial practice. These three CAS dynamics that run through the research evidence demand an appreciation of the managerial role as one that cannot rely only on pre-determined, planned and programmed action, driven by command and control. The need is for an approach based on *managing* policy and its implementation, rather than on policy planning and mechanical implementation.

As discussed earlier in this chapter the managerial role therefore, in a CAS context, emphasizes the navigation of policy-setting and implementation. The importance of achieving a shared (or at least a consensus) project vision is pivotal since this provides the means of establishing direction and outcome. By allowing for the unanticipated adaptations that occur as agents interact, and for the intrinsic unpredictability of emergence and bifurcations, it is more likely that the flexible navigation of the processes will lead to the desired outcome. While the traditional bureaucratic process in public management may have been characterized by disjointed incrementalism, the CAS perspective might be viewed as one that can be based on a notion of complex incrementalism. In such an understanding, vision is a vital centre point. Action in pursuit of that vision may be seen as incremental but 'jointed' in so far as the end remains clear, even when subject to continuing adaptation, so that actions taken remain true to a directional agreement as decision-makers navigate their way through the unexpected and the unpredictable. The implications of such an approach to public management are significant in terms of governance, since so much of present governance and accountability frameworks are based on assumptions of predictability, the elimination of uncertainty by planning and analysis methodologies, and control by compliance. An approach that might be described as 'flexible navigation' demands considerable change in the common assumptions and principles concerning governance, accountability and compliance. Nonetheless, the research illustrates the disparity between 'reality' and many of the normative expectations under which public managers have to work—as well as their own internalized professional expectations of what it is that amounts to 'good practice'. The dissonance is both institutionalized and personalized, and often experienced at great cost.

The research data shows how managerial action took place at different levels in the project systems. Policy-making was located principally at national or even supranational levels. Implementation of policy was specifically located in a physical or organizational geography. Responsibility for delivery was allocated to specific public sector organizations, whose managers could decide to contract out specific elements to the private sector. Such a hierarchy of policy-making and action is a commonplace observation in organizational settings. The observations that have been widely drawn are that policy can only be effectively realized if the various levels are well aligned and are capable of adapting to feedback up and down the hierarchy so that 'the whole' is capable of learning both between and during projects. However, the combination of complexity, and the presence of traditional normative principles about implementation and accountability in the kind of systems explored in this research, makes the management of such policy hierarchies challenging. The complexity introduces some unavoidable uncertainty and the need for frequent adaptation and a real-time approach to navigating emergent reality—at all levels. Traditional approaches to accountability, however, press back against such navigational flexibility and may even prevent necessary adaptation in the name of complying with what was originally promised and planned. When this happens projects easily fail, cynicism is spread and path-dependencies are laid down that set negative initial conditions for subsequent projects.

EMPIRICAL RESEARCH

The book's contribution to the development of a more empirical research tradition in CAS as applied in the social sciences must be judged by the value of the outcomes noted above but also by its lessons for continuing research. These lessons arise from the operationalization of systems and CAS concepts in the form of the '6+4' framework, the deployment of multiple methods for measurement, a multi-level approach to data collection and a demonstration of the potential for research across different jurisdictions.

In order to operationalize the concepts of 'system' and CAS for application in the field research, the '6+4' analytical framework, consisting of the six core elements of system, environmental factors, environmental rules, agents, processes, and outcomes plus the four uniquely CAS dynamics of path-dependency, adaptation, bifurcation and emergence was devised. It proved possible to work with these elements as the bases for data collection and the analysis revealed in the earlier chapters. Identification of the research framework elements was a multi-method undertaking within a case study research design, using extensive secondary source research, exploratory qualitative field interviews, feedback to and from a selection of the actors in the systems, a structured questionnaire survey and extensive face-to-face interviews with system participants. This multi-method approach made it possible to cross-check evidence and interpretation and to make the analysis more robust and reliable.

A focus on specific and quite bounded public sector projects was important to 'forcing' specificity in methodology and to ensuring that the analysis and findings would be firmly grounded, unlike studies that focus on large systems with boundaries of scope and time that are difficult to establish. It was felt that research at this project level was best suited to the development of a working theoretical framework and measures at this stage in pursuing CAS research in this context. This view, it is felt, has been justified by the results. The next stage in pursuing this CAS research offers two possibilities. One is to continue to refine the data collection, measurement and analysis approaches in pursuit of greater methodological effectiveness. Another is to take the '6+4' framework and, based on the findings reported here, to develop a simulation model approach to understanding the same phenomena. CAS modelling based on cellular automata premises offers a direct point of entry to an alternative means of exploring CAS dynamics, assisting researchers in refining constructs and measures, and helping decision-makers to explore the 'navigational space' they may confront. Combining the results of extensive field work such as reported here with a 'harder' modelling initiative offers a route to gaining the best from these different methodologies and developing a more multi-dimensional understanding of public sector management in action.

Notes

NOTES TO CHAPTER 1

1. The private sector includes all privately owned firms or organizations that are operated on a for-profit basis. The non-profit sector includes privately owned organizations operating on a not-for-profit basis (often, but not always, registered as charities in Ireland). The public sector includes statutory and semi-state agencies with mandates to provide housing services. The community sector includes all organizations with a particular location basis, but with a potentially broad range of activities that are aimed at improving the quality of life for people in that location. The policy sector includes all organizations, government departments and political committees or sub-groups that focus on policy development for the specified policy domain.
2. Unemployment as measured by the International Labour Organization (ILO) includes all those who would take a job if offered one, rather than the claimant count.
3. Laeken indicators are a set of measures of poverty and social exclusion established at the European Council in December 2001 in Laekan, Belgium—a suburb of Brussels. They were established in order to assist in the development of European-wide policies to tackle these issues.
4. Clientelism is essentially the exchange of votes for favours—i.e., voters elect a representative with the expectation that their individual and/or local issues/needs will be dealt with expediently and favourably.
5. Pollitt and Bouckaert were referring to the UK Government in this quote, but it is equally relevant to both Irish governments.
6. 'Making Belfast Work' (MBW) was launched in 1988 and aimed at addressing the economic, educational, social, health and environmental problems facing people living in the most disadvantaged areas of Belfast. Thirty-two wards in Belfast (including Clonard and Blackstaff) were identified as target areas for this programme. Since 1988, £275 million has been funneled into over 350 projects under the MBW programme—which is administered out of the Belfast Regeneration Office in the Department for Social Development. The MBW strategy was updated in 1995 following a city-wide consultation process.
7. Vesting means that the NIHE has the legal authority to buy out owner-occupiers/landlords in the targeted area and to relocate social tenants prior to demolition—effectively equivalent to a compulsory purchase order (CPO) in the south.
8. Noble indicators are used in Northern Ireland to measure the extent of social and economic deprivation in an area. Developed by a team of researchers

in Oxford University led by Michael Noble, the indicators span a range of deprivation 'domains' including: income, health, employment, access to services, education and environment.

9. The International Fund for Ireland was established in 1986 by the British and Irish governments 'to promote economic and social advance and to encourage contact, dialogue and reconciliation between nationalists and unionists throughout Ireland. The fund gives priority to projects located in the most disadvantaged areas in Northern Ireland and the six southern border counties. For further information see <http://www.internationalfundforireland.com>.

10. See Power (2000), Norris (2001) and Somerville-Woodward (2002).

11. Now called Dublin City Council.

12. Irish Punt was valued at €1.2697 at date of conversion to Euros in 2000 giving a Euro value of between €63–89 million for this project.

13. The 'Rainbow' coalition was made up of three separate parties sharing power: Labour, *Fine Gael* and the Democratic Left.

14. As of 2006, there were five regions.

15. Revitalising Areas by Planning, Investment and Development (RAPID) was launched in 2001 by the government to focus efforts of regeneration and development in 25 urban areas and 20 provincial towns. Targeted areas are required to form area implementation teams (made up of public, private, non-profit and community groups) to formulate and carry through plans for revitalization. While the programme is currently under the remit of the Department of Community, Rural and Gaeltacht Affairs, its implementation is overseen by a non-profit organization 'Pobal'. Pobal provides guidance to area implementation teams on the objectives and requirements of the programme as well as reporting on progress and performance measures to the Department.

16. Note that 'practical completion' was in May 2004 with all physical development completed by the contractor. Final completion involves drawing up of a 'snag list' by the architect (and residents) to fix small problems and the addressing of those problems by the contractor. This took about a year after practical completion.

17. HL7 stands for 'Health Level 7' and is a messaging protocol that is designed to accommodate all healthcare information requirements and is accredited by the American National Standards Institute (ANSI).

18. See *Quality and Fairness: A Health System for You* (DoHC 2001), *Health Information: A National Strategy* (DoHC 2004) and *Embedding the 'e' in Health: A strategic ICT framework for the Irish health system* (HeBE 2004).

NOTES TO CHAPTER 2

1. Within the geo-political environment of Northern Ireland, 'Catholic' is taken to mean identification with Irish Nationalism and/or Republicanism. By the same measure 'Protestant' is associated with Unionism, and/or Loyalism. This definition is now reflected in a new shorthand, 'PUL' community, meaning Protestant/Unionist/Loyalist, or CNR, meaning Catholic/Nationalist/Republican.

2. Available at <http://www.environ.ie/en/DevelopmentandHousing/Housing/SocialHousingSupport/RegenerationSchemes/> (accessed 7th August 2008).

3. Available at <http://www.environ.ie/en/DevelopmentandHousing/Planning Development/UrbanandVillageRenewal/UrbanVillageRenewalScheme/> (accessed 9th August 2008).
4. Available at <http://www.pobal.ie/Pages/home.aspx> (accessed 20th November 2008).
5. Available at <http://www.seupb.org/about.htm> (accessed 9th August 2008).
6. Pobal, originally called Area Development Management Ltd (ADM), is an intermediary company established in 1992 by the Irish Government in agreement with the European Commission. The main role of ADM is to support integrated social and economic development through managing programmes targeted at disadvantage and exclusion and promoting reconciliation and equality. For further information see <http://www.pobal.ie>.
7. Available at <http://www.gvrt.org/> (accessed 17th December 2007).

NOTES TO CHAPTER 3

1. PRINCE2 stands for PRojects IN Controlled Environments—the second version. It is a set of standard activities and deliverables for managing IT projects and PRINCE2 is a registered trademark of the Office of Government Commerce in the UK.
2. Even when the Assembly was suspended between 2002 and 2007, MLAs remained and were able to lobby British ministers on behalf of their constituents.
3. There is some uncertainty about the remit of this organization. Its web site states that it inspects children's homes, nursing homes and residential care, nursing agencies and private medical provision; however, in August 2008 it carried out an inspection of (public) hospital hygiene standards.
4. Competitive Dialogue is an approach to defining requirements for complex consulting or other service contracts in which the buyer gives only broad guidelines to a limited number of suppliers and then actively engages with these suppliers to develop the proposals ultimately submitted for consideration.

NOTES TO CHAPTER 4

1. Kingdon's (1995) model of the policy process involves three distinctive streams of human activity: the 'problem' stream, the 'policy' stream and the 'political' stream. Each of these streams have their own dynamic and Kingdon refers to the opening and closing of policy 'windows' that allow for the three streams to come together to generate actionable public policy.
2. Quasi-autonomous non-governmental organizations.
3. Casti lists six types of models used for modelling large-scale systems: differential equations, input/output functions, finite state descriptions (equilibrium), potential functions (maxim*ize*/minim*ize* a given output), entropy (measures of disorder) and sets/relations between sets.
4. Morgan's eight metaphors for organizations are: machine, organism, brain, culture, political system, psychic prison, flux and transformation, and instrument of domination.

NOTES TO CHAPTER 5

1. For a comprehensive analysis of the evolution of murals and iconography in the Northern Ireland conflict see <www.cain.ulst.ac.uk>.
2. The surrender grant scheme was a government programme established in 1984 under which social housing tenants who gave up their tenancies received a grant to aid them in purchasing a new home. The take-up of this scheme was largely confined to tenants with moderate incomes and/or other financial means, leaving only those with very low or no incomes to remain in the targeted housing estates.

NOTES TO CHAPTER 6

1. Arnstein (1969: 217) proposes eight 'rungs on a ladder of citizen participation': manipulation, therapy, informing, consultation, placation, partnership, delegated power and citizen control.

NOTES TO CHAPTER 7

1. Market mechanisms in public sector reform include the use of service contracts between public sector organizations, such as those introduced in the UK National Health Service, service level agreements, performance incentives for promotion, etc.
2. In Ireland, 'affordable' housing is a term used to refer to dwellings that are sold at a discount to owner/occupiers. The discount is determined based on a formula applied by local government based on the income of the buyer.
3. Positive feedback refers to the process by which a system generates an output that provides further impetus for the system to create more output and so on in an ever-expanding loop. An example of a positive feedback loop is a run on the banking system, where depositors see one bank fail and then start to pull their savings out of other banks—which causes these banks to fail as well—which causes more depositors to withdraw savings, and so on. Positive feedback is not generally seen as a good thing as it leads to instability and systems spiralling out of control.
4. Quote from interview notes of Fatima Mansions local authority official.
5. The 'network effect' is the impact that additional participants or users have on the value of a technology or service. Classic examples of network effects are the telephone and the Internet as the value (to each user) of these networks increases the more users there are.

NOTES TO CHAPTER 8

1. The NI Executive performed most of the functions of a regional government from November 1999 to October 2002. Exempted functions included policing and security and the power to raise additional revenue through local tax.
2. For a full analysis see Chapter 2.

3. The Katherine Howard Foundation is an independent grant-making foundation whose key function is the provision of small, easily accessible grants to community-based groups throughout Ireland, North and south. Within this provision, the Foundation's particular focus is on projects that provide direct support to children and their families in disadvantaged communities. For further information see <http://www.khf.ie/About_KHF/index.php>.
4. Available at <http://news.bbc.co.uk/1/hi/northern_ireland/4863674.stm> (accessed 7th August 2008).

Bibliography

Ackoff, R. and Emery, F. (1972) *On Purposeful Systems*. London: Tavistock Publications.

Agranoff, R. and McGuire, M. (2003) *Collaborative Public Management: Strategies for Local Government*. Washington, DC: Georgetown University Press.

Anderson, B. (1991) *Imagined Communities*. London: Verso.

Anderson, P.W. (1999) 'Complexity theory and organizational science'. *Organization Science*, 10(3): 216–232.

Arnstein, S. (1969) 'A ladder of citizen participation'. *Journal of the American Institute of Planners*, 35(4): 216–224.

Ashby, W.R. (1956) *Introduction to Cybernetics*. New York, NY: Wiley.

Ballymun Community Action Programme (2000) *On the Balcony of a New Millennium*. Dublin: BCAP.

Ballymun Regeneration Ltd. (2005) *Ballymun Regeneration Progress Report 2003–2004*. Dublin: BRL.

Bannon, M. J. (1999) The greater Dublin region: planning for its transformation and development. In: Killen, J. & MacLaran, A. (eds) *Dublin: Contemporary Trends and Issues for the Twenty First Century*. 11: 1–19. Dublin: Geographical Society of Ireland.

Barzelay M. *et al.* (2003) 'Research on public management policy change in the Latin America region: a conceptual framework and methodological guide'. *International Public Management Review*, 4(1): 20–42.

Beinhocker, E.D. (2007) *Origin of Wealth: Evolution, Complexity, and the Radical Remaking of Economics*. Boston, MA: Harvard Business School Press.

Bertalanffy, L. von (1968) *General Systems Theory*. New York, NY: Braziller.

Birrell, D. (1994) Social policy responses to urban violence in Northern Ireland. In: Dunn, S. (ed.) *Managing Divided Cities*. Keele: Keele University Press.

Blackman, T. (2001) 'Complexity theory and the new public management'. *Social Issues*, 1(2). Online. Available <http://www.whb.co.uk/socialissues> (accessed 3 Sep 2002).

Boal, F.W. (1995) *Shaping a City: Belfast in the Late Twentieth Century*. Belfast: Institute of Irish Studies, Queen's University Belfast.

Boston, J. (2000) The challenge of evaluating systemic change: the case of public management reform. Paper presented at the IPMN *Learning from experience with new public management* conference. Macquarie Graduate School of Management, Sydney, Australia, 4–6 March.

Bowles, S. & Gintis, H. (2002) 'Social capital and community governance'. *The Economic Journal*, 112(November): F419–F436.

Boyle, M. (2005) 'Sartre's circular dialectic and the empires of abstract space: a history of space and place in Ballymun, Dublin'. *Annals of the Association of American Geographers*, 95(1): 181–201.

Brewer, G. (1975) *Politicians, Bureaucrats, and the Consultant: A Critique of Urban Problem Solving*. New York, NY: Basic Books.

Brugha, R. & Varvasovszky, Z. (2000) 'Stakeholder analysis: a review'. *Health Policy and Planning*, 15(3): 239–246.

Brunsson, N. & Olsen, J.P. (1993) *The Reforming Organization*. London: Routledge.

Bryan, D. & Gillespie, G. (2005) *Transforming Conflict: Flags and Emblems*. Belfast: Institute of Irish Studies, Queen's University Belfast.

Burton, P. *et al.* (2004) *What Works in Community Involvement in Area-based Initiatives?: A Systematic Review of the Literature*. London: Home Office.

Caldart, A.A. & Ricart, J.E. (2004) 'Corporate strategy revisited: a view from complexity theory'. *European Management Review*, 1: 96–104.

Campbell, H. (2003) 'Public health—a bond between a government and its people'. Presidential address to the Ulster Medical Society, October 10th, 2002. *Ulster Medical Journal*, 72(1): 4–9.

Carlile, P.R & Christensen, C.M. (2006) *The Cycle of Theory Building in Management Research*. Boston University School of Management Working Paper, 2005–2003.

Casti, J. (1979) *Connectivity, Catastrophe and Complexity in Large-scale Systems*. International Series on Applied Systems Analysis. New York, NY: John Wiley & Sons.

Central Statistics Office (2003–2008) *Ireland North and South: A Statistical Profile*. Dublin, Ireland: CSO.

Chapman, J. (2002) *System Failure: Why Governments Must Learn to Think Differently*. London: Demos.

Checkland, P. (1981) *Systems Thinking, Systems Practice*. New York, NY: John Wiley & Sons.

Chondroleou, G. *et al.* (2005) 'A comparison of local management of regeneration in England and Greece'. *International Journal of Public Sector Management*, 18(2): 114–127.

Clarke, P. (2007) Institutional cooperation: the health sector. In: Coakley, J. & O'Dowd, L. (eds) *Crossing the Border: New Relationships between Northern Ireland and the Republic of Ireland*. Dublin: Irish Academic Press.

Considine, J. & O'Leary, E. (1999) The growth performance of Northern Ireland and the Republic of Ireland: 1960 to 1995. In: Collins, N. (ed.) *Political Issues in Ireland Today*. Manchester: Manchester University Press.

Cooke, P., Roper, S. & Wylie, P. (2003) "The golden thread of innovation' and Northern Ireland's evolving regional innovation system'. *Regional Studies*, 37(4): 365–379.

Coombs, C.R., Doherty, N.F. & Loan-Clarke, J. (2002) The role of user ownership and positive user attitudes in the successful adoption of information systems within NHS community trusts. In: Armoni, A. (ed.) *Effective Healthcare Information Systems*. Hershey, PA: Idea Group Publishing.

Craig Gardner Ltd (1993) *An Evaluation of the Ballymun Refurbishment*. Unpublished report for Dublin Corporation.

Crawford, M., Rutter, D. & Thelwall, S. (2004) *User Involvement in Change Management: A Review of the Literature*. London: National Co-ordinating Centre for NHS Service Delivery and Organisation.

Currie, Graeme and Olga Suhomlinova. 2006. The Impact of Institutional Forces Upon Knowledge Sharing in the UK NHS: The Triumph of Professional Power and the Inconsistency of Policy. Public Administration 84 (1): 1-30.

De Wolf, T. & Holvoet, T. (2004) Emergence and self-organisation: a statement of similarities and differences. In *Proceedings of the International Workshop on Engineering Self-organising Applications 2004*, : 96–110.

Deloitte (2007) *Research into the Financial Cost of the Northern Ireland Divide*. Online. Available <http://www.allianceparty.org/resources/index/External> (accessed 6 August 2008).

Dennard, Linda, Kurt Richardson and Goktug Morcol (2008), *Complexity and Policy Analysis: Tools and Methods for Designing Robust Policies in a Complex World*, Goodyear, AZ, ISCE Publishing

Donaldson, L. (2001) *The Contingency Theory of Organizations*. London: Sage Publications.

Doolin, B. (2004) 'Power and resistance in the implementation of a medical management information system'. *Information Systems Journal* 14: 343–362.

Downey-Ennis, K. & Harrington, D. (2002) 'In search of excellence in Irish health care'. *International Journal of Health Care Quality Assurance*. 15(2): 65–73.

Dublin City Council (2001) *Regeneration/Next Generation*. Dublin: Dublin City Council.

Dunsire, A., Hartley, K. & Parker, D., (1994) Organisational status and performance: summary of the findings. In: McKevitt, D. & Lawton, A. (eds) *Public Sector Management: Theory, Critique and Practice*, London: Sage Publications.

Eason, K. (2006) *A Local Socio-technical Design Approach to Exploiting the Potential of the National Health Service IT programme NPfIT*. London: The Bayswater Institute.

Eisenhardt, K. (1989) 'Building theories from case study research'. *Academy of Management Review* 14(4): 532–550. New York, NY: Academy of Management.

Emmeche, C., Koppe, S. & Stjernfelt, F. (1997) 'Explaining emergence: towards an ontology of levels'. *Journal for General Philosophy of Science*, 28: 83–119.

European Commission (2000) *Charter of Fundamental Rights of the European Union*. Luxembourg: Office for Official Publications of the European Communities.

European Commission (2007) *Together for Health: A Strategic Approach for the EU 2008–2013*. Luxembourg: Office for Official Publications of the European Communities.

Fahey, T. (1999) Summary of findings. In: Fahey, T. (ed.) *Social Housing in Ireland: A Study of Success, Failure and Lessons Learned*. Dublin: Oak Tree Press.

Fatima Community Regeneration Team (2000) *Eleven Acres, Ten Steps*. Dublin: Fatima Groups United.

Finlay, A. (2001) 'Defeatism and northern protestant 'identity''. *Global Review of Ethnopolitics*. 1(2): 3–20.

First Trust (2005) *Economic Outlook and Business Review*. 20(3). Belfast: First Trust Bank.

First Trust (2006) *Economic Outlook and Business Review*. 21(2). Belfast: First Trust Bank.

First Trust (2008) *Economic Outlook and Business Review*. 23(2). Belfast: First Trust Bank.

Fitzpatrick Associates (2006) *Evaluation of the RAPID Programme: Final Report*. Dublin: Fitzpatrick Associates.

Frederickson, G.H. & Smith, K.B. (2003) *The Public Administration Theory Primer*. Boulder, CO: Westview Press.

Gallagher, M. (1999) The changing constitution. In: Coakley, J. & Gallagher, M. (eds) *Politics in the Republic of Ireland*. 3rd Ed. London: Routledge.

Geddes, M. & Bennington, J. (2001) Social exclusion and partnership in the European Union. In: Geddes, M. & Bennington, J. (eds) *Local Partnerships and Social Exclusion in the European Union: New Forms of Local Social Governance?*. London: Routledge.

Gell-Mann, M. (1994) Complex Adaptive Systems. In: Midgley (ed) (2003) *Systems Thinking: Volume 1*. London: Sage Publications.

Gilchrist, A. (2000) 'The well-connected community: networking to the 'edge of chaos''. *Community Development Journal*, 35(3): 264–275.

Gottheil F. (2003) 'Ireland: what's Celtic about the Celtic Tiger?'. *The Quarterly Review of Economics and Finance*, 43: 720–737.

Greer, J. (2001) *Partnership Governance in Northern Ireland: Improving Performance*. Aldershot: Ashgate.

Hazy, J.K., Tivnan, B.F. & Schwandt, D.R. (2003) 'The impact of boundary spanning on organizational learning: computational explorations'. *Emergence*, 5(4): 86–123.

Holland, J.H. (1995) *Hidden Order: How Adaptation Builds Complexity*. Reading, MA: Addison-Wesley.

Holland, J.H. (1998) *Emergence: from Chaos to Order*. Cambridge, MA: Perseus Books.

Hood, C. (1991) 'A public management for all seasons?'. *Public Administration*, 69: 3–19.

Hoos, I.R. (1972) *Systems Analysis in Public Policy: A Critique*. Berkeley, CA: University of California Press.

Hughes, J. (1998) *Partnership Governance in Northern Ireland: The Path to Peace*. Dublin: Oak Tree Press.

Ireland. Acts (1986–1998) *Urban Renewal Acts*. Dublin: Stationery Office.

Ireland. Acts (2000) *Planning and Development Act, 2000*. Dublin: Stationery Office.

Ireland. Department of Health and Children (2001) *Quality and Fairness: A Health System for you*. Dublin: Stationery Office.

Ireland. Department of Health and Children (2001) *Quality and Fairness: A health system for you* Dublin: Stationery Office.

Ireland. Department of Health and Children (2004) *Health Information: A National Strategy*. Dublin: Stationery Office.

Ireland. Department of Health and Children (2008) *Health Information Bill*. Dublin: Stationery Office.

Ireland. Department of the *Taoiseach* (2002) *New Connections*. Dublin: Stationery Office.

Ireland. *Oireachtas* (1999) *National Development Plan 2000–2006*. Dublin: Stationery Office.

Jarman, N. (2004) *Demography, Development and Disorder: Changing Patterns of Interface Areas*. Belfast: Institute for Conflict Research.

Jordan, A. (2006) *Health Systems in Transition: The Northern Ireland Report*. Copenhagen: WHO Regional Office for Europe on behalf of the European Observatory on Health Systems and Policies.

Kauffman, S.A. (1993) *The Origins of Order: Self-organization and Selection in Evolution*. New York, NY: Oxford University Press.

Kauffman, S.A. (1995) *At Home in the Universe: the Search for Laws of Self-organization and Complexity*. New York, NY: Oxford University Press.

Kay, J. (2002) 'The balance sheet'. *Prospect*, 76.

Kingdon, J.W. (1995) *Agenda, Alternatives, and Public Policies*. 2nd Ed. New York: HarperCollins.

Kirby, P. (2002) *The Celtic Tiger in Distress: Growth with Inequality in Ireland*. Basingstoke: Palgrave.

Kirby, P. (2004) 'Globalization, the Celtic Tiger and social outcomes: is Ireland a model or a mirage?'. *Globalizations* 1(2): 205–222.

Kitchen, P. (2002) 'Identifying dimensions of urban social change in Dublin– 1986 to 1996'. *Irish Geography*, 35(2): 156–174.

Koppenjan, J. & Klijn, E-H. (2004) *Managing Uncertainties in Networks*. London: Routledge.

Kornai, J. (1999) *The System Paradigm*. Collegium Budapest: Institute for Advanced Study working paper.

KPMG *et al.* (1996) *Study on the Urban Renewal Schemes*. Dublin: Stationery Office.

Lane, J-E, (1993) *The Public Sector: Concepts, Models & Approaches*. London: Sage.

Lane, J-E (2000) *New Public Management*. London: Routledge.

Layte, R., Nolan, A. & Nolan, B. (2007) Health and Health Care. In: Fahey, T., Russell, H. & Whelan, C. (eds) *Best of Times? The Social Impact of the Celtic Tiger*. Dublin: Institute of Public Administration.

Lindblom, C.E. (1959) 'The science of muddling through'. *Public Administration Review*, 19(1): 79–88.

Lorenzi, N.M. & Riley, R.T. (2003) 'Organizational issues = change'. *International Journal of Medical Informatics*, 69: 197–203.

Lukes, S. (1974) *Power: A Radical View*. London: Macmillan.

Lynn, L. Jr., Heinrich, C. & Hill, C. (2001) *Improving Governance: A New Logic for Empirical Research*. Washington, D.C.: Georgetown University Press.

MacLaran, A. (1999). Inner Dublin: change and development. In: Killen, J. & MacLaran, A. (eds) *Dublin: Contemporary Trends and Issues for the Twenty First Century*. Dublin, Geographical Society of Ireland. 11: 21–33.

Marchal, J.H. (1975), 'On the Concept of a System', *Philosophy of Science*, vol. 42, pp. 448–468

McAuley, J. *et al.* (1999) Developing the interface between centre and periphery as an agent for organisational learning: issues of strategy and local knowledge. Paper presented at the *Organisational Learning Conference*, University of Lancaster, UK.

McCready, S. (2001) *Empowering People: Community Development and Conflict 1969–1999*. Belfast: HMSO.

McEvoy, R., Keenaghan, C. & Murray, A. (2008) *Service User Involvement in the Irish Health Service: A Review of the Evidence*. Dublin: Stationery Office.

Meade, R. (2005) 'We hate it here, please let us stay! Irish social partnership and the community/voluntary sector's conflicted experiences of recognition'. *Critical Social Policy*, 25(3): 349–373.

Meredith, J.R. & Mantel, S.J. (2006) *Project Management: A Managerial Approach*. 6th Ed. Hoboken, NJ: John Wiley & Sons.

Midgley, G. (2000) *Systemic Intervention: Philosophy, Methodology and Practice*. New York, NY: Kluwer.

Moe, R.C. (1994) 'The 'reinventing government' exercise: misinterpreting the problem, misjudging the consequences'. *Public Administration Review*, 54(2): 111–122.

Morgan, G. (1986) *Images of the Organization*. London: Sage.

Moynihan, D.P. (2006) 'Managing for results in state government: evaluating a decade of reform'. Public Administration Review, 66(1): 78–90.

Mueller, K. (1996) *General Systems Theory: History, Methodology and Social Science Heuristics of a Program of Science*, trans from *Allgemeine Systemtheorie: Geschichte, Methodologie und Sozialwissenschaftliche Heuristik eines Wissenschaftsprogramms*. Opladen, Germany: Westdeutscher Verlag.

Muir, J. (2004) 'Public participation in area-based urban regeneration programmes'. *Housing Studies* 19(6): 947–966.

Muir, J. & Rhodes, M.L. (2008) 'Vision and reality: community involvement in Irish urban regeneration'. *Policy & Politics*, 36(4): 497–520.

Murie, A. (2001) Housing policy and administration in Northern Ireland: 1945–1990. In: Paris, C. (ed) *Housing in Northern Ireland and comparisons with the Republic of Ireland*. Coventry: Chartered Institute of Housing.

Murphy, P.W. & Cunningham, J. (2003) *Organizing for Community Controlled Development: Renewing Civil Society*. Thousand Oaks, CA: Sage.

Murtagh, B. (2002) *The Politics of Territory: Policy and Segregation in Northern Ireland*. Basingstoke: Palgrave.

Myers, M.D. & Young, L.W. (1997) 'Hidden agendas, power and managerial assumptions in information systems development'. *Information Technology and People*, 10(3): 224–240.

Nolan, B. & Maître, B. (2007) 'Economic Growth and Income Inequality: Setting the Context'. In: Fahey, T., Russell, H. & Whelan, C.T. (eds) *Best of Times? The Social Impact of the Celtic Tiger*. Dublin: Institute of Public Administration.

Northern Ireland Statistics and Research Agency (2002) 'Mental Health and Wellbeing'. *Northern Ireland Health and Social Wellbeing Survey 2001*. Belfast: NISRA.

Northern Ireland Statistics and Research Agency (2005) Online. Available <http://www.dhsspsni.gov.uk/adult_death_rates2005.pdf> (accessed 8 August 2008).

Northern Ireland. Acts (1946) *Health Services Act (NI), 1946*. Belfast: HMSO.

Northern Ireland. Acts (1971) *Housing Executive Act, 1971*. Belfast: HMSO.

Northern Ireland. Department for Social Development (2001) *Shaping Our Future*. Belfast: DSD.

Northern Ireland. Department for Social Development (2003) *Northern Ireland's Strategy for Neighbourhood Renewal*. Belfast: DSD.

Northern Ireland. Department of Health, Social Services and Public Safety (2004) *A Healthier Future: a Twenty Year Vision for Health and Wellbeing in Northern Ireland 2005–2025*. Belfast: DHSSPS.

Northern Ireland. Department of Health, Social Services and Public Safety (2005) *HPSS ICT Programme—From Vision to Reality: Implementing the ICT Strategy*. Belfast: DHSSPS.

Northern Ireland. Department of Health, Social Services and Public Safety (2005) *Information and Communications Technology Strategy*. Belfast: DHSSPS.

O'Gorman, A. (2000) *Eleven Acres, Ten Steps*. Dublin: Fatima Groups United.

O'Reilly, D. & Browne, S. (2001) *Health and Health Service Use in Northern Ireland: Social Variations*. Belfast: DHSSPS.

Ó Riain, S. (2000) 'The flexible developmental state: globalization, information technology, and the 'Celtic Tiger''. *Politics and Society*, 28(2): 157–193.

Osborne, D. & Gaebler, T. (1992) *Reinventing Government: How the Entrepreneurial Spirit is Transforming the Public Sector*. Reading, MA: Addison Wesley.

Osborne, S. (ed) (2010) *The New Public Governance: Emerging Perspectives on the Theory and Practice of Public Governance*. London: Routledge.

Power, A. (1993) *Hovels to High Rise: State Housing in Europe since 1850*. London: Routledge.

Prager, J. (1994) 'Contracting out government services: lessons from the private sector'. *Public Administration Review*, 54(2): 176–84.

Propper, C., Burgess, S. & Green, K. (2004) 'Does competition between hospitals improve the quality of care? Hospital death rates and the NHS internal market'. *Journal of Public Economics*, 88(7–8): 1247–1272.

Punch, M., Redmond, D. & Kelly, S. (2007) 'Uneven development, city governance and urban change– unpacking the global-local nexus in Dublin's inner city'. In: Hambleton, R. & Gross, J.S. (eds) *Governing Cities in a Global Era: Urban Innovation, Competition, and Democratic Reform*. London: Palgrave.

Putnam, R.D. (2000) *Bowling Alone: the collapse and revival of American community*. New York: Touchstone.

Quinn, B.J. (1980) *Strategies for Change: Logical Incrementalism.* Homewood, IL: Irwin.

Rhodes, M.L. (2005) 'Agent based modelling for policy analysis: exploring the Irish housing system'. *Proceedings of the ISCE Workshop on Complexity & Policy Analysis.* Cork, Ireland, 22 to 24 June.

Rhodes, M.L. (2008) 'Complexity and emergence in public management: the case of urban regeneration in Ireland'. *Public Management Review*, 10(3): 361–379. London: Routledge.

Rhodes, M.L. & Haynes, P. (2004) Social housing in Ireland: a study. Paper presented at *Complexity, European Network of Housing Research Conference.* Cambridge, UK, 3 July.

Rhodes, M.L. & Keogan, J. (2005) 'Strategic choice in the non-profit housing sector: an Irish case study'. *Irish Journal of Management*, 122–135.

Rhodes, M.L. & MacKechnie, G. (2003) 'Understanding public service systems: is there a role for complex adaptive systems theory?'. *Emergence*, 5(4): 58–85.

Rhodes, M.L. & Murray, J. (2007) 'Collaborative decision-making in urban regeneration: a complex adaptive systems perspective'. *International Public Management Journal*, 10(1): 79–101. London: Routledge.

Rhodes, R.A.W. (1988) *Beyond Westminster and Whitehall: the Sub-central Governments of Britain.* London: Unwin Hyman.

Rich, R. & Merrick, K. (2006) 'Cross-border health care in the European Union: challenges and opportunities'. *Contemporary Health Law and Policy*, 23(1): 64–105.

Romanelli, E. & Tushman, M.L. (1994) 'Organizational transformation as punctuated equilibrium: an empirical test'. *Academy Of Management Journal*, 37(5): 1141–1166.

Rosenhead, J. (1998) *Complexity Theory and Management Practice.* Online. Available <http://www.human-nature.com/science-as-culture/rosenhead.html> (accessed 7 August 2008).

Ryan, H., Lios Geal Consultants & Healy, M. (2007) *eHealth strategy and implementation activities in Ireland.* Online. Available <http://www.ehealth-era.org/database/documents/ERA_Reports/Ireland_eHealth-ERA_country_report_final2.pdf> (accessed 7 August 2008).

Scott, W.R. (1995) *Institutions and Organizations.* Thousand Oaks, CA: Sage Publications.

Shine, K.T. & Norris, M. (2006) *Regenerating Local Authority Housing Estates: Review of Policy and Practice.* Dublin: Centre for Housing Research.

Shirlow, P. (2001) 'Devolution in Northern Ireland/Ulster/the North/Six Counties: Delete as Appropriate'. *Regional Studies*, 35(8): 743–752.

Shirlow, P. (2001) 'Fear and Ethnic Division'. *Peace Review* 13(1): 67–74.

Shirlow, P. & Murtagh, B. (2006) *Belfast: Segregation, Violence and the City.* Contemporary Irish Studies. London: Pluto Press.

Shuttleworth, I. & Lloyd, C. (2008) *Mapping Segregation on Belfast NIHE Estates.* Belfast: Northern Ireland Housing Executive.

Skelcher, C., McCabe, A. & Lowndes, V. (1996) *Community Networks in Urban Regeneration: 'It all depends who you know . . !'.* Bristol: The Policy Press.

Somerville-Woodward, R. (2002) *Ballymun: A History, Volume 2, c.1960–2001.* Dublin: BRL.

Somerville, P. (2005) 'Community governance and democracy'. *Policy & Politics*, 33(1): 117–44.

Stacey, R.D. (2000) *Strategic Management and Organisational Dynamics: The Challenge of Complexity.* 3rd Ed. London: Prentice Hall.

Stacey, R.D. & Griffin, D. (eds) (2006) *Complexity and the Experience of Managing in the Public Sector.* London: Routledge.

Stacey, R.D., Griffin, D. & Shaw, P. (2002) *Complexity and Management: Fad or Radical Challenge to Systems Thinking?*. London: Routledge.

Stillman, R.J. (2000) *Public Administration: Concepts and Cases*. 7th Ed. New York, NY: Houghton Mifflin Co.

Taylor, M. (2003) *Public Policy in the Community*. Basingstoke: Palgrave Macmillan.

Taylor, M. (2007) 'Community participation in the real world: opportunities and pitfalls in new governance spaces'. *Urban Studies*, 44(2): 297–317.

Teisman, G. & Klijn, E-H. (2008) 'Complexity theory and public management: an introduction'. *Public Management Review*, 10(3): 287–297.

Tushman, M. & Scanlon, T. (1981) 'Boundary spanning individuals: their role in information transfer and their antecedents'. *Academy of Management Journal*, 24(2): 89–305.

Umbach, E. (2000) 'The Fundamental Tasks of Systems Science'. In *Proceedings of the World Congress of the Systems Sciences*, July 2000.

Walsh, J. (2001) 'Catalysts for change: public policy reform through local partnership in Ireland'. In: Geddes, M. & Benington, J. (eds) *Local Partnerships and Social Exclusion in the European Union: New Forms of Local Social Governance?*. London: Routledge.

Weber, J. (2005) 'Introduction to chaos, complexity, uncertainty and public administration: a symposium'. *Public Administration Quarterly*, 29(3): 262–267.

Weber, M. (1948) 'Bureaucracy'. In: Wright Mills, C. (ed) *Max Weber: Essays in Sociology*. London: Routledge.

Weick, Karl (1969) *The Social Psychology of Organizing*. Reading, MA: Addison Wesley.

Whelan, C.T., Nolan, B. & Maître, B. (2006) 'Trends in Economic Vulnerability in the Republic of Ireland'. *The Economic and Social Review*, 37(1): 91–119.

Whittington, R. (2001) *What is Strategy—and Does it Matter?* 2nd Ed. London: Thompson Learning.

Wiener, N. (1948) *Cybernetics: Or Control and Communication in the Animal and the Machine*. Cambridge, MA: MIT Press.

Wiley, M. (2005) 'The Irish health system: developments in strategy, structure, funding and delivery since 1980'. *Health Economics*, 14: S169–S186.

Yin, R.K. (1993) *Applications of Case Study Research*. Newbury Park, CA: Sage Publishing.

Yin, R.K. (2002) *Case Study Research: Design and Methods*. 3rd Ed. Beverly Hills, CA: Sage Publishing.

Young-Hoon, K. (2005) A brief history of Project Management. In: Carayannis, E.G. *et al.* (2005) *The Story of Managing Projects*. 9th Ed. Westport, CT: Greenwood Publishing Group.

Index